"Samantha Miller provides a sch[ ] scholars are willing to tackle. The topic of demons doesn't get a lot of press in the West, perhaps because we have enough other distractions that lure our attention away from God. The study is well grounded in the precursors of Greco-Roman and Jewish thought, as well as early Christian literature before Chrysostom. It also includes a discussion about free will which, like Chrysostom himself, borders on the synergistic. But Miller pushes back, pointing out that such discussions about synergism and soteriology largely came after Chrysostom's time. While this is a debatable point, her assertion that Chrysostom held that 'neither God nor the devil compels,' is nonetheless quite compelling on its own. Chrysostom noted that just as humans have limits, so do demons. They are not as strong as they pretend to be—but neither are they to be trifled with, which is why Chrysostom insisted that Christians must be trained in virtue in order to do battle. This book will provide a window into that spiritual battle as well as provide an added dimension to scholarship on Chrysostom and early Christian spirituality and soteriology."

Joel C. Elowsky, professor of historical theology at Concordia Seminary, St. Louis, Missouri

"I am often surprised when I preach how often listeners want to talk about demons. The liberal in me wants to demythologize. Samantha Miller, drawing on St. John Chrysostom, shows me a better way. Demons can't make you do anything. In fact, God uses our struggle against evil to hasten salvation. What a timely word she brings, addressing even the prosperity gospel and Americans' present penchant for demonizing one another."

Jason Byassee, Butler Professor of Homiletics and Biblical Hermeneutics at the Vancouver School of Theology

"Samantha Miller clearly lays out John Chrysostom's demonology, but more importantly, she demonstrates how, for Chrysostom, demonology is a kind of practical theology because of the way it becomes part of his overall systematic theology, especially anthropology and soteriology, and because of the way Chrysostom uses his teaching on demons to drive his audience toward virtue. Miller shows how to respond to a world where people are tempted to claim, 'the devil made me do it,' by countering as Chrysostom did with a healthier view of spiritual warfare and human freedom, regardless of one's present view of the demonic. Miller is a careful and thorough scholar, but also eminently readable, and she has the gift of making nuanced analysis accessible to the scholar and nonscholar alike. This is a very satisfying book. It covers all the bases and checks all the boxes."

James L. Papandrea, professor of church history and historical theology, Garrett-Evangelical Theological Seminary

"In an age when we have lost the ability to discern the principalities and powers, Miller's *Chrysostom's Devil* is a welcome intervention. She offers a historically substantive demonology and its place in the theology of the early church, particularly that of Chrysostom. As important as the historical analysis is, this work offers much more. It is a profound investigation into moral theology. The discussion of *proairesis* is brilliant. Given its ongoing importance for theological and philosophical ethics, her work should be required reading for anyone interested in a theological rendering of human action and practical reasoning. Miller not only shows us why we should have 'no sympathy for the devil,' she shows us how we can avoid it."

D. Stephen Long, Cary M. Maguire University Professor of Ethics, Southern Methodist University

"Miller connects the dots from Chrysostom's demonology to the fundamental questions of what it means to be human and to be saved. By opening the door into the moral imagination of early Christian demonology, Miller breaks open the hard shell that Western thought has encased around it. This book will help Western Christians learn, not only from these ancient voices but from much of global Christianity today."

Amy Oden, visiting professor of early church history and spirituality, Saint Paul School of Theology at Oklahoma City University

"In this well-written account, Miller fills an important gap in our understanding of John Chrysostom's theology: demons and personal responsibility. In a somewhat surprising conclusion, she argues persuasively that this early Eastern preacher speaks directly to the concerns of Western charismatic and evangelical Christians today. Delightful turns of phrase, such as '[The devil] will put [sin] in a tuxedo and make it dance so that it is enticing' and 'A monk who is content and has no sweet tooth will not be tempted, even if the dessert is a three-tiered chocolate cake,' illustrate the argument and make an otherwise dry topic accessible to the student and more general reader."

Wendy Mayer, associate dean for research at Australian Lutheran College, University of Divinity

"*Chrysostom's Devil* takes us on a captivating journey through the spirit world of late antiquity as described by one of the most prolific Christian authors in history. Miller aptly demonstrates how John Chrysostom engages with the culture of his day by providing significant correctives to how people understood demons and demonology in their lives. But *Chrysostom's Devil* also brings John into conversation with modern-day deliverance theology for the very first time, proving that today's church can—and should—still learn a great deal from ancient Christian wisdom."

Chris L. de Wet, University of South Africa, author of Preaching Bondage: John Chrysostom and the Discourse of Slavery in Early Christianity

"*Chrysostom's Devil* is an example of how crucial historical theology of early Christian texts is for modern theology. Demonology is not one of those fields of study that tends to take up much, if any, space in modern Western conversations of theology. Samantha Miller helps create some needed space through engagement with the great fifth-century preacher, John Chrysostom. The theological connections he makes in his sermons and catechetical writings between demons and anthropology, soteriology, and ecclesiology demonstrate Chrysostom's deep pastoral concern that his flock live without fear and choose lives of virtue. Miller's expansive and close reading of Chrysostom's texts (and other ancient texts) both illuminates the late-antique world in which demons are a granted reality and offers a starting point for shared ecumenical understanding today. For Pentecostals or charismatic Christians, discussions of the demonic might be commonplace but would benefit from Chrysostom's deeply theological integration of demonology, free will, and virtue. For other Christians who are either unfamiliar with demonology or who rebuff such discussions for whatever reason, *Chrysostom's Devil* offers a fascinating and accessible entry point."

Amy Brown Hughes, assistant professor of theology at Gordon College, coauthor of *Christian Women in the Patristic World*

"This succinct yet thorough account offers a window, not only into John Chrysostom's views on demons, but also into his thinking on persons human and divine. Drawing on texts from across John's corpus, Miller deftly limns the ancient contexts, practices, and intellectual traditions shaping John's perspectives, even while relating his thinking to contemporary movements and assumptions. Anyone interested in demonology, John Chrysostom, or early Christian anthropology should read this thoughtful, engaging, and celestially clear book."

Han-luen Kantzer Komline, assistant professor of church history and theology at Western Theological Seminary

NEW EXPLORATIONS IN THEOLOGY

CHRYSOSTOM'S DEVIL:

DEMONS, THE WILL, AND VIRTUE IN PATRISTIC SOTERIOLOGY

SAMANTHA L. MILLER

An imprint of InterVarsity Press
Downers Grove, Illinois

InterVarsity Press
P.O. Box 1400, Downers Grove, IL 60515-1426
ivpress.com
email@ivpress.com

InterVarsity Press® is the book-publishing division of InterVarsity Christian Fellowship/USA®, a movement of students and faculty active on campus at hundreds of universities, colleges, and schools of nursing in the United States of America, and a member movement of the International Fellowship of Evangelical Students. For information about local and regional activities, visit intervarsity.org.

Scripture quotations, unless otherwise noted, are from the New Revised Standard Version of the Bible, copyright 1989 by the Division of Christian Education of the National Council of the Churches of Christ in the USA. Used by permission. All rights reserved.

Cover design: Cindy Kiple
Interior design: Beth McGill

ISBN 978-0-8308-4917-8 (print)
ISBN 978-0-8308-5116-4 (digital)

Printed in the United States of America ∞

InterVarsity Press is committed to ecological stewardship and to the conservation of natural resources in all our operations. This book was printed using sustainably sourced paper.

Library of Congress Cataloging-in-Publication Data
A catalog record for this book is available from the Library of Congress.

P	25	24	23	22	21	20	19	18	17	16	15	14	13	12	11	10	9	8	7	6	5	4	3	2	1
Y	37	36	35	34	33	32	31	30	29	28	27	26	25	24	23	22	21	20							

For my parents

and

For all my teachers

This is fruit of your work and your love.

Contents

Acknowledgments

A TRUE INTROVERT, I never expected to desire the company of people as much as I have while writing this book. Though it was born out of countless hours holed away in the library, I have never been alone in this process. My gratitude runs deep, and I could not hope to thank everyone who deserves it, but I offer here what thanks I can.

The gift A Foundation for Theological Education provided in choosing me as a John Wesley Fellow is immeasurable. Their financial support made my work in graduate school and the first iteration of this book possible, and the fellowship with other Wesleyan scholars has buoyed my soul throughout each successive stage.

Dr. Michel René Barnes, Dr. Deirdre Dempsey, Dr. Wanda Zemler-Cizeweski, Fr. Joseph Mueller, Dr. Steve Long, and Fr. Alexander Golitzen have my thanks for all of the helpful comments, answered questions, and general direction as I wrote the first draft. My colleagues and students at Anderson University have contributed to revisions through their conversations and questions. Nathan Willowby graciously read drafts of revised conclusions and has been ever supportive.

One of the great gifts of my doctoral program is the wonderful community of scholars and friends it gave me. Stephen Waers, Tim Gabrielson, Nathan Lunsford, and Nathan Thiel through conversations, multiple readings, and encouragement have made this book better for their input. Jakob Rinderknecht, Anne Carpenter, and Ryan Hemmer also deserve special mention among those who are not only colleagues but also friends, whose conversations about work and life, potlucks, old movie nights, and games of catch have made this experience richer and have helped me to maintain my humanity.

I also owe a debt of gratitude to the people of Calvary Presbyterian Church in Milwaukee, with special thanks to the members of the Wednesday night Bible study group, who kept me well-fed both physically and spiritually throughout my writing. An even more special thanks goes to Mark and Maggie McDonough for unbelievable generosity, for conversations, and for occasional bags of groceries. Kent Busman and the UFS at Camp Fowler embody the best of all the virtue I write about, and they have kept me afloat with their encouragement, laughter, friendship, and a sock puppet parody titled "The Dessert Daddies." Christina Jager also proofread this manuscript and made the writing stronger, cleaner, and generally more comprehensible.

Finally, and perhaps most importantly, to my family I say, "Thank you." You have never wavered in your support of me, nor in your love for me. What you called "stubbornness" when I was a child you now call "determination," and this is the result. You refuse to let me take myself too seriously, and I love you for it.

Abbreviations

OTP	*Old Testament Pseudepigrapha.* Edited by James H. Charlesworth. 2 vols. New York: Doubleday, 1983–1985.
PG	Patrologia Graeca [= Patrologiae Cursus Completus: Series Graeca]. Edited by Jacques-Paul Migne. 162 vols. Paris, 1857–1886.
PO	Patrologia Orientalis
SC	Sources chrétiennes
SJC: CS	St. John Chrysostom: Commentaries on the Sages
SVTQ	*St. Vladimir's Theological Quarterly*
TLG	*Thesaurus Linguae Graecae: Canon of Greek Authors and Works.* Edited by Luci Berkowitz and Karl A. Squitier. 3rd ed. New York: Oxford University Press, 1990.
VC	*Vigiliae Christianae*
y.	Jerusalme tractate
ZNW	*Zeitschrift für die neutestamentliche Wissenschaft und die Kunde der älteren Kirche*

CHRYSOSTOM'S WORKS[1]

Ad eos qui scand.	*Ad eos qui scandalizati sunt* (often called *On Providence*)
Ad Stag.	*Ad Stagirium a daemone vexatum*
Ad Theod.	*Ad Theodorum lapsum*
Ad vid. iun.	*Ad viduam iuniorem*
Adv. Iud. or.	*Adversus Iudaeos or. 1-8*
Adv. opp. vit. mon.	*Adversus oppugnatores vitae monasticae*
Cat.	*Catecheses ad illuminandos*
Cat. ult. ad bapt.	*Catechesis ultima ad baptizandos*
Comm. in Iob	*Commentarius in Iob*
Comp. reg. et mon.	*Comparatio regis et monachi*

---

[1]I follow the list compiled by Wendy Mayer at the Centre for Early Christian Studies at Australian Catholic University since this list was created in the hope of beginning to standardize abbreviations among Chrysostom scholars. The full list can be found at www.cecs.acu.edu.au/onlineresources _chrysostomabbreviations.html.

De Bab. c. Iul. et gent.	*De s. Babyla contra Iulianum et gentiles*
De diab. tent. hom. 1 =	
De eleem.	*De eleemosyna*
De incompr. hom.	*De incomprehensibili dei natura hom.* 1-3
De laud. Paul. hom.	*De laudibus sancti Pauli homiliae* 1-7
De poen. hom.	*De poenitentia homiliae* 1-9
De proph. obsc. hom.	*De prophetiarum obscuritate hom.* 1-2
De proph. obsc. hom. 3	*De diabolo tentatore hom.* 1
De res. dom.	*De resurrectione domini nostri*
	Iesu Christ homilia
De sac.	*De sacerdotio*
De stat.	*De statuis homiliae* 1-21
Dom., non est in hom.	*In illud: Domine, non est in homine*
ep. ad Olymp.	*Epistulae 1-17 ad Olympiadem*
Exp. in ps. 4–150	*Expositiones in psalmos*
Illum. cat. 1	*Ad illuminandos catechesis* 1
Illum. cat. 2	*Ad illuminandos catechesis* 2
In Act. apost. hom.	*In Acta apostolorum hom.* 1-55
In Col. hom.	*In epistulam ad Colossenses hom.* 1-12
In Eph. hom.	*In epistulam ad Ephesios hom.* 1-24
In 1 Cor. hom.	*In epistulam I ad Corinthios hom.* 1-44
In 1 Thess. hom.	*In epistulam I ad Thessalonicenses hom.* 1-11
In 1 Tim. hom.	*In epistulam I ad Timotheum hom.* 1-18
In Gen. hom.	*Homiliae 1-67 in Genesim*
In Gal. comm.	*In epistulam ad Galatas commentarium*
In Heb. hom.	*In epistulam ad Hebraeos homiliae* 1-34
In Ioh. hom.	*In Iohannem hom.* 1-88
In Matt. hom.	*In Matthaeum hom.* 1-90
In Rom. hom.	*In epistulam ad Romanos hom.* 1-32
In 2 Cor. hom.	*In epistulam II ad Corinthios hom.* 1-30
In 2 Thess. hom.	*In epistulam II ad Thessalonicenses hom.* 1-5
In Tit. hom.	*In epistulam ad Titum hom.* 1-6
Inan. glor. et ed. lib.	*De inani gloria et de educandis liberis*
Ne tim. hom.	*In illud: Ne timueritis homiliae*
Quod nem. laed.	*Quod nemo laeditur nisi a seipso*

Works by Ancient Authors
Aeschylus
Ag.   *Agamemnon*
Aristotle
Eth. eud.   *Ethica eudemia / Eudemian Ethics*
Eth. nic.   *Ethica nicomachea / Nicomachean Ethics*
Athanasius
Letters   *Letters of St. Antony*
Augustine
Civ. Dei   *The City of God*
Lib.   *De libero arbitrio*
Trin.   *De Trinitate / The Trinity*
Aulus Gellius
Noct. att.   *Noctes atticae / Attic Nights*
Basil of Caesarea
Ep.   *Epistluae 1-366*
Hom. adv. ira.   *Homilia adversus eos qui irascuntur*
Hom. invid.   *Homilia de invidia*
Hom. in Ps.   *Homiliae super Psalmos*
Calcidius
Comm.   *Commentarius*
Diogenes
Lives   *Lives of Eminent Philosophers*
Epictetus
Diatr.   *Diatribai (Dissertationes)*
Gregory of Nazianzus
Carm.   *Carmina Dogmatica*
Epig.   *Epigrammata*
Or.   *Orationes*
Gregory of Nyssa
Anim. et res.   *Dialogus de anima et resurrectione*
In cant. cant.   *In Canticum canticorum*
Or. catech.   *Oratio catechetica*
Lucif. res.   *In luciferam sanctam domini resurrectionem*

Irenaeus

Haer.   *Adversus haereses / Against Heresies*

Methodius

Autex.   *Peri tou autexousiou*

Origen

Cels.   *Contra Celsum / Against Celsus*

Comm. Matt.   *Commentarium in evangelium Matthaei*

Princ.   *De principiis (Peri archōn) / First Principles*

Seneca

Ep.   *Epistulae morales*

Tertullian

Apol.   *Apology*

Introduction

WHEN I WAS BAPTIZED in the United Methodist Church, my parents renounced the "spiritual forces of wickedness" and rejected the "evil powers of this world" on my behalf. My Catholic friends got to renounce "Satan and all his pomps" at their daughter's baptism last year, and I watched my Orthodox friends spit on the devil when their son was baptized. Even in less liturgical traditions, there is at baptism a recognition of the turn away from sin and toward Christ. So those of us who have been baptized have rejected evil, perhaps even Satan by name, but I dare say most of us do not give this a second thought. I have never heard my parents bring it up. In fact, when I was interviewing for faculty positions with my work on John Chrysostom's demonology, I was advised by one of my professors to have an answer prepared for when deans and provosts asked me whether I believed in the devil.[1] The realm of the demonic is something that a lot of the modern, Western church (excluding the more charismatic branches) is uncomfortable with. Demons make us nervous in this part of the world.

The ancient world, however, was populated with spirits: some good, some evil, some indifferent or even ambiguous. Though Jews, pagans, and Christians told different narratives about what these *daimones* (δαίμονες) were, where they came from, and how they interacted with human beings, most people in the ancient world understood the same thing by the term.

---

[1]The reply D. Stephen Long gave me was, "Go with Karl Barth: 'I believe against him.'"

Daimones were the spirits active in the world around them. Most people also understood this invisible population to be worthy of fear. *Daimones* could and often did cause physical harm: illness, poverty, pregnancy complications, even death. In response, people of late antiquity employed amulets, magic bowls, and magical papyri to protect themselves and their families from the threat demons posed. The fear was not debilitating however. It was just a way of life. Fourth-century Christians and Jews, intellectuals and the uneducated, rich and poor, all ancient Mediterranean people participated in such anti-*daimones* magic as a part of life. It was what one did.

In this world lived John Chrysostom (c. 347–407 CE). Raised in Antioch by his mother as a Christian and educated in classical rhetoric under the pagan orator Libanius, Chrysostom then apprenticed himself to Diodore of Tarsus to learn theology. Chrysostom became a monk after his mother died and lived in such extreme asceticism in the mountains outside Antioch that he damaged his health and was forced to return to the city. On his return, he was ordained a deacon (381) and then a priest (386). Chrysostom served as priest in Antioch for about eleven years and gained his reputation (and nickname) as the "golden-tongued." In 397 he was appointed the bishop of Constantinople, where he served until 407, when Empress Eudoxia exiled him for the second time. His health was too ravaged, and Chrysostom died on the forced march.

CHRYSOSTOM'S DEMONOLOGICAL DISCOURSE

Chrysostom's world, and that of his congregants, was populated by *daimones*, just like all of his neighbors' worlds. Unlike in the works of Chrysostom's contemporaries, however, demons run rampant through his preaching: "How many demons are carried about in this air? How many opposing powers? If God permitted them to show their frightening and joyless faces, we would lose our minds."[2] "Do you not know how many demons are in this space . . . how many evil spirits? Therefore if we have that light, they will not be able to do us any harm; but if we put it out, they will conquer us quickly, they quickly rob us of everything."[3] Before I continue, I want to make one

---

[2]Chrysostom, *Exp. in ps.* 41.5 (PG 55.162). Unless otherwise noted, translations are my own.
[3]Chrysostom, *In 1 Thess. hom.* 11.1 (PG 62.462).

note about terminology. From here on I will use *demons* when discussing Chrysostom's thought in particular or Christian thought more generally and reserve *daimones* for accounts of pagan demonologies. Christians believed the *daimones* to be agents of the devil and their aim the hindering of salvation. That is, *daimones* were always evil, and *demons* denotes this particular Christian understanding of demons with which this work is concerned.

In many instances Chrysostom's concern is that his congregants know that demons are not as dangerous as they think. He preaches, "Some would be so bold as to say that demons govern our affairs."[4] "[The devil] does not conquer with force, nor with tyranny, nor by compelling, nor by being violent. If this were the case, he would have destroyed all people."[5] Yet elsewhere Chrysostom preaches that demons are *more* dangerous than they think: "The enemy is at war with us, not simply, nor openly, but craftily. . . . I mean something like this: he never sets sins before us plainly; he does not speak of idolatry, but he dresses it up differently, using craftiness, that is, making up a plausible argument, using disguises."[6] The congregants need to be on their guard against all this craftiness. Chrysostom urges his audience, "Mighty and violent, the devil presses in, besieging our salvation on every side."[7] It is not merely the flu or a bad reputation that is at stake but salvation itself.

Much of this demonological discourse takes place in the context of discussions about suffering and the origin of evil. Chrysostom's congregants think the devil and his demons are responsible for the suffering they experience and see in the world. In response to their fear, Chrysostom tells his audience not to be afraid. Demons may, in fact, be responsible, but if they do cause suffering, it is with God's permission and within God's providence, for God is the one governing the world, not the devil. Moreover, these illnesses, destructions, and deaths are not true harm. Applying categories he borrows from Stoic philosophy, Chrysostom says that these sufferings are only apparent harm; the only true harm is harm to the soul: sin. It is sin that Christians should fear, and neither the devil nor his demons can cause this, for each person has control of her own *proairesis* (προαίρεσις), her choice.

---

[4]Chrysostom, *De proph. obsc. hom.* 3.6 (PG 49.253).
[5]Chrysostom, *De diab. tent. hom.* 1.1 (SC 560bis, 122).
[6]Chrysostom, *In Eph. hom.* 22.3 (PG 62.158).
[7]Chrysostom, *In Ioh. hom.* 23.1 (PG 59.137).

Everyone has a *proairesis*, a faculty of the soul that is an ability to choose, which is free and what makes a human self-determining. Since it is free, neither demons nor God can compel a person's *proairesis*. It is entirely within a person's own control. The devil attacks and deceives, dressing up sins in fancy clothes, and for this reason Christians must be vigilant that they not lose their salvation.[8]

When Chrysostom uses demonological discourse in places other than these conversations about suffering, the demonological is still usually related to questions of human virtue. This relationship is particularly apparent in Chrysostom's baptismal homilies. He tells his catechumens not to be afraid but to be ready to engage in a struggle, for the whole of the Christian life is a contest with Satan. Chrysostom preaches, "These thirty days are like the practices and gym exercises in some wrestling school. Let us learn in this time to overcome that wicked demon. For we are about to strip for that [struggle] after the baptism."[9] Yet, because the contest is rigged, Christians need not fear this struggle. Christ has bound the devil and is "wholly with us."[10] Even more, Chrysostom says that he is going to talk of demons in order to prepare them to defend.[11] Baptism is about the change from being the devil's captive to joining Christ's service. For Chrysostom, every baptized Christian is in battle with the devil daily, and they all need sermons about the devil so that they can defeat him with their virtue.[12]

What becomes clear in reading Chrysostom's discussions about demons is that he does not discuss them in order to speculate where they come from or what their composition is; Chrysostom discusses demons for the purpose of encouraging his congregation to be virtuous. Chrysostom insists that demons are not as dangerous as people assume and that there is no need for magic to repel them; humans are in themselves stronger than the devil.

---

[8]Chrysostom, *In Gen. hom.* 8.6 (PG 53.75): "Therefore, let us not think too little of our salvation. For nothing is as important as virtue, beloved. For this virtue snatches us out of Gehenna in the coming age and gives us the enjoyment of the kingdom of heaven . . . and it even makes us stronger than the enemy of our salvation—I mean the devil."

[9]Chrysostom, *Illum. cat.* 1.16 (SC 366bis, 144).

[10]Chrysostom, *Cat.* 3.9 (SC 50bis, 156).

[11]Chrysostom, *De diab. tent. hom.* 1.1 (SC 560bis, 122).

[12]Chrysostom, *Cat.* 4.3 (SC 50bis, 183): "Yesterday and the day before, they were slaves of sin and without freedom, and under the tyranny of the devil; like captives they were led around and around. Today they have been received into the order of sons."

Demons, in fact, are powerless to cause any sort of true harm because humans have *proairesis*, an innate ability to choose their actions.

Humans are meant to exercise their *proairesis* against temptation and against sin. This *proairesis* is the locus of moral responsibility and the reason virtue can be virtue, for only thoughts, words, and deeds that one chooses can be sin or virtue. Additionally, only things a person chooses to say, think, or do can be punished or praised. Commenting on the parable of the sheep and the goats in Matthew 25:31-46, Chrysostom preaches, "How then was the end [of each group] not the same? Because the *proairesis* did not allow it. For this alone created the division. For this reason the one set went to Gehenna, but the other to the Kingdom. . . . Again, do you see that the *proairesis* is the cause of the end, not the devil?"[13] In this way Chrysostom's demonological discourses become anthropological discourses, and, because virtue is a key aspect of salvation for Chrysostom, they become soteriological as well. In examining Chrysostom's thought, one cannot treat demons without also treating the nature of human beings and their salvation.

The literature on Chrysostom has tended either to ignore his demonology or to engage with it in one of two ways. The first way is as part of Chrysostom's baptismal liturgy, as in Thomas Finn's *The Liturgy of Baptism in the Baptismal Instructions of St. John Chrysostom* and Dayna Kalleres's "Exorcising the Devil to Silence Christ's Enemies: Ritualized Speech Practices in Late Antique Christianity."[14] These studies tend to focus on the function of catechetical exorcisms. The second way scholars engage Chrysostom's demonology is in relation to demon possession and mental illness, as in Claire Salem's "Sanity, Insanity, and Man's Being as Understood by St. John Chrysostom."[15] The exception to this pattern is Dayna Kalleres's *City of Demons: Violence, Ritual, and Christian Power in Late Antiquity.*[16] Kalleres

---

[13]Chrysostom, *De diab. tent. hom.* 2.3 (SC 560bis, 174).

[14]Thomas M. Finn, *The Liturgy of Baptism in the Baptismal Instructions of St. John Chrysostom* (Washington, DC: Catholic University of America Press, 1967); and Dayna S. Kalleres, "Exorcising the Devil to Silence Christ's Enemies: Ritualized Speech Practices in Late Antique Christianity" (PhD, Brown University, 2002).

[15]Claire Elayne Salem, "Sanity, Insanity, and Man's Being as Understood by St. John Chrysostom" (PhD diss., Durham University, 2010).

[16]Dayna S. Kalleres, *City of Demons: Violence, Ritual, and Christian Power in Late Antiquity* (Berkeley: University of California Press, 2015).

argues that Chrysostom, Ambrose of Milan, and Cyril of Jerusalem used demonological rhetoric as part of their projects to Christianize the cities where they served. In Chrysostom's section, the argument is that the diabolization of various behaviors is Chrysostom's strategy to turn his congregants away from these behaviors and to create a fully Christianized city, his ideal *politeia* (πολιτεία).

What all of these approaches have in common is scholarship that is primarily sociohistorical in nature and provides a picture of Chrysostom as a fiery preacher concerned with using a Christian *philosophia* (φιλοσοφία) to transform Antioch or Constantinople into a Christian *politeia*.[17] Demons appear only briefly in the scholarship as part of this program, though the devil and his demons appear frequently in Chrysostom's rhetoric. The work does involve Chrysostom's anthropology and soteriology, but still missing is a theological account that makes sense of Chrysostom's moral-philosophical program. It is this theological framework that I aim to provide here.[18]

In what follows, I argue that Chrysostom understands demons to be created beings who cannot harm human beings without their consent. Therefore, Chrysostom's demonology and account of self-determination exert a mutual influence on one another: self-determination is necessary for virtue, and virtue is integral to salvation. That is, Chrysostom's demonology highlights—through its relation to his account of virtue and self-determination—the depth to which humans are responsible for their own salvation. These are the internal logic and theology that undergird

---

[17]For examples, see Jaclyn L. Maxwell, *Christianization and Communication in Late Antiquity: John Chrysostom and His Congregation in Antioch* (Cambridge: Cambridge University Press, 2006); and Margaret M. Mitchell, "John Chrysostom," in *The Sermon on the Mount Through the Centuries*, ed. Jeffrey P. Greenman, Timothy Larsen, and Stephen R. Spencer (Grand Rapids: Brazos, 2007), 19-42.

[18]There has, however, been a recent reappraisal of his theology among scholars like David Rylaarsdam, Wendy Mayer, and Chris de Wet. On the reappraisal of Chrysostom as a sophisticated thinker and theologian, see especially Wendy Mayer, "Shaping the Sick Soul: Reshaping the Identity of John Chrysostom," in *Christians Shaping Identity from the Roman Empire to Byzantium: Studies Inspired by Pauline Allen*, ed. Wendy Mayer and Geoffrey Dunn (Leiden: Brill, 2015), 140-64; Mayer, "Mania and Madness in the Works of John Chrysostom: A Snapshot from Late Antiquity," in *The Concept of Madness from Homer to Byzantium: Manifestations and Aspects of Mental Illness and Disorder*, ed. Hélène Perdicoyianni-Paléologou (Amsterdam: Hakkert, 2016), 349-73; and Chris L. de Wet and Wendy Mayer, eds., *Revisioning John Chrysostom: New Approaches, New Perspectives* (Leiden: Brill, 2019).

Chrysostom's rhetoric of diabolization that he deploys in Christianizing the city. Therefore, Chrysostom's actions and rhetoric are better understood when the complex interactions between his demonology, anthropology, and soteriology are taken into account.

My first task in this effort is descriptive. Chapter one sets the scene of late antique demonology in order to place Chrysostom within his context and its trajectories of thought. Chrysostom's particular understanding of demonology is a forceful rejection of the ideas of the laity in his congregation so it is important to describe the demonological milieu in order both to understand the target of his rejection and to understand how unique Chrysostom was. This first chapter is a broad treatment of the pagan, Jewish, and Christian demonologies from Origen to Chrysostom that provide context for Chrysostom's own treatment of the demons' (non)influence on human sin. This broad outline provides only specific and concentrated treatments of those sources and traditions that are necessary for understanding Chrysostom's context.

Chapter two is an exploration of Chrysostom's demonology in two parts. The first part is an outline of Chrysostom's demonology proper: How does Chrysostom understand the origin, nature, and activities of demons, and how does his understanding compare to that of his predecessors? The second part looks at the rhetorical function demonology serves for Chrysostom. He does not discuss demons for the sake of speculating about demons' origins or what they are composed of the way that Origen does; Chrysostom discusses demons for the sake of encouraging his congregants to virtuous lives. Chrysostom's demonological discourse is overwhelmingly practical. Demons are real, and demons can also be useful. Chrysostom employs demonic rhetoric often when he exhorts his congregation to a given act, virtue generally, or a way of life.

Similar to the descriptive task of chapter one, chapter three examines the place of *proairesis* in Stoic theological anthropology and the possible philosophical sources of Chrysostom's anthropology. This background sets up and gives depth to the argument of chapter four, which explores Chrysostom's theological anthropology with a particular emphasis on his account of human virtue. This chapter demonstrates that Chrysostom uses demonology to highlight anthropology. Demons are limited, created beings, unable to harm a human unless given permission by God and freely followed by the human himself. In Chrysostom's discussions of the devil and his demons,

Chrysostom's account of the demons' powerlessness in the face of the Christian's *proairesis* becomes clear.[19] Humans have the ability to choose good and to resist the devil and thus to "defeat" him. The devil cannot harm a human being; a human being can only harm himself by choosing to follow the devil, that is, by choosing to do evil, to sin. Chrysostom draws on what appear to be Stoic categories for discussing "harm" to humans, distinguishing between true and apparent harm. The only true harm, he says, is harm to the soul, that is, sin; everything else—poverty, unemployment, natural disaster, disease—is only apparent harm.[20]

Sin is avoidable in Chrysostom's understanding because every person has a *proairesis*. The term has a history in both Aristotle and Epictetus's ethics, and Chrysostom uses it to refer to the faculty of a person's soul that God created within the person's own control, which cannot be compelled by either God or the devil. Therefore, the *proairesis* is the locus of moral responsibility. God created everyone with freedom and self-determination, lodged in each person's *proairesis*, and for this reason a demon cannot, however much he tempts or deceives, compel a person to sin. By the same token, one must exercise one's *proairesis* for an act to be virtuous. This is further significant because there are people in Chrysostom's congregation who claim the devil has caused their sins. Chrysostom attempts to correct his people's errant understandings by explaining the limitations of the demons' power.

Responding to misplaced blame for sin is not Chrysostom's only objective, however. He is also offering a theodicy. In responding to the suffering in the world and among his congregants, Chrysostom argues that neither God nor the devil is responsible; humans are responsible for suffering. In the line of Methodius, the Cappadocians, and others, Chrysostom

---

[19] Though many translators will approximate προαίρεσις with "free will," I leave it untranslated for two reasons. First, it is of such importance to Chrysostom's thought that it is better to explain how Chrysostom uses it (see below and chap. 5) than to approximate it with a baggage-laden phrase like "free will." Second, "free will" encourages the importation of ideas Chrysostom did not necessarily have, being prior to the Pelagian controversy. Both προαίρεσις and αὐτεξούσιος in Chrysostom's works refer to a lack of compulsion, and for this reason "self-determination" is a better choice than "free will." Where I do not leave it untranslated, τὸ αὐτεξούσιον will be rendered "self-determination," and I will not use the phrase "free will."

[20] This is not to say that these things are not suffering, for they are, and Chrysostom addresses them as such. Yet they are not the cause of true injury, which is sin alone, since sin prohibits salvation and is entirely avoidable.

answers questions of theodicy by having recourse to anthropology. If evil is not God's fault—and Christians hold that it cannot be—then whose fault is it? Chrysostom answers first with his distinction between true and apparent harm and second with his claim that all true harm is the responsibility of the human. What makes Chrysostom different from his predecessors is his injection of demons into the conversation. Demons, like God, are not responsible for true injury (sin), however much they seem to be.

Chapter five is an exegesis of a passage from Chrysostom's *Homiliae in Genesim* 8.6. This passage is a typical homily-ending exhortation to virtue, and it ties together all the themes here discussed. By concluding with this close reading, I intend to show that the purpose of all this information about demons, virtue, and responsibility is aimed at salvation. Chrysostom tells his congregants to use this information to attain their salvation. Moreover, this homily-ending exhortation is typical, which adds insight into the purpose of Chrysostom's homily-ending exhortations to virtue: they are exhortations against temptation and toward salvation.

The exegesis of *Homiliae in Genesim* 8.6 will show that Chrysostom portrays the Christian life as one of struggle with the devil for virtue and salvation. When a person is tempted, she is supposed to remember that she has *proairesis*, spit in the devil's face, and stand tall and virtuous. This is important to Chrysostom because for him virtue is an integral part of salvation. Salvation is a cooperative venture between God and the human being wherein God's work is sufficient, all-encompassing, and primary, but salvation also requires something of the human. God's work is the incarnation, death, and resurrection of Christ, and the human contribution is a virtuous life. This virtue is made possible by God's work, but a person must still make a choice for his salvation and struggle to maintain it in the face of the attacks of the devil, who is the enemy of our salvation. By tempting Christians to sin, the devil and his demons are trying to thwart salvation, but salvation is a matter of a person's *proairesis*.

The study concludes with a reflection on the significance of Chrysostom's narrative for modern Christianity. I look at the current American climate of fear, especially fear of the other, and what Chrysostom's virtuous demonological discourse has to contribute to the conversation. I also touch on the deliverance movement and prosperity gospel in global Christianity.

I raise questions about how Chrysostom might respond to these two strains, given his understanding of demons, responsibility, and salvation. For Chrysostom, everything is connected and the story is simple. Though God woos and the devil tempts, neither God nor the devil compels: God because he does not, and the devil because he cannot. A person must make an active choice. Christ and the devil each try to lead people to their respective homes, and it is up to the Christian to choose whom to follow home each day.

1

Jewish, Pagan, and Christian
Demonology Before Chrysostom

D*AIMŌN* (Δαίμων) is an ambiguous term and an ambiguous spirit in the ancient world. Pagans, Jews, and Christians agreed that spirits called *daimones* (δαίμονες) existed, but they did not agree about what these spirits were or what they did. Some pagans used *daimōn* as a synonym for *theos* (θεός), some used it to refer to the souls of the dead, and some used it to indicate something like a person's conscience. Some ancient writers claimed all *daimones* were good and others that *daimones* were capable of being either good or evil. Jews believed *daimones* to be evil spirits, ontologically similar to angels but in a state of rebellion against God. Christians began with intertestamental understandings of *daimōn* and used the term to refer only to evil spirits. Though ancient Christians' demonologies were not uniform, they did believe all *daimones* to be evil, the enemies of God and of human beings. Christian authors had different narratives about the origin of demons, different ideas about the nature of demons, and different emphases with regard to demonic activities.

There are extant writings from Jewish, pagan, and Christian traditions, and there is also much archaeological evidence of magical artifacts that provide a window into the popular spirituality of the time. There are papyri, gems, amulets, bits of metal, bowls, and other objects inscribed with spells for every realm of life from headaches and fevers to love to protection against evil demons. Most significantly, not only have these items been found in pagan traditions, but there are items distinctly Jewish and Christian as well. Spirits were everywhere in the ancient world, and people wanted to control them. There were also voices that wanted to subdue this magical trade, primarily Christian preachers and bishops. Christian ascetics, even as they too saw a world inhabited by spirits and demons who wanted to harm them at every moment, had an entirely different way of controlling the demons.

This was the lively spirituality John Chrysostom encountered as a fourth-century preacher in Antioch and then Constantinople.[1] Such traditions constituted the ideological milieu in which Chrysostom's congregation lived and in which Chrysostom spoke. Therefore, in order to understand Chrysostom's demonology well, it is necessary to survey Chrysostom's demonological context. This is particularly true because Chrysostom's most elaborate articulation of his demonology is a forceful rejection of the ideas of the laity in his congregation.

JEWISH DEMONOLOGIES

Jewish demonology in the fourth century focused on the activities of demons against human beings more than on their origin or nature, and the spirits known as *daimones*, or demons, were evil.[2] All activities of these spirits were for harm. The demons' maliciousness is explained in both primary narratives of demonic origins, both of which developed in intertestamental literature. The most prominent of these, and that which Chrysostom explicitly rejects, is in 1 Enoch 6–11, expanding on Genesis 6:2. The narrative, called the watchers myth, recounts that Semjaza, the chief angel, saw the daughters of men on earth and lusted after them. Semjaza

---

[1]For more background on the demonological milieu of fourth-century Antioch, see Dayna S. Kalleres, *City of Demons: Violence, Ritual, and Christian Power in Late Antiquity* (Berkeley: University of California Press, 2015), 25-50; and Robert L. Wilken, *John Chrysostom and the Jews: Rhetoric and Reality in the Late 4th Century* (Berkeley: University of California Press, 1983), 12-29. I focus on Antioch because it is where Chrysostom preached *De diab. tent. hom.*, *De proph. obsc.hom.* 3, and the *Cat.*, but the demonology of pagans, Jews, and Christians would not have been markedly different from that in Antioch at this time.

[2]One important exception to the use of δαίμων in an exclusively negative manner was Philo, who used δαίμων as the pagans did, referring to deities and even, at times, to the souls of the dead. Philo also used δαίμων in reference to biblical angels, which Philo further claims were souls: "It is Moses' custom to give the name of angels to those whom other philosophers call demons (or spirits), souls that is which fly and hover in the air" (*On the Giants* 2.6, translation from F. H. Colson and G. H. Whitaker, *Philo*, LCL [Cambridge, MA: Harvard University Press, 1929], 227:449). Philo's influence on Origen makes this a notable point.

convinced a large number of other angels to go down with him and to have intercourse with the women. The rogue angels joined Semjaza and went to earth to sin with women. The sin was not about the lust and intercourse alone, however. Semjaza, Azazel, and Ezeqeel, the three archangels who transgressed, also revealed knowledge of things like astrology and metallurgy to the humans. The author of 1 Enoch writes that the fallen angels "revealed to them [humans] all kinds of sins. And the women have borne giants, and the whole earth has thereby been filled with blood and unrighteousness" (1 Enoch 9:9b-10).[3] These events were a further corruption. Michael was charged with hunting down the fallen angels, binding them, and throwing them into a pit where they will be until the final judgment, when they will go into eternal fire.

The other prominent narrative comes from the Greek *Life of Adam and Eve* 12-17. *Life* claims the devil's jealousy of Adam and Adam's place in creation, and the devil's attempt to make the angels worship him instead, as the reason for the resulting punishment of his fall. In this section of the *Life*, the devil (*ho diabolos* [ὁ διάβολος]) tells the story:

> And when Michael kept forcing me to worship, I said to him, "Why do you compel me? I will not worship one inferior and subsequent to me. I am prior to him in creation; before he was made, I was already made. He ought to worship me." When they heard this, other angels who were under me refused to worship him. . . . And the Lord God was angry with me and sent me with my angels out from our glory; and because of you [Adam], we were expelled into this world from our dwellings and have been cast onto the earth.[4]

The devil's refusal to worship Adam caused his fall. Similar in theme to this story is a verse from the apocryphal Wisdom of Solomon: "Through the devil's envy death entered the world, and those who belong to his company experience it" (Wisdom of Solomon 2:24).

These two origin narratives are the most common in Jewish literature and the two that most often appear in early Christian literature as an explanation for demons' existence. By the fourth century, Jewish literature assumes these

---

[3]Unless otherwise noted, English translations for all pseudepigrapha are from James H. Charlesworth, ed., *Old Testament Pseudepigrapha*, 2 vols. (Garden City, NY: Doubleday, 1983–1985). This quotation is found in Charlesworth, *OTP*, 1:17.
[4]Greek *Life of Adam and Eve* 14:3–16:2, quotation from Charlesworth, *OTP*, 2:262.

narratives and does not speak much about them. Demons exist, and there are reasonable explanations for their existence, but fourth-century Jews were primarily concerned about the activities in which demons engaged, the things for which they were feared.

One account of the nature of demons will suffice to demonstrate the way demons' natures relate to their ability to induce fear. In the Babylonian Talmud Berakhot, the rabbis describe demons as innumerable, invisible, and responsible for difficulties:

> If the eye had the power to see them, no creature could withstand the demons. Said Abaye, "They are more numerous than we and stand around us like the ridge around a field." Said R. Huna, "At the left hand of each one of us is a thousand of them, and at the right hand, ten thousand." Said Raba, . . . "The fact that the clothing of rabbis wears out from rubbing comes on account of them, the bruising of the feet comes from them. If someone wants to know that they are there, take ashes and sprinkle them around the bed, and in the morning he will see something like the footprints of a cock."[5]

Though these demons are invisible, they make footprints in ashes. Footprints imply bodies, as does "rubbing against" the scholars' clothes and wearing them out. Therefore the demons are not incorporeal, even as they are invisible and, according to other statements, spiritual. Note, too, the dark and foreboding tenor of this passage. "No creature could endure seeing them" likely because they were so awful to behold; the demons "surround us," implying an inability to escape the demons. There is a note of fear here, or at least a description of corporeal, though spiritual, demons and their physical harm that are both worth fearing, a theme repeated in this period.[6]

---

[5]b. Berakhot 6a (Neusner, *Talmud*, 1:53). All translations of the Talmud are from Jacob Neusner, ed., *The Talmud of Babylonia: An American Translation*, 36 vols., BJS (Chico, CA: Scholars Press, 1984–1994) unless specified otherwise. The passage quoted continues on to explain how a person can see the demons: "If one wishes to see them, let him take the after-birth of a black she-cat, the offspring of a black she-cat, the first-born of a first-born, let him roast it in fire and grind it to powder, and then let him put some into his eye, and he will see them. Let him also pour it into an iron tube and seal it with an iron signet that they should not steal it from him. Let him also close his mouth, lest he come to harm."

[6]For an excellent survey of the Mishnah's and Talmud's speculation on the nature of demons, see Everett Ferguson, *Demonology of the Early Christian World* (Lewiston, NY: Mellen, 1984), 87-95. Note that the corporeality or incorporeality of demons is not uniform across the sources. This passage is an account of bodily spiritual beings, but other passages describe incorporeal spiritual

The primary feature of the Talmud and Midrash that differs from earlier Jewish sources is that increasingly more sins are attributed to the work of Satan, here a chief demon, than in previous sources.[7] Babylonian Talmud Shabbat claims Satan was responsible for people worshiping the golden calf: "At the end of forty days Satan came along and confounded the world" and convinced the Israelites that Moses was dead.[8] Babylonian Talmud Sanhedrin attributes David's sin with Bathsheba to Satan: "Bath Sheba [*sic*] was shampooing her hair behind a screen. Satan came to [David] and appeared to him in the form of a bird. He shot an arrow at [the screen] and broke it down, so that she stood out in the open, and he saw her."[9] In both cases, Satan makes sin possible, though in neither is Satan the cause of sin. He is responsible only indirectly, for example, for breaking the screen and exposing Bathsheba, but not for possessing David or forcing him to commit adultery. In fact, the rabbi says that David asked God to be tested as Abraham was tested, and God obliged, suggesting a sanctioned adversarial role for Satan not unlike the one in the story of Job. In the case of the golden calf, Satan works independently of God, inciting Aaron for his own purposes rather than for God's. Thus, in terms of agency, Satan tempts and deceives, but the human being commits the sin. The Talmud also records demonic temptations of rabbis, not only interpretations of scriptural narratives:

> R. Meir would ridicule sinners. One day Satan appeared to him on the op-
> posite side of a canal in the form of a woman. There being no ferry, he grabbed

---

beings. In Midrash Rabba, Genesis 7:5, 5d, demons were left "without bodies" because the Sabbath interrupted creation. Whether this passage means only that the demons are spiritual rather than physical or whether it means they are also incorporeal is unclear.

[7]The association of the adversarial *satan* of the Old Testament with the chief demon, the enemy of humanity, has a complex history. Intertestamental literature uses various names for the chief demon: Mastema in Jubilees, Semjaza in 1 Enoch, and Belial in the Dead Sea Scrolls and the *Testament of the Twelve Patriarchs*. Christians would combine the function of the *satan* in the Old Testament with various narratives of the chief demon or fallen angel in intertestamental literature as well as with the New Testament understanding of Satan and the devil, the two terms used interchangeably. This New Testament understanding is that the devil is a being (again the chief opponent) wholly devoted to humanity's destruction, whom Jesus says he saw fall like lightning from heaven (Lk 10:18). The result is the devil of Christian demonology: the leader of a band of fallen angels, the great enemy of God, of God's will, and of humanity.

[8]b. Shabbat 89a (Neusner, *Talmud*, 2C:87).

[9]b. Sanhedrin 107a (Neusner, *Talmud*, 23C:187).

a rope and got across. As he had reached half way down the rope, Satan released him.[10]

Demons appear as instigators of sin, not at all unlike what we will see in Christian monastic literature.

Jews understood demons to be malicious spirits. One talmudic warning reads, "It is forbidden to a man to greet another by night for fear that he is a demon."[11] Demons can also be the explanation for any kind of misfortune, from disease[12] to robbery to death, and for this reason it was not uncommon for Jews in late antiquity to carry amulets or to use incantation bowls and other devices for repelling demons.[13] Jews, no less than pagans—or Christians—worried about what demons could do to a person, what (primarily physical) harm they could inflict, and took the necessary precautions. These amulets and talismans, found in graves, private homes, public spaces, and even in synagogues, demonstrate what precisely people feared demons were capable of doing.[14] Many of the Jewish magical items were either for exorcising demons afflicting a patient or for preventing harm from demons in general, such as in this inscription on an incantation bowl:

---

[10]b. Qiddushin 81a (Neusner, *Talmud*, 19B:171).

[11]b. Megillah 3a. Translation from Isidore Epstein, ed., *The Babylonian Talmud* (London: Soncino, 1961), 4:12.

[12]The most extensive talmudic discussion of demons and ailments they can cause is b. Pesahim 110a-112b. The Talmud also has sections of instructions for remedies for various maladies considered to be the work of demons. For one such representative list, see b. Gittin 69a.

[13]For modern discussion, see J. N. Ford, "Phonetic Spellings of the Subordinating Particle *d(y)* in the Jewish Babylonian Aramaic Magic Bowls," *Aramaic Studies* 10, no. 2 (July 2012): 215-47; Markham J. Geller, "Eight Incantation Bowls," *Orientalia Lovaniensia Periodica* 17 (1986): 101-17; Geller, "Tablets and Magic Bowls," in *Officina Magica: Essays on the Practice of Magic in Antiquity*, ed. Shaul Shaked (Leiden: Brill, 2005), 53-72; Ronald H. Isaacs, *Ascending Jacob's Ladder: Jewish Views of Angels, Demons, and Evil Spirits* (Northvale, NJ: Aronson, 1998), 92-97; Charles D. Isbell, "Story of the Aramaic Magical Incantation Bowls," *BA* 41 (1978): 5-16; Shaul Shaked, "Transmission and Transformation of Spells: The Case of the Jewish Babylonian Aramaic Bowls," in *Continuity and Innovation in the Magical Tradition*, ed. Gideon Bohak, Yuval Harari, and Shaul Shaked (Leiden: Brill, 2011), 187-217; Hershel Shanks, "Magic Incantation Bowls," *Biblical Archaeology Review* 33 (2007): 62; and Edwin M. Yamauchi, "Magic Bowls: Cyrus H. Gordon and the Ubiquity of Magic in the Pre-modern World," *BA* 59 (1996): 51-55. A helpful collection of incantations and inscriptions on amulets, bowls, and other artifacts is Joseph Naveh and Shaul Shaked, *Magic Spells and Formulae: Aramaic Incantations of Late Antiquity* (Jerusalem: Magnes Press, Hebrew University, 1993).

[14]Gideon Bohak describes the various locations in which archaeologists have discovered magical items: Gideon Bohak, *Ancient Jewish Magic: A History* (Cambridge: Cambridge University Press, 2008), 151. See also Giancarlo Lacerenza, "Jewish Magicians and Christian Clients in Late Antiquity: The Testimony of Amulets and Inscriptions," in *What Athens Has to Do with Jerusalem: Essays on Classical, Jewish, and Early Christian Art and Archaeology in Honor of Gideon Foerster*, ed. Leonard V. Rutgers (Leuven: Peeters, 2002), 393-419.

This is the figure of the *mbklt'*-demon who appears in dreams, and in images. Gabriel and Suriel appear to him. This bond is from this day and forever, amen, amen, selah. This strong seal and guarding and sealing of Solomon is for Pana'-Hormiz bar Resanduk and for Bustai bat Givat . . . and for all of their household, their possessions, their food, and all their houses, that they might have favorable healing from heaven in the name of El Saddai.[15]

Other incantations are more specific: "To heal . . . the body of Marian daughter of Sarah and of her fetus that is in her belly . . . Afflictions and enemies . . . That they may have power neither over Marian nor over her fetus."[16] Another reads, "Exorcise the fever and the shiver, the female demons (and) the spirits from the body of Ya'itha the daughter of Marian."[17] And, "I adjure you evil spirit, whether flying or resting, that you should not touch Habibi son of Herta, and that you should not appear to him by any likeness by which you appear to people."[18] These imply that pregnancy complications, fevers, and appearing to people in various guises were common actions of demons.[19] These are all offenses against individuals. Illness is the foremost affliction caused by demons, but there are amulets and bowls for protection of a person's house and for protection against thieves as well, and even one accusing a demon of murder and asking protection against further killing.[20] The magical objects do not refer to natural disasters or events against large communities. The attacks are also primarily, though not exclusively, physical; some refer to dreams, as in the quotation above about "the demon who appears in dreams and in images." Another amulet reads, "I adjure you, spirit . . . you should not be seen to Shlamsu daughter of . . . neither at night nor at daytime."[21]

Such frequent use of these objects and practices led to the Jews having a reputation as magicians.[22] To Jewish clients, Jewish magicians could offer a

---

[15]Aaron Bowl A. Translated and transcribed in Geller, "Eight Incantation Bowls," 106-7.

[16]Amulet 28. Translation from Naveh and Shaked, *Magic Spells and Formulae*, 97.

[17]Amulet 2. Translation from Joseph Naveh and Shaul Shaked, *Amulets and Magic Bowls: Aramaic Incantations of Late Antiquity* (Jerusalem: Magnes Press, Hebrew University, 1985), 45.

[18]Amulet 26. Naveh and Shaked, *Magic Spells and Formulae*, 89.

[19]Other amulets seek protection from premature births. See amulet 30, Naveh and Shaked, *Magic Spells and Formulae*, 102.

[20]Amulet 15. Naveh and Shaked, *Amulets and Magic Bowls*, 105-22.

[21]Amulet 11. Naveh and Shaked, *Amulets and Magic Bowls*, 95.

[22]I admit that *magician* is a freighted term, but I use it here to indicate the extrabiblical nature of these practices. Gideon Bohak begins with the question of whether there can be such a thing as

"kosher" version of magic, and to non-Jewish clients, Jewish magicians could promise powerful and effective techniques and names they had not encountered in their pagan contemporaries. Even Christians were known to seek them out for magical remedies for illnesses or other needs.[23] The world was populated with spirits that could harm physically and sometimes mentally, and people hoped the spirits would not harm them or their families. People wanted protection, a way to ward off these spirits who cause bruises, diseases, and miscarriages.

PAGAN DEMONOLOGIES

Iamblichus (c. 245–325 CE) and Calcidius (early fourth century CE) provide a sketch of fourth-century pagan demonologies. In his *De mysteriis*, Iamblichus describes the various inhabitants of the cosmos: gods, archangels, angels, *daimones*, heroes, and souls. *Daimones* are intermediaries connecting gods with souls since the order and harmony of the universe require that the extremes—gods and souls—be linked.[24] Iamblichus does not explain how *daimones* link gods and souls, but we know that it is not, as for Calcidius a few years later, because *daimones* are immortal like gods but subject to the passions like human beings.[25] Iamblichus is adamant that none of the superior beings—*daimones* included—are passible: "They [superior beings] completely transcend the distinction between passible and impassible, because they do not even possess a nature that is susceptible to passion."[26] Furthermore, Iamblichus is concerned with the spectrum between gods and souls, all "superior beings," rather than gods and humans, as Calcidius is. Iamblichus understands that *daimones* have been given

"Jewish magic" at all (*Ancient Jewish Magic*, 8-69) since it appeals to spiritual beings other than God to act against God's will, seemingly opposing the foundational monotheism of Judaism. Moreover, magic is forbidden by the Torah. Bohak concludes that Jews were practitioners of magic just as much as their contemporaries in the ancient world, as seen in the evidence of Jewish amulets and magic papyri that differ little, and in some cases not at all, from pagan or Christian models.

[23]In fact, this was a major motivation for Chrysostom's homilies *Against the Judaizing Christians* (see especially *Adv. Iud. or.* 1.1; 4.4-5; 8.5, 7). Chrysostom spoke against the false belief Christians had that the Jews' "magic" was more powerful than the Christians' own worship.

[24]Iamblichus, *De mysteriis* 1.5. Translation from Emma C. Clarke, John M. Dillon, and Jackson P. Hershbell, eds., *Iamblichus: De mysteriis* (Leiden: Brill, 2004), 22-23.

[25]Calcidius, *Commentarius* 131. Translation from J. den Boeft, *Calcidius on Demons: (Commentarius Ch. 127–136)* (Leiden: Brill, 1977), 26.

[26]Iamblichus, *De mysteriis* 1.10. Clarke, Dillon, and Hershbell, *Iamblichus*, 42-43.

administration "over certain restricted portions of the cosmos," and they are also in service to the gods and must do what they command.[27]

Iamblichus claims that *daimones*, like the other "superior beings," are able to manifest themselves to human beings, and he spends considerable time describing the effects of such a manifestation so that humans may be able to recognize when they are seeing a *daimōn*. *Daimones* may appear in any shape or size, will be accompanied by "tumult and disorder," will be obscure, and "glow with smouldering fire." There are both good and wicked *daimones*, but most of Iamblichus's work concerns *daimones* in general. Toward the end of *De mysteriis*, Iamblichus explains the personal *daimōn* each person's soul has, which the soul has chosen to be its guide:

> It [the *daimōn*] stands over it as the fulfiller of the various levels of the life of the soul, and as the soul descends into the body it binds it to the body, and it supervises the composite living being arising from it, and personally regulates the particulars of the life of the soul; and all our reasonings we pursue thanks to the first principles which it communicates to us, and we perform such actions as it puts into our minds; and it continues to direct men's lives up to the point at which, through sacred theurgy, we establish a god as the overseer and leader of our soul; for then it either withdraws in deference to the superior principle, or surrenders its administrative role, or subordinates itself so as to contribute to the god's direction of the soul, or in some other way comes to serve it as master.[28]

The *daimōn* is a guide that directs the soul where it needs to go, even so far as putting thoughts in a person's mind, until it can deliver the soul to a being higher than itself, to a god. Here is a guiding *daimōn* who is good, an echo of Socrates's *diamonion*.

Calcidius, too, like Iamblichus, claims that *daimones* have charge over humanity. As mentioned, Calcidius also understands *daimones* as necessary intermediary beings, though between the extremes of gods and humans rather than gods and souls.[29] *Daimones* are immortal and passible, and their passible nature is what makes them care for humans.[30] Calcidius even gives a definition of *daimones*: "A demon is a rational, immortal, sensitive, ethereal

---

[27]Iamblichus, *De mysteriis* 1.20. Clarke, Dillon, and Hershbell, *Iamblichus*, 76-79.
[28]Iamblichus, *De mysteriis*, 9.6. Clarke, Dillon, and Hershbell, *Iamblichus*, 334-37.
[29]Calcidius, *Comm.* 131. Boeft, *Calcidius*, 26.
[30]Calcidius, *Comm.* 131. Boeft, *Calcidius*, 26-27.

living being taking care of men."[31] Like the beings Jews call angels, *daimones* take humans' prayers to God and make God's will known to humans.[32] Calcidius is primarily concerned with these good *daimones*, who watch over and take care of humanity, but he does mention wicked ones also, who can act as avengers of "crimes and impiety according to the sanctions of divine justice."[33] This description of wicked *daimones'* activities—the only one Calcidius provides—implies a limit: they are subject to "the sanctions of divine justice." Thus, though the moral status of *daimones* is ambiguous, even the wicked *daimones* are not unrestrainedly wicked. Calcidius prefers to speak of the good *daimones* who watch over humanity.

Beyond the more formal descriptions of Iamblichus and Calcidius, there were popular expressions of demonology as well. Pagan cults were still in existence, though sacrifices and mystic rituals were much less common than they had been in prior centuries. Libanius, Chrysostom's own teacher, was a strong advocate for classical pagan worship.[34] Another of Libanius's students, Emperor Julian (c. 331–363), was mocked even by pagans for his excessive piety. Julian saw himself as returning the empire to its old religion and promoted sacrifices, cults, and other rituals intended to seek the favor of the gods. In his *Letter to a Priest*, Julian tells the priest his job is to "take care to exhort men not to transgress the laws of the gods, since those are sacred."[35] Just prior to this, Julian writes about evil demons who punish those who do not sacrifice to the true gods:

> The tribe of evil demons is appointed to punish those who do not worship the gods. . . . Some men there are also who . . . seek out desert places instead of cities, since they have been given over to evil demons. . . . And many of them have even devised fetters and stocks to wear; to such a degree does the evil demon to whom they have of their own accord given themselves abet them in all ways, after they have rebelled against the everlasting and saving gods.[36]

[31]Calcidius, *Comm.* 135a. Boeft, *Calcidius*, 36.

[32]Calcidius, *Comm.* 132. Boeft, *Calcidius*, 28.

[33]Calcidius, *Comm.* 135b. Boeft, *Calcidius*, 37.

[34]Christine Kondoleon, *Antioch: The Lost Ancient City* (Princeton, NJ: Princeton University Press, 2000), 17-20; and Aideen M. Hartney, *John Chrysostom and the Transformation of the City* (London: Duckworth, 2004), 6-7.

[35]Julian, *Letter to a Priest* 288c. Translation from Wilmer Cave France Wright, ed., *The Works of the Emperor Julian*, LCL 29 (New York: Macmillan, 1913), 2:298-99.

[36]Julian, *Letter to a Priest* 288b. Wright, *Works of the Emperor Julian*, 2:296-97.

Julian sees demons as servants of the gods. Though the first part of the letter has been lost, Julian's designation of the punishing demons as "evil" suggests that he believed there were also good demons.

People used *daimōn* to refer to any divine or occult power when it was impossible or undesirable to attribute a given event to a specific deity.[37] *Daimones* caused illness, disease, and natural disaster. Additionally, *diabolos* (διάβολος) does not appear in ancient pagan literature, nor does a concept of a chief *daimōn*. The devil is a peculiarly Judeo-Christian figure. People made sacrifices to *daimones* in order to placate them and to curry favor since the *daimones* could not only cause evil to befall a person but were also capable of conferring prosperity. Just as the amulets do in Jewish traditions, various Greek magical papyri and other magical texts allow a glimpse at popular Greek religion. Common were curse tablets, or *defixiones*, thin sheets of lead or other metal with a magic inscription, often rolled or folded and either worn or deposited somewhere said to be effective for the particular kind of spell. Often these spells were either for inducing a person to fall in love with the spell caster or for invoking harm to one's enemies.[38] For instance, one *defixione* reads, "Rouse yourselves, you *daimones* who lie here and seek out Euphemia. . . . Let her not be able to sleep for the entire night, but lead her until she comes to his feet, loving him with a frenzied love, with affection and with sexual intercourse."[39] This particular example has a lengthy inscription, invoking the *daimones* several times to bring the desired woman to the man who used this *defixione*. Some of the *defixiones* seem to be written by amateurs, possibly by the user himself, but others appear to be written by professional scribes, often even written in advance, with a blank left for the name of the client.[40] Magic texts were a common trade. Many of

---

[37]Ian Kidd suggests that it was the vagueness of the term δαίμων that made it so useful among pagans. Ian Kidd, "Some Philosophical Demons," *Bulletin of the Institute of Classical Studies* 40, no. 1 (1995): 218.

[38]See the introduction to John G. Gager, ed., *Curse Tablets and Binding Spells from the Ancient World* (Oxford: Oxford University Press, 1992), for nuances in the various uses of such *defixiones* and spells. For instance, Gager notes that some *defixiones* have been found nailed to the floor at a racetrack, implying that people believed the spirits could interfere at the races.

[39]No. 30, quoted in Gager, *Curse Tablets*, 103.

[40]An excellent book on the magicians and sorcerers themselves is Matthew W. Dickie, *Magic and Magicians in the Greco-Roman World* (London: Routledge, 2001). Dickie surveys what kinds of people were engaged in peddling magical items as well as who was accused of magical practices. He concludes that though sorcerers were often women, they did come from every demographic:

these tablets called on the gods, not *daimones*, but many were left in or near graves, with the understanding that the souls of the departed would help carry out the curse or spell. They speak to the magical world populated with spirits in which the Greeks lived, spirits who constantly interact with human beings but whose actions may be either malicious or beneficent and require proper attention from humans to ensure good treatment.

CHRISTIAN DEMONOLOGIES

At the popular level, Christians thought about demons much the same way their Jewish and pagan neighbors did. Demons were the spirits who populated their world and could be assuaged or incited, so Christians, like their neighbors, used various magical items to control demons and keep them from causing harm. Christian theologians, bishops, and other leaders, on the other hand, developed more formal demonologies and tried to temper their audiences' background fear of demons. For simplicity, I divide these leaders into theologians and ascetics.[41] Origen and the Cappadocian fathers serve as representatives of the theologians, and Antony and various collections of sayings serve as the ascetics. Both groups are voices heard by Chrysostom and his congregation.[42]

Origen. Though he is not a fourth-century writer, Origen's (c. 182–254 CE) influence on the Greek theologians of the fourth century and Chrysostom's relation to the Origenist controversies, as well as his significance in the development of Christian demonology, make his demonology worth noting in brief. Origen wrote the first developed, explicit Christian demonology, and this account is a fusion of pagan, Jewish, and Christian thought about demons. His biggest contribution to Christian demonology regards the

---

women, men, poor, rich, uneducated, educated, pagan, Jewish, Christian. This may be one more reason to think the clients also came from all manner of society.

[41]I do not, by this distinction, imply that ascetics are not theologians or that theologians do not have ascetic practices and inclinations. By *theologians* I refer to the group of writers who wrote formally of theology, often using philosophical language, and by *ascetics* I refer to those referred to as monks, who wrote little but had much written about them.

[42]I mean by this that traditions and ways of thinking of the Cappadocians and ascetics were known to Chrysostom and his congregation rather than that any particular writing was known. Scholars still debate any direct link between the Cappadocians and Chrysostom, and much of the written accounts of ascetics came about after Chrysostom's death. However, I use these groups as representatives. Given the similarity of thought between them, I claim that they are voices Chrysostom and his audience would have heard in some capacity.

origin of demons. Origen accepts that demons are some kind of fallen spiritual being, but his origin narrative has a distinctively pagan flavor to it. Instead of a narrative similar to intertestamental accounts and those told by first- and second-century Christians, where the fall of Satan and his angels occurs after the creation of the earth, Origen, in his *De principiis* 3.2, claims that the rogue angels' fall was pre-cosmic. Origen has a theory of preexistent minds or intelligences (*noes*, νόες) that rebelled against God, their creator, and thus fell. What the minds became when they fell depended on how deep their sin was. The worst minds became demons, the next became souls, and the best became angels. Origen writes,

> Before the ages minds were all pure, both daemons and souls and angels, offering service to God and keeping his commandments. But the devil, who was one of them, since he possessed free-will, desired to resist God, and God drove him away. With him revolted all the other powers. Some sinned deeply and became daemons, others less and became angels; others still less and became archangels; and thus each in turn received the reward for his individual sin. But there remained some souls who had not sinned so greatly as to become daemons, nor on the other hand so very lightly as to become angels. God therefore made the present world and bound the soul to the body as a punishment.[43]

In telling of preexistent minds that fell and became angels, demons, and souls, Origen's narrative resembles pagan narratives, in particular the Plutarchian narrative, more than 1 Enoch's description.[44] Plutarch recounts the movements of souls that enter bodies, depart bodies, and sometimes enter new bodies; 1 Enoch tells of spiritual beings, not minds, who look on the creatures of earth and who lust. First Enoch's fallen angels initially descend to earth voluntarily, whereas Plutarch's souls waft around in the air and

---

[43]Origen, *De principiis* 1.8.1. Translation from Origen, *On First Principles: Being Koetschau's Text of the* De principiis, trans. G. W. Butterworth (1936; repr., Gloucester, MA: Peter Smith, 1973), 67. Greek text from *Origenes Werke*, ed. Paul Koetschau, GCS 22 (Leipzig: Hinrich, 1899), 5:96. Critical edition is Origen, *Traité des principes*, ed. and trans. Henri Crouzel and Manlio Simonetti, 5 vols., SC 252-53, 268-69, 312 (Paris: Cerf, 1978). The issues of the reliability of the *Princ.* text are well known. Can Rufinus's translation be trusted to give us Origen's unmodified thought? Scholars disagree. With regard to the passages at hand, I use a comparison of the Greek text to the critical edition in order to use the best scholarship has to offer at present. At any rate, I am interested in Chrysostom's appropriation of the tradition more than Origen's thought in itself.

[44]Plutarch's demonology is located primarily in *De facie lunae* 28-30 and *De defectu oraculorum* 39.

hope not to fall too low. Origen's demons, like Plutarch's, sinned above the earth, not on its surface. Origen's narrative is also similar to Plutarch's in that the degree of descent is proportional to the degree of sin, or ethical behavior, just as the just and unjust souls ascend or descend according to their deeds.[45] After Origen, the standard Greek Christian demonological narrative is that demons are "fallen angels," and the fall occurred before the creation of the rest of the world. Competing narratives about where demons come from disappear at this point. The fall was a rebellion of angels against God; the angel's motive of rebellion was pride; the watchers myth plays no part in the narrative. This is a significant point for demonology. In the watchers myth, according to some Christian readings, Justin Martyr's among them, demons are the progeny of miscreant angels and human women, which means that demons are born evil. In Origen's explanation, demons were created good by God but became evil by their own will. Following Origen, Christians would hold that demons are not evil by nature, only by choice.

By contemporary standards Origen gives a lengthy description of the nature of demons, and his description is similar to pagan descriptions. Origen writes that demons have ethereal or "airy" bodies and that they feed on the smoke of sacrifices: "This body is by nature a fine substance and thin like air."[46] The more they feed, the fatter they become; the fatter they become, the farther they fall. If the demons fall too close to earth, they become dangerous, because that is when demons are able to do harm to human beings. Thus, Origen says, do not feed the demons by sacrificing (presumably to pagan gods). Origen has continued the Jewish-Christian demonological tradition of holding that demons are evil spiritual beings and identified with pagan gods, but he adds that demons have bodies, or that they are not incorporeal just because they are invisible.[47]

About the activities of demons Origen has nothing new to add to prior Jewish-Christian accounts, and theologians will continue to ascribe the same activities to demons. Origen writes, "We must now see how, according

[45]An excellent article comparing Origen's demonology with Plutarch's is Toshio Mikoda, "A Comparison of the Demonologies of Origen and Plutarch," in *Origeniana Quinta: Papers of the 5th International Origen Congress, 1989*, ed. Robert J. Daly (Leuven: University Press, 1992), 326-32.
[46]Origen, *Princ.* preface 8. Butterworth, *On First Principles*, 5.
[47]Origen, *Princ.* 5.

to the scriptures, the opposing powers and the devil himself are engaged in a struggle with the human race, provoking and inciting men to sin."[48] Similar to Irenaeus and Tertullian, Origen asserts that demons are able to tempt but not force human beings to sin. Origen also emphasizes the Christian's free will and responsibility, though he does list Judas's betrayal of Christ as an act of a demon, probably because of John's statement that "after he received the piece of bread, Satan entered into him" (Jn 13:27). Origen also says that "Christ was crucified by 'the princes of this world,' who are 'coming to nought.'"[49] After cataloging demonic activities that, apart from entering Judas and crucifying Christ, involve only temptation, deception, and persuasion at the acquiescence of humans, Origen writes,

> Through all these instances, therefore, the divine scripture teaches us that there are certain invisible enemies fighting against us, and it tells us that we must be armed to meet them. This leads the simpler sort of believers in Christ the Lord to suppose that all the sins that men have committed come from the persistent influence of the contrary powers on the sinners' minds, because in this invisible contest the powers are found to be superior.[50]

The "simpler" folk believe the devil and his demons are too persistent; they wear down the weaker human beings. The invisible powers seem to such folk to be superior to anything a human being can do, so the devil and his demons win, and humans sin. Origen says that demons are not stronger than humans: "We however, who look more carefully into the reason of things, do not think that this is so."[51] Demons do fight against human beings, but they are not stronger.

---

[48]Origen, *Princ.* 3.2.1. Butterworth, *On First Principles*, 211.
[49]Origen, *Princ.* 3.2.1. Butterworth, *On First Principles*, 213. Origen is quoting from 1 Cor 2:6-8: "Yet among the mature we do speak wisdom, though it is not a wisdom of this age or of the rulers of this age, who are doomed to perish. But we speak God's wisdom, secret and hidden, which God decreed before the ages for our glory. None of the rulers of this age understood this; for if they had, they would not have crucified the Lord of glory." The immediate context of 1 Cor 2 suggests the "rulers of this age" are the earthly authorities, but Origen reads the passage in conjunction with Eph 6:12: "For our struggle is not against enemies of blood and flesh, but against the rulers, against the authorities, against the cosmic powers of this present darkness, against the spiritual forces of evil in the heavenly places." This juxtaposition leads him to understand "rulers of this age" to mean "the cosmic powers of this present darkness" and to suggest that these were the true agents of Christ's crucifixion.
[50]Origen, *Princ.* 3.2.1. Butterworth, *On First Principles*, 213.
[51]Origen, *Princ.* 3.2.2. Butterworth, *On First Principles*, 213.

The Cappadocians. The Cappadocian fathers were predecessors of Chrysostom who also lived and wrote in Asia Minor. Basil of Caesarea, Gregory of Nyssa, and Gregory of Nazianzus wrote less about demons than did the ascetic traditions, and, as with most of their predecessors, the demonic rhetoric they did use is scattered throughout their writings. However, a few relevant things may be said about their demonology. First, Satan is the chief demon who was created good by God but who fell by pride or envy— Gregory of Nazianzus alone cites both motives—and caused others to fall with him.[52] Also as with their predecessors, the Cappadocians identified the pagan gods as demons.[53] All three Cappadocians held that God won victory over demons in Christ, that God allowed demons still to roam the earth willing evil, and that God would have final victory over the demons at the end of all things.[54] Most significant here is that the Cappadocians believed God allowed humans to cooperate with demons to do evil, a theme that Chrysostom will emphasize. Basil writes, "The demons, who are enemies of all that is good, use for their own ends such [human] free acts (*proaireseis*, προαιρέσεις) as they find congenial to their wishes."[55] Humans have the *proairesis* to work with demons, and demons take full advantage of it with constant temptations.

As with prior Christian tradition, the Cappadocians know the demons' primary objective is to prevent humans' salvation. Gregory of Nazianzus writes, "[The devil] utterly hates the wise of heart, and shuts off all heaven's

---

[52]Gregory of Nazianzus, *Carm.* 1.1.7.68-69, 73-77 (PG 37.443) (pride): "After arrogance destroyed him [the devil] there fell with him a multitude"; 1.1.7.56-66 (PG 37.443) (envy): "Because of this he cast them out of paradise, the envier, in his lust for a glory equaling God's." English from Gregory of Nazianzus, *On God and Man: The Theological Poetry of St. Gregory of Nazianzus*, trans. Peter Gilbert (Crestwood, NY: St. Vladimir's Seminary Press, 2001), 59, 60. Compare Gregory of Nyssa, *Lucif. res.* 4 (GNO 9:311); *In cant. cant.* (GNO 6:166, 421); *Or. catech.* 5-8 (GNO 3/4:15-36). The first two cited passages of Nyssa's accounts speak only of a fall, not of the fall's cause. In the *Or. catech.* 5-8, however, envy is given as the reason for Satan's fall.

[53]For a sample, see Nazianzus, *Or.* 31.16; Basil of Caesarea, *Ep.* 8.3; *Ep.* 217.81; Nyssa, *Or. catech.* 18 (GNO 3/4:50-52).

[54]The three Cappadocians do not agree about the details of this final victory. Gregory of Nyssa follows Origen and argues all demons will be transformed and redeemed in the end (Nyssa, *Anim. et res.* [PG 46:72]); Basil rejects Origen's universalism and claims God will use demons as the agents of his eternal wrath (Basil, *Hom. in Ps.* [PG 29:369]); and Gregory of Nazianzus also argues that demons are "God's agents of punishment in hell" (Morwenna Ludlow, "Demons, Evil and Liminality in Cappadocian Theology," *JECS* 20, no. 2 [2012]: 185) and those against whom humans struggle in this life in order to be purified (Nazianzus, *Carm.* 1.1.6.88-95).

[55]Basil, *Hom. invid.* (PG 31:380; FC 9:470).

ways, maddened at his disfigurement. Nor did he wish God's creature to draw near to the divinity whence he'd fallen, since he longed to have humans with him in a common sin and darkness."[56] According to Gregory of Nyssa, Gregory Thaumaturgus refers to the devil as "the demon who is the enemy of the true religion."[57] And Basil writes in his *Homiliae super Psalmos*, "Plotting as an enemy, again he deceives the victims of his plots into thinking that they should flee to him as to a protector. Consequently, a twofold evil surrounds them, since they are either seized by force or destroyed by deceit. Therefore, the unbelievers flee to demons and idols, having the knowledge of the true God snatched away by the confusion which is produced in them by the devil."[58]

Demons could also take up residence in one's soul in the form of demonic possession. Speaking of postbaptismal sin and referring to Luke 11:24-26, Gregory of Nazianzus writes,

> But if it [the evil spirit] finds the place in you "swept and adorned," empty and unused, equally ready to receive whoever takes it first, it bursts in, enters and dwells there with a larger entourage. And "the last condition becomes worse than the first," inasmuch as then there was hope of correction and safety, but now evil is manifest, the flight from the good attracts the bad, and because of this the inhabitant's possession is somehow more secure.[59]

Gregory uses the case of demons taking up residence in the soul as a direct contrast to God's divine indwelling, spoken of a few lines earlier.

---

[56]Gregory of Nazianzus, *Carm.* 1.1.7.61-65 (PG 37.443; Gilbert, 59). Gregory writes in *Or.* 40.37 that there are two kinds of light: "The one is a lamp for our directive faculty, making straight our steps according to God. The other is deceptive and meddling and opposed to the true light while pretending to be that light, that it may defraud through its appearance" (SC 358bis, 282). English from Gregory of Nazianzus, *Festal Orations: St. Gregory of Nazianzus*, trans. Nonna Verna Harrison (Crestwood, NY: St. Vladimir's Seminary Press, 2008), 132.

[57]Gregory of Nyssa, *V. Gr. Thaum.* (PG 46:937; FC 98:71-72).

[58]Basil, *Hom. in Ps.* 45 (PG 29:416-17; FC 46:298).

[59]Gregory of Nazianzus, *Or.* 40.35 (SC 358bis, 27; Harrison, *Festal Orations*, 131). Dayna S. Kalleres focuses on Gregory's understanding of the human being as an impression to say that Gregory was concerned with the thoughts, words, logic, and other sophistries demons used to snatch away a person's salvation and restoration to the divine image. Kalleres does not mention the possibility of possession in the sense of a demon entirely taking over a human's soul and body but emphasizes the intellectual nature of demonic attacks. Though her argument about Gregory's understanding of demonic attacks is sound, it is deficient for delineating a more complete understanding of possession, i.e., what Gregory means by demons inhabiting the soul. See Dayna S. Kalleres, "Demons and Divine Illumination: A Consideration of Eight Prayers by Gregory of Nazianzus," *VC* 61 (2007): 157-88.

Where Christ indwells a person, the evil spirit cannot enter. In contrast to Gregory's understanding of an external spirit taking possession of a person's soul in a literal reading of Scripture, Basil's talk of possession has a tendency to use the terms *daimōn* and *pathos* (πάθος) ambiguously, so it is unclear whether the demon of anger is a demon or a passion *in* the soul, as in his *On Those Prone to Anger*:

> [Anger] is a malady upon the soul, a dark mist over the reason. It brings es-
> trangement from God. . . . It is a wicked demon coming to birth in our very
> souls, taking prior possession of our interior . . . and barring entrance to the
> Holy Spirit. Whenever there are enmities, strifes, bursts of anger, intrigues,
> rivalries, causing restless agitation in the soul, there the Spirit of Meekness
> does not take His rest.[60]

Here, too, God and a demon cannot simultaneously indwell a human being.

Antony. Asceticism had a strong influence on the popular imagination in the fourth and fifth centuries. People often went out to see the monks in their "natural habitat," either as a trip to view exotic Christians out of curiosity or as a form of pilgrimage to see the holy men and learn from them. Many accounts speak of Christians visiting monks in order to receive general spiritual wisdom, advice about a specific problem, or even a judgment on a dispute. The collections of sayings and lives, then, were also popular. With so much interaction, the popular imagination absorbed some aspects of ascetic demonologies. Moreover, ascetic traditions had great influence on Chrysostom. He spent years as a monk himself in the mountains outside Antioch, and Chrysostom exhorted his congregation to visit the monks on the outskirts of the city, learning from them as exemplars of virtue.

Antony the Great, considered the "father of desert monasticism," holds a place of prominence in the ascetic tradition.[61] Patristic literature presents us

---

[60]Basil, *Hom. adv. ira.* (PG 31:372; FC 9:460-61).

[61]I spend this time on Antony because of the prominence of the Antony tradition in asceticism rather than because of any known influence on Chrysostom. Though a definitive link between Egyptian and Syrian ascetic traditions has not been established, it is likely that Chrysostom knew both the *Life* and *Sayings* traditions of Antony through his own contact with asceticism and Syrian monasticism. In particular, Chrysostom's own understanding of Job and in what way demons are powerless are similar enough to what Athanasius reports in the *Life of Antony* that Chrysostom either knows the source, knows another work that knows the source, or shares a common tradition with the source. It is impossible to know whether Chrysostom had knowledge of Antony's letters.

with three very different Antonys:[62] (1) Antony the author of the *Letters of Antony*; (2) Antony as portrayed by Athanasius in his *Life of Antony*; and (3) Antony the Great as presented in the various collections of the *Sayings of the Desert Fathers*. I treat the first two here, but because the Antony of the *Sayings* is not different in any significant way from the other abbas mentioned in the collection, I treat that Antony as part of the sayings tradition.

Antony's sixth letter focuses on demonology and shows a distinct Origenian influence. Antony writes, "They [demons] are, moreover, all from one (source) in their spiritual essence; but through their flight from God great diversity has arisen between them since their deeds are varying. Therefore all these names have been imposed on them after the deeds of each one."[63] Antony goes on to say that those who "kept the will of their Creator" are named "archangels . . . thrones and dominions, principalities, powers and cherubim," but "due to the wickedness of the conduct of others it was necessary to name them devil and Satan. . . . Others are called demons, evil and impure spirits, spirits of seduction and powers of this world, and there are many other varieties among them."[64] Antony even talks of a categorization of names for classes of humans, which also resulted from this fall: "patriarchs . . . prophets and kings and priests and judges and apostles."[65] This echoes Origen's description of the minds that fell to different degrees as a result of various degrees of sin, resulting in diversity. Antony's

---

[62]Current scholarship holds that the historical Antony was born about 252 CE at Koma in Heracleopolis in Middle Egypt, a fact scholars draw from Sozomen's recording (*Historia Ecclesiastica* 1.13, 2), and both the *Life* and Jerome record Antony's death in 356. Other events and the movements of Antony's life—from the outskirts of his village to a tomb to Alexandria—are reconstructed from the *Life*, but very few details are known with certainty. A good summary of the historical Antony is found in Vincent Desprez, "Saint Anthony and the Beginnings of Anchoritism," *American Benedictine Review* 43 (1992): 72-73; and an excellent critical discussion about both the historical Antony and the scholarship on him is Samuel Rubenson, *The Letters of St. Antony: Monasticism and the Making of a Saint* (Minneapolis: Fortress, 1995), 9-12.

[63]Antony, Letter 6. Translation from Rubenson, *Letters of St. Antony*, 220. Rubenson makes the case that Antony's letters were originally written in Coptic and quickly translated into Greek; we have fragments in both Coptic and Greek. The only full versions we have are in Arabic, Georgian, and Latin. Rubenson made his English translation from a critical comparison and use of all extant manuscripts ("on the basis of all the extant versions"), and so I do not hesitate to use the English here. For a full discussion of both the extant versions and Rubenson's own translation, see Rubenson, *Letters of St. Antony*, 15-34, 196. Rubenson's book is the definitive work on Antony's letters.

[64]Antony, Letter 6. Rubenson, *Letters of St. Antony*, 220.

[65]Rubenson, *Letters of St. Antony*, 220.

explanation makes no mention at all of the watchers myth or envy-of-Adam tradition. Athanasius's Antony, when speaking to a group of the brothers about demons, mentions that the demons "were not always called 'demons' and did not come into being as demons, for God has made nothing bad. No, they too came into being good, but when they fell from heavenly wisdom, from that time on they wandered the earth."[66] In the next sentence, Antony further refers to heaven as "the place from which they fell."[67] This is vague, but it shows that Antony considers demons to be fallen angels, created good. Athanasius also writes, "There is . . . a great crowd of them [demons] in the air around us. . . . There are great differences among them."[68] This, too, sounds not unlike Origen's diversity of fallen minds.

Antony is also similar to Origen regarding the nature of demons. Antony's sixth letter speaks of demons as invisible and spiritual, but if the monk does not put on his rational mind and be vigilant, if he gives the demon a place, the monk will become the demon's body: "They are not visible bodily. But you should know that we are their bodies, and that our soul receives their wickedness; and when it has received them, then it reveals them through the body in which we dwell."[69] In the *Life*, Antony, again in his speech to the brothers, says that the demons have bodies "more subtle than humans possess."[70] Demons can pretend to prophesy, or to predict the future, by running exceedingly fast because they are so subtle and thin. Antony says, "If someone begins to walk from the Thebaid . . . the demons do not know before he sets out walking whether he will walk. But when they see this person on his way, they run on ahead and, before he arrives, report it."[71] From Athanasius's Antony we also learn that demons are invisible but can become visible. They can take the form of women, "black boys," beasts, and all kinds of creatures.

The stories of physical struggle against demons in the *Life of Antony* provide a glimpse of demonic interaction with human beings. As with prior

[66] Athanasius, *Life of Antony* 22.1-2 (Greek *Life*, SC 400bis, 194-196). English from Athanasius, *Life of Antony*, trans. Tim Vivian and Apostolos N. Athanassakis with Rowan A. Greer (Kalamazoo, MI: Cistercian, 2003), 111. All subsequent references will be to the Greek rather than the Coptic *Life* for simplicity.
[67] Athanasius, *Life of Antony* 22.1-2 (SC 400bis, 194-196; Vivian and Athanassakis, *Life of Antony*, 111).
[68] Atanasius, *Life of Antony* 21.4 (SC 400bis, 194; Vivian and Athanassakis, *Life of Antony*, 109).
[69] Antony, Letter 6 (Rubenson, *Letters of St. Antony*, 219).
[70] Athanasius, *Life of Antony* 31.2 (SC 400bis, 220; Vivian and Athanassakis, *Life of Antony*, 129).
[71] Athanasius, *Life of Antony* 31.5 (SC 400bis, 222; Vivian and Athanassakis, *Life of Antony*, 129).

Jewish and Christian tradition, Antony understands the demons' goal to be the thwarting of salvation. Athanasius has Antony say to the brothers, "The [demons] envy us Christians and create all sorts of disturbances, wishing to impede us on our way to heaven."[72] Antony continues to speak of the various wiles by which the demons attempt their hindrance: suggesting filthy thoughts to the monks; fabricating apparitions of women, beasts, reptiles, and armies; pretending to prophesy; deception; throwing their voices or speaking without becoming visible; appearing as monks in order to deceive.[73] In addition to these machinations, the *Life* speaks of the physical brutality the demons wrought on Antony, beating him without mercy.[74] Thus, in the *Life*, demons' activities are both external and internal to the monk. By contrast, the Antony of the *Letters* says that the demons' attacks are all internal, that is, psychological or spiritual. Letter 6 gives a long list of psychological means that demons use. It includes

> evil counsel, their secret persecution, their subtle malice, their spirits of seduction, their fraudulent thoughts, their faithlessness which they sow in our hearts every day . . . all their wrath, the mutual slander which they teach us, our self-justifications in our deeds, and the condemnations they sow in our hearts . . . the contempt they send into our hearts through pride so that we become hard-hearted and despise one another . . . and they incite us to do things which we are unable to do and whose time it is not, and make us weary of things we do and which are good for us.[75]

Both the *Letters* and the *Life*, though, insist that the demons are powerless. As with Origen, Athanasius's Antony claims that the demons only cause wickedness in persons when they open their souls to the demon. He says that demons "make us their slaves" through deceit and "fill our hearts with all these [evil thoughts and inclinations]," but this happens because "we feed on them and they become our food."[76] Antony tells the brothers, "We have

---

[72]Athanasius, *Life of Antony* 22.2 (SC 400bis, 194-96; Vivian and Athanassakis, *Life of Antony*, 111).

[73]Athanasius, *Life of Antony* 23.1-25.4 (SC 400bis, 198; Vivian and Athanassakis, *Life of Antony*, 111-19).

[74]Athanasius, *Life of Antony* 8.1-10.4 (SC 400bis, 156-64; Vivian and Athanassakis, *Life of Antony*, 79-85).

[75]Antony, Letter 6 (Rubenson, *Letters of St. Antony*, 218).

[76]Antony, Letter 6 (Rubenson, *Letters of St. Antony*, 218). In Stoic terms, demons can make an "impression" that triggers an impulse, but they cannot make a person consent to that impulse. Antony is neither using Stoic vocabulary nor making any explicit reference to Stoic thought, but

no need to fear them [demons], even if they seem (*dokōsi*, δοκῶσι) to be assaulting us, even if they are threatening us with death, for they are weak and are unable to do anything but make threats."[77] The demons only "seem" to be assaulting the monks, including Antony.[78]

Antony then speaks of Job to explain further the demons' powerlessness. In the *Life*, Job's function is to highlight God's superiority over the devil, for

---

the Stoic way of explaining this motion is helpful for understanding. For more Stoic echoes in Antony, see David Brakke, *Demons and the Making of the Monk: Spiritual Combat in Early Christianity* (Cambridge, MA: Harvard University Press, 2006), 52-55. Brakke draws from Barnes's analysis in Michel R. Barnes, "Galen and Antony: Anger and Disclosure," in *Studia Patristica: Biblica et Apocrypha, Ascetica, Liturgica*, ed. E. A. Livingstone, vol. 30 (Leuven: Peeters, 1996), 136-43. This vocabulary will be further helpful as we see resonances of Stoic anthropology in Chrysostom's works.

[77] Athanasius, *Life of Antony* 27.5 (SC 400bis, 210; Vivian and Athanassakis, *Life of Antony*, 121).

[78] Most often Athanasius uses some form of the verb δύναμαι with the negative μή or οὐ to explain that the demons are unable to do something or anything. For example, μηδὲν δυνάμενος (*Life of Antony* 28.2) or μηδὲν δύνασθαι ποιεῖν (*Life of Antony* 28.6). Athanasius will also say that demons are "weak" (ἀσθενεῖς) or "not strong" (εἰσι μηδὲν ἰσχύοντες, *Life of Antony* 28.5). However, most readers would understand the demons' ability to inflict πληγάς on Antony as a form of power. Athanasius's Antony appears to say that demons are powerless to harm. Athanasius provides the logic: "[Demons] desire to do evil and are ready to do harm. . . . Nevertheless, we are still alive; what is more, we live our lives in opposition to them. Therefore, they clearly have no power at all" (*Life of Antony* 28.5; SC 400bis, 212; Vivian and Athanassakis, *Life of Antony*, 123). The Greek is Εἰσὶ δὲ κακοθελεῖς καὶ πρὸς τὸ βλάπτειν ἕτοιμοι. . . . ζῶμεν δὲ νῦν ἡμεῖς καὶ μᾶλλον κατ᾿αὐτοῦ πολιτευόμεθα, δῆλοί εἰσι μηδὲν ἰσχύοντες. Vivian and Athanassakis translate the κατ᾿αὐτοῦ as "against them," when properly it should be "against him." In the excised portion, Antony includes a quotation from Jesus about the devil, and it seems that the κατ᾿αὐτοῦ immediately following this refers to living in opposition to the devil, whereas the following εἰσι refers to the demons again. The translation, however technically inaccurate, does capture the sense of the statement, which is that humans live in opposition to the devil and his demons, who are powerless against them. Still, the question is whether the beatings Antony received from demons constitutes harm. Antony says, "There is nothing they [demons] care more about than doing harm to those who love virtue and worship God. But because they are unable to act, they do nothing except make threats" (Athanasius, *Life of Antony* 28.5; SC 400bis, 212; Vivian and Athanassakis, *Life of Antony*, 123). This is why the demons "sport about like actors on the stage, changing their shapes" (Athanasius, *Life of Antony* 28.9; SC 400bis, 214; Vivian and Athanassakis, *Life of Antony*, 125). They try to frighten by apparitions because they are powerless to do more. Athanasius does not address the question of whether the beatings Antony received constitute a case of the demons' visiting τὸ βλάπτειν on him, but later in this speech he has Antony speak of the devil's attack on Job as an example of Satan's weakness since Satan must ask permission from God before he can afflict Job. It is possible that Antony understood his own beatings in a similar fashion—or, at least, that Athanasius did. Antony may have viewed his beatings as an attack allowed by God for his strengthening, or to display virtue to the demons; thus, God was responsible, not the demons. The *Life of Antony* is ambiguous about whether the demons harmed Job, but it does say that things happened to Job and to his cattle, possessions, and so on. At the very least, then, one can say that Antony's understanding of εἰσὶ . . . πρὸς τὸ βλάπτειν ἕτοιμοι is complex and dependent on his understanding of God's will. Ultimately, this understanding is not explicitly consistent.

in the *Life* demons are powerless to cause harm of their own volition: only with God's permission can demons act against a human being with more than threats and apparitions.[79] Christians thus have no need to fear demons. The demons may harbor all kinds of ill will toward Christians, but demons are not able to act on their ill will except by God's permission. Notably, the *Life* does not address how, when, why, or whether God might grant a demon permission to harm a person. It is assumed that God is purely good and any action God takes, even allowing suffering to befall a human, is good.[80] Therefore, though God can and does give permission for the devil to physically harm humans, as in the case of Job, Antony thinks one has no reason to fear demons because God is still governing the universe, and God is good.[81]

The *Letters* do not draw on Job's story at all, as the focus in the *Letters*, particularly Letter 6, is human resistance to demonic works. Demons attempt to bring about evil, but only when a person cooperates and allows a demon to work in him can the demon do anything. Rather than employing Job, Antony speaks of God's superiority over demons by telling his audience to pray for help in resisting, for Jesus "died because of them in this world, and prepared for them to inherit Gehenna."[82]

A few texts in the *Life* and *Letters* offer three further dimensions of demonic interaction with human beings. First, demons are able to suggest, tempt, and even deceive monks in an attempt to get the brothers to abandon their ascetic discipline and do wrong.[83] Antony says, "They drag [*helkysōsi*,

---

[79]Speaking about Job as example and proof of the devil's weakness, Antony says, "If he had had power, he would not have asked. But when he asked, not once but twice, he showed that he was weak and unable to do anything. It is not remarkable that the Devil had no power against Job, seeing that nothing would have happened even to Job's cattle if God had not consented. The Devil did not have authority even over pigs! But 'they begged' the Lord, as it is written in the Gospels, saying, 'Allow us to depart into the swine.' If the demons have no authority over pigs, how much less authority do they have over human beings, who have been created in the image of God!" (Athanasius, *Life of Antony*, 29.3-5; SC 400bis, 216-18; Vivian and Athanassakis, *Life of Antony*, 125-27).

[80]Note that the devil is able to kill Job's children, cattle, and so on, even though he cannot kill Job. Neither Antony nor Athanasius comments on this apparent injury to humans but assumes that Job is the exemplar and so focuses on demonic interaction with Job, not with Job's family. This aspect of Athanasius's exegesis will be seen in Chrysostom's exegesis of Job as well.

[81]Admittedly, for most people this thought is unlikely to eliminate fear. If God has allowed harm in the past, God could allow harm in the future. Demons can still cause suffering, and now they have divine permission. It is no wonder people remained afraid of demons.

[82]Antony, Letter 6 (Rubenson, *Letters of St. Antony*, 218).

[83]Athanasius, *Life of Antony* 23.1-26.6 (SC 400bis, 198-208; Vivian and Athanassakis, *Life of Antony*, 112-21).

ἑλκύσωσι] away wherever they wish those who have been deceived by them."[84] When a demon successfully deceives a person, she is under the demon's power and will be "dragged" wherever the demon wishes, regardless of the person's wishes. Second, demons characteristically provoke fear. Antony's continual refrain as he speaks to the monks is "do not fear" the demons.[85] They can deceive, yes, but only if the person allows it. They are not nearly so frightening as people think; indeed, people *ought not* fear demons. Antony's concern is to empower and encourage the monks, but he has also made way for later writers like Chrysostom to argue that demons should not be an excuse for sin. Since demons can only tempt and deceive, not coerce, any wrongdoing is the Christian's own fault. This is the third dimension of demonic interaction, and Antony's letters speak even more about the human's responsibility for his own sin than does the *Life*. Antony writes, "We are called sensible, but have put on an irrational mind, so that we are ignorant of how the secret contrivances and manifold crafts of the devil work, and how they might be known." "If you neglect [*neglegatis*] yourselves and do not discern your works, you fall into the hands of the devil."[86] Christians who are neglectful or who choose "to put on an irrational mind" bring harm on themselves. Negligence is an important theme in Letter 6. If the demons do anything, it is through a Christian's own negligence. Christians have no excuse for their sin or their resulting enslavement by the devil and suffering in Gehenna. This third dimension will be a particular emphasis of Chrysostom's.

Other ascetic demonologies. Other ascetic demonologies reflect themes similar to those found in *Life of Antony*, especially the focus on a constant struggle against demons and the demons' inability to cause sin.[87] Vigilance becomes a key theme among Antony's successors, and Job comes to a place

---

[84]Athanasius, *Life of Antony* 25.3 (SC 400bis, 206; Vivian and Athanassakis, *Life of Antony*, 117).

[85]Athanasius, *Life of Antony* 27.5: Οὐ δεῖ δὲ φοβεῖσθαι αὐτούς (SC 400bis, 210); 28.8: Ἔπειτα κἀκεῖνο λογίζεσθαι χρή, πρὸς τὸ μὴ φοβεῖσθαι τούτους (SC 400bis, 214); 30.1: Τὸν θεὸν ἄρα μόνον δεῖ φοβεῖσθαι, τούτων δὲ καταφρονεῖν καὶ μηδ᾽ ὅλως αὐτοὺς προσποιεῖσθαι (SC 400bis, 126).

[86]Antony, Letter 6 (Rubenson, *Letters of St. Antony*, 217, 224).

[87]An excellent treatment of ascetic thought about demons is Brakke, *Demons and the Making of the Monk*. Brakke argues that the development of monks and demons cannot be understood apart from the antagonistic relationship they have with one another, though the particular character of the struggle and development varies between monks and traditions. Brakke also explores the various functions of demons in ascetic literature.

of prominence as an example for emulation of the virtuous man who with-
stood all that the demon tried. There are various collections of sayings and
lives of the desert fathers and ascetics; most were written after people had
been going to the desert for some time. Most were also written after Chrysostom had died. The exception is the anonymous *A History of the Monks of
Egypt*, likely written about 400 CE, just after Chrysostom came to Constantinople and just before he was exiled for the first time.[88] Since this is the case,
Chrysostom did not know these works as collections or completed works.
However, since the collections were compiled from oral traditions, and since
Chrysostom himself spent a substantial amount of time among the monks
outside Antioch,[89] it is reasonable to think that Chrysostom did know the
tradition, if not every story recorded in the various collections.[90]

These collections of sayings and lives of desert fathers offer nothing about
the origin of demons. The stories assume demonic existence but do not
ponder where they come from. Even with regard to demons' composition
there is little to say.[91] Monks assumed that the devil and his demons existed,

---

[88]Brakke, *Demons and the Making of the Monk*, 128.

[89]For more on the particular brand of asceticism practiced by Chrysostom, see J. N. D. Kelly,
Golden Mouth: The Story of John Chrysostom—Ascetic, Preacher, Bishop (London: Duckworth,
1995), 18-20; Jean M. Leroux, "Saint Jean Chrysostome et le monachisme," in *Jean Chrysostome
et Augustin*, ed. Charles Kannengiesser (Paris: Beauchesne, 1975), 125-44; and Wendy Mayer,
"Monasticism at Antioch and Constantinople in the Late Fourth Century: A Case of Exclusivity
or Diversity?," in *Prayer and Spirituality in the Early Church*, ed. Pauline Allen, Wendy Mayer,
Lawrence Cross, and B. Janelle Caiger (Everton Park, Queensland: Australian Catholic University, 1998), 275-88.

[90]Brakke, *Demons and the Making of the Monk*, 88. In particular, Theodoret of Cyrrhus's *A History
of the Monks of Syria* is dated 437–448 CE and is said to be a record of oral tradition, reports
from bishops Theodoret knew, and Theodoret's own observations. Written only a few decades
after Chrysostom's death, the *History* recounts stories of past generations of Syrian monks, and
it is possible Chrysostom also knew these stories from his own time as an ascetic. Even so, the
influence of Egyptian asceticism on Syrian forms is unclear. What can be said is the Syrian form
of asceticism Theodoret describes in his *History* is more theatrical, individualistic, and extreme
than the Egyptian form described in the *Sayings of the Desert Fathers* and even the *History of the
Monks of Egypt*. As Peter Brown phrases it, "Syria was the great province for ascetic stars" (Peter
Brown, "The Rise and Function of the Holy Man in Late Antiquity," *Journal of Roman Studies* 61
[1971]: 82). I only suggest that there are similarities between Chrysostom's thought and the
ideas in ascetic literature to which we have access, and that it is possible Chrysostom knew of
the traditions.

[91]There is no philosophical reflection on the subtlety of demons' bodies or on demons' feeding
habits as in Origen or even Antony's letters, but the reader is able to infer a few things from the
stories. For one, demons are spirits. Sometimes the stories give demons physical powers, such
as when a demon tried to drag a man bodily from the temple (Elias 7, *Apophthegmata Patrum*,
alphabetical collection). Palladius also describes instances of a demon beating a monk

that they were evil, and thus they focused their instruction on the demons' various tactics: how demons interact with monks, what harm this interaction threatens, and what this interaction has the potential to accomplish. The demons' purpose, just as for Antony, is to disturb the Christian's soul and to destroy human beings morally, for moral destruction leads to damnation.[92] Also as in the Antony tradition, the demons use all manner of temptations, deceptions, and apparitions in order to achieve this goal.

The narratives often portray demons as "afraid" (*phobeō*, φοβέω) of the monks who are virtuous. In fact, a monk's virtue can drive the demons away. For instance, Isidore the Priest refused an invitation to a meal, and when a brother questioned him about it, asking if he was afraid to leave his cell, Isidore replied that he was afraid to go because of the devil and the way the devil is always prowling like a lion for prey. Isidore continues, "When someone gives himself a drink, he will not escape being attacked by thoughts. Lot, indeed, being constrained by his daughters, got drunk with wine, and through the effect of drunkenness, the devil easily brought him to a shameful act of fornication."[93] Isidore seems to be saying of the devil what is said in a children's story: "If you give a mouse a cookie, he will want a glass of milk."[94] That is, once a monk allows the devil a place by his own momentary weakness, the devil will lead the monk on to much graver sins, and so the monk must choose not even to leave his cell lest he give the devil a foothold. In another story, Moses the Ethiopian suffers repeated attacks by a demon, and finally a most holy man is able to drive the demons away. About this holy man Palladius writes, "He was deemed worthy of a divine gift over demons."[95] This

---

physically, just as Athanasius records having happened to Antony (Palladius, *The Lausiac History* 38.12; 71.2), and there is a narrative of a demon attempting to enter Theodore of Pherme's cell by force but being unable to do so. Theodore binds the demon and keeps it out of his cell (Theodore of Pherme 27, *Apophthegmata*). In contrast to Evagrius, who seems to internalize or psychologize the demons by referring to different passions as demons, the collections of sayings allow for external demons as well.

[92]Theodoret of Cyrrhus, *A History of the Monks of Syria* 21.28; Heraclides 1, *Apophthegmata*; and Syncletica 7, *Apophthegmata*.

[93]Isidore the Priest 1, *Apophthegmata* (PG 65.236). English translation is from Benedicta Ward, trans., *The Sayings of the Desert Fathers: The Alphabetical Collection* (Kalamazoo, MI: Cistercian, 1975), 106.

[94]Laura Numeroff, *If You Give a Mouse a Cookie*, illustrated by Felicia Bond (New York: Harper, 1985).

[95]Κατηξιώθη δὲ οὗτος χαρίσματος κατὰ δαιμόνων. Palladius, *Lausiac History* 19.11. Critical edition: Edward Cuthbert Butler, ed., *The Lausiac History of Palladius: A Critical Discussion Together with Notes on Early Egyptian Monachism* (Nendeln, Liechtenstein: Kraus Reprints, 1967), 62.

particular platitude is repeated about Innocent, who "was deemed worthy of the gift of power against demons."[96] Theodoret also records a story about Marcianus, who was able to drive a demon out of a girl from four days' journey away. According to the story, "[Marcianus] ordered [for the father of the girl to return a flask], the demon who was four days' journey away cried out at the power of the one who was driving him out."[97]

One interesting nuance to the desert collections that does not appear in Antony or other earlier works is that demons are not able to create temptations; demons are able only to exacerbate or "flare up" an existing temptation.[98] Abba Poemen (d. 450 CE) tells a disciple, "[Demons] do not fight against us at all as long as we are doing our own will. For our own wills become the demons, and it is these which attack us in order that we may fulfill them."[99] Though one may understand this saying as a symbolic interpretation of demons that yields a simple psychological explanation, many of Poemen's other sayings, which refer to demons external to the monk, preclude such an interpretation. In this case, however, it seems that a person's will can become like a demon, demanding attention and attacking the Christian. Elsewhere, when a brother comes to Poemen seeking help because of a demon who keeps trying to get the brother to blaspheme, Poemen says, "Everything that the soul does not desire [*thelei*, θέλει], does not long remain."[100] For a demon's temptation to have traction, the sinful desire must already be present in the monk's soul. Theodoret of Cyrrhus (c. 393–457 CE) writes in the prologue to his *History of the Monks of Syria*,

> Not having thoughts that give away the interior and being deprived of the cooperation [*synergias*, συνεργίας] of human limbs, [demons] are not able to wage war. For the devil borrows our own limbs as weapons against us. For if the eyes are not enticed nor the hearing bewitched nor touch kindled nor the mind receptive to evil plans, the zeal of those plotting injury is in vain.[101]

---

[96]Palladius, *Lausiac History* 44.3 (Butler, *Lausiac History*, 131). English translation is from Palladius, *The Lausiac History*, trans. Robert T. Meyer, ACW 34 (New York: Newman, 1965), 121.

[97]Theodoret, *History of the Monks of Syria* 3.9 (SC 234bis, 264).

[98]That is, a demon can place dessert before a monk, but it is only a temptation if the monk already desires dessert. A monk who is content and has no sweet tooth will not be tempted, even if the dessert is a three-tiered chocolate cake.

[99]Poemen 67, *Apophthegmata* (PG 65.337; Ward, *Sayings of the Desert Fathers*, 176).

[100]Poemen 93, *Apophthegmata* (PG 65.345; Ward, *Sayings of the Desert Fathers*, 180).

[101]Theodoret, *History of the Monks of Syria*, prologue 6 (SC 234bis, 132-34).

Theodoret here claims the demons are unable to wage war at all if a person does not already have wicked thoughts. More than the necessity of some preexistent inclination toward sin, this statement indicates the necessary cooperation of a human being with a demon in order for sin to occur. Theodoret asserts that no amount of demonic zeal is effective unless the human offers his limbs to the demon's cause. Here again, then, the ascetic tradition upholds the notion that demons cannot make people do anything they do not want to do, which reinforces the idea that being tempted by demons is not a valid excuse for human sin. Demons tempt and deceive, but a Christian only sins if he or she assents to the demons' temptations or is negligent enough to be deceived.

This matter of demonic-human cooperation also poses a question about whether a demon can access a person's soul or mind at all.[102] One of the stories about Abba Arsenius records a brother coming to Arsenius and saying, "My thoughts trouble me, saying, 'You can neither fast nor work; at least go and visit the sick, for that is also charity.'" The story continues, "But the old man, recognizing the suggestions of the demons, said to him, 'Go, eat, drink, sleep, do no work, only do not leave your cell.'"[103] Here the troubled brother cannot distinguish his own thoughts from those given to him by demons, though the holy man can discern the spirits for the brother, demonstrating that demons are able not only to suggest thoughts to the

---

[102]Jeffrey Russell argues that ascetics thought demons were unable to enter a person's soul (Jeffrey B. Russell, *Satan: The Early Christian Tradition* [Ithaca, NY: Cornell University Press, 1981], 181). Peter Brown explains that demons could implant thoughts in a monk's mind. In fact, Brown claims there was a point at which the monk could not distinguish his own thought from that suggested by the devil (Peter Brown, *The Body and Society: Men, Women, and Sexual Renunciation in Early Christianity* [New York: Columbia University Press, 1988], 228-29). Moreover, desert literature does recognize demoniacs and those who have been possessed, but it is not clear which part of a person needs to be accessed and taken over or controlled in order for the person to be considered "possessed." Those who talk of demon possession, however, seem to mean something different from suggesting thoughts to the mind; they seem to mean total possession of a person, a taking over of all faculties. For instance, Palladius recounts that the monk Innocent "was deemed worthy of the gift of power against demons. Once we ourselves saw brought to him a young man who was paralyzed and possessed. . . . He prayed over the young man from the third to the ninth hour and then returned him healed to his mother the same day, as he had driven out both the paralysis and the demon" (Palladius, *Lausiac History* 44.3-4; Meyer, *Lausiac History*, 121). The ambiguity in the desert literature leaves scholars without a clear consensus on which parts of a person a demon could access and what constitutes possession rather than influence.

[103]Arsenius 11, *Apophthegmata* (PG 65.89; Ward, *Sayings of the Desert Fathers*, 10).

mind but also to do it in such a subtle way as to convince the monk a demonic thought is his own. This suggests that demons have some kind of access to a human's mind, though the mechanics of how a demon implants a thought are unclear.

Still, the monks could resist the thoughts of the demons. Poemen says that if the soul does not desire a thought, the thought will not remain. In another saying Poemen states that a monk can cause evil thoughts suggested by demons to disappear through patience.[104] In addition, Theodoret writes in the prologue to his *History of the Monks of Syria*, "It is impossible for the demons that are waging war from outside to prevail a soul encircled by divine grace, unless the easiness of some thought open some small gate in our senses and receive the enemy inside it."[105] All these examples indicate some faculty of the monk that the devil and his demons cannot penetrate unless allowed in. The monk's will is significant in this, for the monk must choose to resist, or if the monk does not exercise his will against the demon, the demon will gain entrance and the monk cooperate with the demon's scheme.

It is significant that so much of monastic literature in both Egypt and Syria is concerned with the demons' attempts to destroy morally rather than physically. People, especially in Syria, came to the monks for blessings and protections against the physical harm demons could inflict; this physical harm was the primary fear regarding demons.[106] In spite of this,

---

[104]Poemen 21, *Apophthegmata* (PG 65.728).

[105]Theodoret, *History of the Monks of Syria*, prologue 6 (SC 234bis, 134).

[106]Theodoret recounts, "The wife of a nobleman fell sick with gluttony, and some called the illness a work of demons, but others thought it a sickness of the body. Whether the former or the latter . . . her relatives took pity on her and begged that divine man. He came and prayed, and by placing his hand over water, tracing the sign of salvation, and telling her to drink, healed the illness" (Theodoret, *History of the Monks of Syria* 13.9, SC 234bis, 490-92). Peter Brown argues that one of the primary characteristics of the ancient holy man was his power. He writes, "To visit a holy man was to go to where power was" (Brown, "Rise and Function of the Holy Man," 87). That power was demonstrated most acutely in exorcisms, where a holy man stands in the midst of demonic abuse; the holy man's ability to drive out demons was a "dramatic articulation" of his power (Brown, "Rise and Function of the Holy Man," 89). Brown even goes so far as to argue that the holy man was a replacement of amulets and the like since the blessing of a holy man could ward off demons. With the holy man's blessing, amulets were unnecessary (Brown, "Rise and Function of the Holy Man," 100). For stories from Theodoret, *History of the Monks of Syria*, see 3.9, where Marcianus tries to hide his power and is reluctant to reveal it to the many people who come to him, and 3.22, where a noble woman "ran to [Marcianus] from Antioch and begged him to help her daughter who was being attacked by

the majority of what authors chose to record was sayings and stories about the moral, rather than physical, attacks, as well as the human's ability to resist those attacks. The authors attempted a shift in focus and a deemphasizing of physical harm caused by demons, implying that they understood the true danger of demons to be in their attempts to destroy a person's virtue. This is a redefinition of harm, just as we will see Chrysostom provide. Physical harm is not true harm, even though the monks address this harm as well; true harm is harm done to one's virtue, and this is the monks' emphasis. It is an implicit theodicy: demons are not the source of true suffering, humans are.[107]

This shift in emphasis is also the monks casting their anthropology in terms of demonology. A holy person is one who resists the devil, one who has power over demons. A Christian is a person who struggles against the devil's attacks. A Christian is *able* to resist the devil, which implies something about the spiritual makeup of a Christian. Ascetic demonology highlights ascetic anthropology.

Popular demonologies. Origen, Antony, and the ascetic tradition all emphasize the ability of humans to resist demonic attacks. That several different writers address the limits of demonic powers and emphasize the Christian's ability to resist demons is evidence that there were significant populations living in fear of demons and what they could do. More than the words of priests, bishops, and theologians, though, there is archaeological evidence to provide a view of popular beliefs about demons. Incantation bowls found with Christian inscriptions or crosses indicate Christian use.[108] For example,

---

a demon" (SC 234bis, 258-60, 286). See also Theodoret, *History of the Monks of Syria* 9.4, 9, 10; 13.10; 16.2, for a sample.

[107]In the next chapter I show Chrysostom emphasizing the same concern to his congregation, an audience that appears to be more afraid of what harm a demon can cause physically than of spiritual harm from demons. Instead, Chrysostom consistently warns his audience against the moral attacks a demon makes and argues that demons are attempting a greater destruction than the audience realizes: destruction of the soul.

[108]For various examples of Christian magical items with translated inscriptions, see Theodore S. De Bruyn, "Appeals to Jesus as the One 'Who Heals Every Illness and Every Infirmity' (Matt 4:23, 9:35) in Amulets in Late Antiquity," in *Reception and Interpretation of the Bible in Late Antiquity*, ed. Lorenzo DiTommaso and Lucian Turcescu (Leiden: Brill, 2008), 65-81; De Bruyn, "The Use of the Sanctus in Christian Greek Papyrus Amulets," in *Studia Patristica: Liturgia et Cultus, Theologica et Philosophica, Critica et Philologica, Nachleben, First Two Centuries*, ed. F. Young, M. Edwards, and P. Parvis, vol. 40 (Leuven: Peeters, 2006), 15-19; Geller, "Eight Incantation Bowls," 101-17; Philippe Gignoux, "A New Incantation Bowl Inscribed in Syriac

bowl 26 in Naveh and Shaked's *Magic Spells and Formulae* is in Syriac and has a distinct cross in the center. Part of the inscription reads,

> May it [the house] be bound and sealed by the seal by which the heaven and the earth are sealed, and by the seal by which Noah sealed his ark, and by the seal of Solomon, by which the demons and the dews are sealed and by the great seal. May there be sealed, sealed [*sic*], girded and scattered these amulets that were written for the healing and the preservation of Khusrau son of Qaqay and Shelta daughter of Qayumta. . . . Hallelujah. By your name, living god, the god who annuls all demons and devils. Healing, health, cure, sealing, existence, and the preservation of life from heaven. I have written and God cures. Amen. Now and forever. Yes, and Amen, Amen, Amen, Selah.[109]

Such items were used to ward off the devil and his demons, to protect the Christian from harm.

There are also papyri, metal amulets, and various talismans whose inscriptions and pictures leave little doubt as to their Christian origin.[110] One Christian jasper amulet from the third or fourth century has a figure of a fish-shaped boat with the word ΙΧΘΥΣ (*ICHTHUS*) underneath.[111] Ascetic literature speaks often about the power of Jesus' name to repel demons; it is possible amulets and incantations that call on the name of Jesus belong to a similar tradition. What may have begun as a call on Christ who has defeated the devil and is able to protect a person from demons became a sort of "magic word."

As with Jewish and pagan texts, many spells concerned medical ailments or were for general healing, as in this text:

> I invoke you, [god] of heaven and god of the earth and [god] of the saints through [your blood] . . . who has come through Gabriel in the womb of the virgin Mary, who was born in Bethlehem and raised in Nazareth, who was

(National Museum of Oriental Art, Rome)," *East and West* 34 (1984): 47-53; and James A. Montgomery, "A Syriac Incantation Bowl with Christian Formula," *American Journal of Semitic Languages and Literatures* 34 (1918): 137.

[109]Naveh and Shaked, *Magic Spells and Formulae*, 140.

[110]R. W. Daniel, "A Christian Amulet on Papyrus," *VC* 37 (1983): 400-404; H. Gitler, "Four Magical and Christian Amulets," *Studii Biblici Franciscani Liber Annuus* 40 (1990): 365-74; and Lucas Van Rompay, "Some Remarks on the Language of Syriac Incantation Texts," in *V Symposium Syriacum, 1988, Katholieke Universiteit, Leuven, 29-31 août 1988*, ed. René Lavenant (Rome: Pontifical Oriental Institute, 1990), 369-81.

[111]Gitler, "Four Magical and Christian Amulets," 373-74. ΙΧΘΥΣ was common on amulets; the letters are initials for Ἰησοὺς Χριστὸς Θεοῦ Υἱὸς Σωτήρ, Jesus Christ, Son of God, Savior.

crucified. . . . The sovereigns [and] the powers and the world-rulers of darkness, whether an unclean spirit or a demon falling at the hours of midday, or a chill, or a mild fever or a shivering fever, or ill treatment from people, powers of the adversary—may they not have power against the figure.[112]

Although many of the spells are for protection against demons and for healing of various kinds, there are also Christian spells for inducing love or for cursing and hurting an enemy, and even some for the most mundane aspects of life, like a good singing voice or silencing a dog.[113] The number of these artifacts that are distinctly Christian is smaller than those considered to be Jewish, but there are plenty of bowls and amulets to provide support for the idea that Christian use of such items was common. From this evidence, popular demonology was one of fear that led to the use of material repellants. For pagans, Jews, and Christians alike, demons were real, and demons could do real harm, causing disease or other suffering.[114]

J. Kevin Coyle suggests that by the fourth century Christians—lay, ascetic,[115] and clergy alike—assumed the standard accounts of the origins and natures of demons that had been developed by earlier thinkers like Justin Martyr or Tertullian and therefore did not spend time discussing demonic origins themselves.[116] Coyle further suggests that the absence of such

---

[112]Cairo, Egyptian Museum 10263, translated and quoted in Marvin W. Meyer and Richard Smith, eds., *Ancient Christian Magic: Coptic Texts of Ritual Power* (San Francisco: HarperSanFrancisco, 1994), 35-36.

[113]For a sample of these, see Meyer and Smith, *Ancient Christian Magic*. The spells for a singing voice and silencing a dog are at pp. 246-50.

[114]In addition to this archaeological evidence, Chrysostom's lack of attempts to convince his congregation that demons exist suggests the popular assumption of demonic reality. As we shall see, Chrysostom takes the devil and demons' existence and wickedness as his starting point, just as do all other writers of his time. Though it is an argument from silence, this silence could indicate a common understanding.

[115]Ascetics were members of the laity, but I separate them here because ascetics had a different way of life than the nonascetic lay Christian and a somewhat different thought-world.

[116]J. Kevin Coyle, "Early Monks, Prayer, and the Devil," in Allen, Mayer, and Cross, *Prayer and Spirituality in the Early Church*, 229-49. Coyle cites the insight of Dwayne E. Carpenter regarding this point: "By the time that the Desert Fathers were writing (or being written about), at least certain basic conceptions of the Devil and of evil in general had been accepted by the Church. . . . The Desert Fathers' treatment of the Devil is based upon a theological foundation constructed by earlier Christian apologists and theologians" (Dwayne E. Carpenter, "The Devil Bedeviled: Diabolical Intervention and the Desert Fathers," *American Benedictine Review* 31, no. 2 [1980]: 183). Neither Coyle nor Carpenter suggests particular earlier thinkers they believe the desert fathers to be assuming, but Carpenter does speak of the watchers myth and also of Tertullian, indicating a perceived reliance on Justin and Tertullian.

explanations or discussions about the existence of demons illustrates how commonplace demons were in the thought-world of early Christians. So common, that is, that the presence of demons required as much explanation in the fourth century as cars do in the twenty-first.[117] Peter Brown makes a similar statement regarding Augustine's own fourth-century context: "Augustine grew up in an age when men thought that they shared the physical world with malevolent demons. They felt this quite as intensely as we feel the presence of myriads of dangerous bacteria."[118] As both Coyle and Brown point out, demons were so much a part of the world that most people, however they interacted with demons, did not need to comment on them; they lived with them.

We are also able to reconstruct the demonological views of Chrysostom's congregation from Chrysostom's sermons. Using the comments Chrysostom made to his congregation, we gain a picture of what the congregation believed. He writes in *De prophetiarum obscuritate*, "As bright as the sun is, the providence of God is clearer. But still some dare to say that demons manage our affairs."[119] The devil is the "ruler of the power of the air" (Eph 2:2), and the "ruler of this world" (Jn 12:31). The devil and his demons are evil, having rebelled against God and having as their single purpose the destruction of God's work. Natural disasters, famine, and the like are large events outside the control of humanity. It is reasonable that these beliefs

---

[117]Coyle, "Early Monks," 231.

[118]Peter Brown, *Augustine of Hippo: A Biography* (Berkeley: University of California Press, 1967), 41. E. R. Dodds makes the same claim: "Virtually everyone, pagan, Jewish, Christian or Gnostic, believed in the existence of these beings and in their function as mediators, whether he called them daemons or angels or aions or simply 'spirits.'" E. R. Dodds, *Pagan and Christian in an Age of Anxiety: Some Aspects of Religious Experience from Marcus Aurelius to Constantine* (Cambridge: Cambridge University Press, 1965), 37-38.

[119]Chrysostom, *De proph. obsc.* 3.6 (PG 49.253). Following Peleanu's argument, what the *NPNF* [1] (vol. 9) lists as the first homily of *De diabolo tentatore*, I list (with Peleanu) as the third homily of *De prophetiarum obscuritate*. For Peleanu's argument for regrouping the homilies, see Adina Peleanu, "Deux séries chrysostomiennes : Sur l'impuissance du diable et Sur l'obscurité des prophéties," *Revue d'études augustiniennes et patristiques* 57 (2011): 89-108. Six years prior to Peleanu's article, Mayer makes a similar argument: "As indicated by a comparison of the opening to *De diab. tent. hom. 1* [Montfaucon's numbering] and the contents of *De prophetiarum obscuritate hom. 2*, the first was delivered a few days after the Sunday on which the latter was preached. From the third of the homilies it is also clear that *hom. 3* was delivered two days after *hom. 2*. The interval between *hom. 1* and *2*, however, is by no means certain, as is the question of whether *hom. 1* actually preceded *hom. 2*" (Wendy Mayer, *The Homilies of St John Chrysostom: Provenance, Reshaping the Foundations* [Rome: Pontifical Oriental Institute, 2005], 77). Thus far there is no critical edition of *De prophetiarum obscuritate*, so I use Migne's Patrologia Graeca.

would work together in a person's mind toward the conclusion that demons cause natural evils. Moreover, the pagans believed that evil demons caused natural disasters, illness, and disease—even, in some cases, death.[120] In this world spirits were active in all manner of earthly occurrences.

CONCLUSION

In the late fourth century the demonological milieu was vast and complex. The "average" person—pagan, Jewish, or Christian—saw evidence of demons running rampant through the world. For the most part, people understood the same kind of being indicated by the term *daimōn*. In short, *daimones* were spiritual beings ontologically inferior to God or the gods yet superior to human beings. They were invisible to humans, though their invisibility did not hinder the *daimones*' ability to interact with humans. *Daimones* attended the mystic rituals of the Greeks, received pagan sacrifices, and provided the oracles. Christians, too, believed these to be functions of the demons. What these things implied was an ability to interfere with human lives. Countless spells and amulets of every religion sought to ward off the evil actions of demons, and pagan magic often sought to bring demons into the service of human aims. Christians believed demons could cause physical harm—note the stories of Job and Antony—or even, according to Origen, "plagues, or barrenness, or tempests, or similar calamities."[121]

Since demons could cause such enormous harm, the natural response was fear. *Daimones* could at any moment bring an earthquake or a famine. Demons

---

[120]Porphyry writes, "One thing especially should be counted among the greatest harm done by the maleficent *daimones*: they are themselves responsible for the sufferings that occur around the earth (plagues, crop failures, earthquakes, droughts, and the like), but convince us that the responsibility lies with those who are responsible for just the opposite" (Porphyry, *On Abstinence from Killing Animals*, trans. Gillian Clark [Ithaca, NY: Cornell University Press, 2000], 2.40, p. 71). Sometimes the source of an event is not named an evil *daimon* but only a god or a spirit, as in the poetry of Aeschylus. In his *Agamemnon*, Cassandra cries, "This revel-band drinks human blood, thus emboldening itself, and then remains in the house, hard to send away—the band of the house's kindred Furies" (Aeschylus, *Ag.*, 1188-90, LCL 146:141-43). This line of verse speaks of a world filled with spirits, and its tenor includes hints of fear ("drinks human blood," "hard to send away"). Further, it was common among pagans to blame Christians for various natural occurrences, as noted by both Tertullian and Augustine: "If the Tiber rises as high as the city walls . . . if there is an earthquake, a famine, a plague—straightway the cry is heard: 'Toss the Christians to the lion!'" (Tertullian, *Apol.* 40; FC 10:102), and "If there is a drought, blame the Christians" (Augustine, *Civ. Dei* 2.3; FC 8:78). The pagans blamed the Christians for offending the gods by their "atheism," thus calling down droughts, floods, and earthquakes.

[121]Origen, *Cels.* 1.31; ANF 4:409. See also *Cels.* 8.31, 54, for similar statements.

could cause a person, or a person's loved one, to fall deathly ill or to be in a fatal accident. For Christians, demons could, even beyond causing physical harm, deceive a person or tempt him and cause him to sin, and if a person sinned, he could be in danger of suffering the fires of hell. This fear must have been overwhelming to some, perhaps merely troubling to others, but it was common among the laity. Beyond this the commonality begins to break down. Unlike the pagans, for whom *daimones* were ethically ambiguous, capable of bringing either fortune or disaster, Jews and Christians knew that *daimones* were without exception evil. *Daimones* meant only harm, and the severest harm. *Daimones* tried to prevent a person's salvation.

Pagans, Jews, and Christians all drew on their own long histories of demonological development as they came to their own understandings of the moral character of *daimones*. Still, among all these groups living together in Antioch, there was some transfer of ideas. Pagans had sacrifices and rituals with which to placate their *daimones*, Jews were known as magicians, and even the Christians had amulets, papyri, and other magical paraphernalia similar to their neighbors' but calling on the name of Christ. Christians knew the demons were wholly evil and there was no placating them, but they did try to gain God's protection from them. If the theologians whose writings are extant can be believed, one thing can be said, that the "average" Christian feared demons. "Average" Christians felt powerless against demons, unable to resist not only the physical harm demons could bring but also the temptation they wrought. It is this fear, and its resulting lack of understanding and trust in the gospel, that Chrysostom would address.

2

Chrysostom's Demonology

Cⁿᴿʏꜱᴏꜱᴛᴏᴍ ᴜɴᴅᴇʀꜱᴛᴏᴏᴅ ᴛʜᴇ ꜰᴇᴀʀ that plagued his con-
gregation. Demons were spiritual beings in league with the devil, seeking to
harm Christians in every way possible. This much both clergy and laity
agreed on. Exactly how dangerous the demons were and what precisely they
aimed to do was another matter. Whereas the congregants feared physical
harm or claimed that demons caused their sin, Chrysostom insisted that
demons, though they aimed to do harm, were incapable of causing true
injury. Chrysostom makes this refutation most often as he addresses his
congregants' questions of suffering. Since his demonology is thus bound up
with his theodicy, I begin with an overview of that theodicy.

Cⁿᴿʏꜱᴏꜱᴛᴏᴍ'ꜱ Tʜᴇᴏᴅɪᴄʏ: Aɴ Oᴠᴇʀᴠɪᴇᴡ

The traditional title of *De prophetarium obscuritate* (*De proph. obs.*) 3 is *That
Demons Do Not Govern the World*, and *De diabolo tentatore* (*De diab. tent.*), often
translated *On the Powers of Demons*, argues that demons are neither as powerful
as the congregation thinks nor the cause of all suffering and sin in the world. In
Quod nemo laeditur nisi a seipso, translated *That No One Can Harm the One
Who Does Not Harm Himself*, Chrysostom's most explicit theodicy, demons are
less prominent but do appear as part of Chrysostom's argument. When
Chrysostom speaks of the question of evil, he speaks of demons. My primary
text for this overview is Chrysostom's *Commentary on Job* (*Comm. in Iob*).[1] The

---

[1]Not even the SC volume suggests a possible date for the *Comm. in Iob*, though there is a lengthy
investigation of both the manuscript tradition and whether it is authentic to Chrysostom. Henri

book of Job is widely regarded as a work of theodicy itself, so it is not surprising that Chrysostom finds here an answer to the question of the origin of evil.

The goal in Christian theodicies is often to protect God from accusations that he is the author of evil. In this regard, Chrysostom is no different from his predecessors, contemporaries, and successors. In the case of the *Commentarius in Iob*, this is almost easy: the devil is the cause of Job's suffering.[2] Job, however, does not know that so Chrysostom says that Job believes God to be the author of his suffering. This does not trouble Chrysostom; he explains that God can indeed be the cause of a person's suffering. That is, God can be the cause of poverty, disease, or loss. According to Chrysostom, God is the ruler of all things, and for this reason all events and misfortunes can be attributed to him. Because God is just and loving, however, Chrysostom says that these misfortunes are not evil. They are either punishments or tests, both intended pedagogically. In another homily, Chrysostom preaches, "Therefore whenever you see that famines have occurred, and plagues, and droughts . . . or any other of the kind of things that chastise human nature, do not be troubled, nor give up in impatience, but worship him who made them. . . . For he who does these things is the same one who chastises the body so the soul may be corrected."[3] In *Quod nemo laeditur nixi a seipso*, Chrysostom argues that God punishes "because of the evil of those who act wickedly."[4] Some suffering, then, is God's chastisement and therefore not true evil. Job's suffering is not this chastisement but a test: "He seems to me to be hinting here that he did not suffer such because of his sins (for if God strikes someone, is it not uncertain that he suffers because of sins? This is the case here also), but for testing and greater crowns."[5]

Sorlin and Louis Neyrand, editors of the SC volume, conclude that Chrysostom is the author. Henri Sorlin and Louis Neyrand, eds., *Commentaire sur Job*, vol. 1, chaps. 1–14, SC 346 (Paris: Cerf, 1988), 33-69.

[2]Translator Hill explains that the term διάβολος, the LXX translation of "Satan," would "carry for [Chrysostom's] congregation the overtones of a malignant, demonic person" rather than the adversary or any other role it would have for the Hebrews (Robert C. Hill, *St. John Chrysostom Commentary on Job*, SJC: CS 1 [Brookline, MA: Holy Cross Orthodox Press, 2006], 7). Though Hill is judging Chrysostom's commentary by modern historical-critical standards of interpretation, he is right to point out that it would not have occurred to Chrysostom to interpret διάβολος as anything other than the being he often writes about, the enemy of humanity's salvation.

[3]Chrysostom, *De proph. obsc.* 3.4 (PG 49.250).

[4]Chrysostom, *Quod nem. laed.* 4 (SC 103bis, 78).

[5]Chrysostom, *Comm. in Iob* 19.4 (SC 348bis, 40).

For Chrysostom, theodicy is a matter of understanding events correctly. He writes, "People, and especially the masses, judge things that happen naively and as fate."[6] Chrysostom is clearer in *De prophetiarum obscuritate* 3.5:

> There is then evil, that is really evil: prostitution, adultery, greed, and the myriad such worse things worthy of accusation and punishment. Again there is evil which really is not evil but is called so: famine, plague, death, disease, and other things like that. . . . Were they evils, they would not be the cause of good for us, bringing us back to our senses, checking our laziness, and spurring us on to zeal, making us more attentive.[7]

Suffering that leads to good, even to virtue, is not evil. Therefore, though God causes these disasters or other forms of suffering, since they are not truly evil, God has not caused evil. God is still both sovereign and innocent.

Those things listed as true evil are sins, and their origin is in the person who commits them. The way Chrysostom often begins to explain this is by demonstrating that true evil is separate from external circumstances; it is instead a matter of a person's *gnōmē* (γνώμη), their disposition or mindset, and *proairesis* (προαίρεσις). These terms will be discussed at length in chapter four, but for now it is enough to know that they are both aspects of the free part of a human, that part which makes a person self-determining and which allows a person to be the cause of her own actions. Chrysostom begins the *Commentarius in Iob* by establishing Job's righteousness, which Chrysostom describes as "perfect virtue."[8] An important part of his argument is that Job was virtuous both when he was wealthy and when he was in poverty:

> He was wealthy so that you might learn that he had wealth as an inclination toward evil, and that wealth is not the cause [*aitios*, αἴτιος] but γνώμη [*gnōmē*]. See him also in poverty lest you also believe that poverty is a cause of folly [*aitia agnōmosynēs*, αἰτία ἀγνωμοσύνης]. See him both in wealth and in poverty, and see in both cases a great athlete, for he was God-fearing. . . . Clearly it was from his own resources [*oikothen*, οἴκοθεν].[9]

Job's virtue is something independent of his external, in this case financial, circumstances. Judas is another of Chrysostom's examples, since Judas had

---

[6]Chrysostom, *Comm. in Iob* 6.1 (SC 346bis, 260).

[7]Chrysostom, *De proph. obsc.* 3.5 (PG 49.251).

[8]ὁλόκληρος ἀρετή. Chrysostom, *Comm. in Iob* 1.1 (SC 346bis, 84).

[9]Chrysostom, *Comm. in Iob* 1.1 (SC 346bis, 88).

all the "right" external circumstances in his favor and yet was still wicked.[10] Neither virtue nor vice is a matter of one's outward situation but of human choice and action.

In this way, Chrysostom answers the question of the origin of evil by having recourse to anthropology. Evil is a result of human choice. All the way through his *Commentarius in Iob*, Chrysostom upholds Job as virtuous because he remained faithful to God in spite of all of his suffering. The circumstances of Job's suffering, which Job believed to be caused by God, were not evil but tests. Evil would have been the choice to curse God, as Job's wife recommended. Chrysostom's answer to the origin of evil is even clearer in *Quod nemo laeditur nisi a seipso*, of which the primary argument is that the only person who can cause true harm is the person herself since true harm is harm to the soul through vice.

So far, Chrysostom is not different from his predecessors and contemporaries in any substantial way. It is an established practice to answer theodicy with anthropology.[11] The point at which Chrysostom diverges from traditional theodicy is his addition of demons to the discussion. The devil and his demons play an important role in Chrysostom's discussions of theodicy, though not as free agents who are able to defy God. In *Commentarius in Iob*, for all Job thinks that his suffering is caused by God, his suffering is actually caused by the devil, even as Chrysostom allows that much of the suffering in the world is a result of God's action. Though the devil is a character in the book of Job only in the first two chapters, Chrysostom devotes fully one quarter of his commentary to a discussion of the devil and his role in Job's story. Chrysostom is concerned to point out that the devil, who afflicts Job with poverty, destruction, and the loss of children, is only able to act against Job with God's permission. The devil is powerful in that he is able to cause death and disease, but he is also powerless because he is only able to do these things when God allows: "Let us learn from this that he is able to do as much as he does with consent, that even if overcome, he does not quit; he is always attempting greater things. But it is of God to allow or not to allow."[12] The

---

[10]Chrysostom, *Quod nem. laed.* 11 (SC 103bis, 114).

[11]We will look more closely at Methodius's and Gregory of Nyssa's works on this matter in chap. 4.

[12]Chrysostom, *Comm. in Iob* 2.5 (SC 346bis, 164). Chrysostom also writes, "See the magnitude of the devil's power, how he moved such nations [the Chaldeans who carried off Job's camels]" (*Comm. in Iob* 1.19 [SC 346bis, 132-34]). Also, "Do you see that he [the devil] does not attack

devil makes periodic appearances throughout the remainder of the commentary as well, as when Chrysostom understands Job's friends to be in league with the devil: "See them [Job's friends], not only bringing no encouragement, but even doing the opposite, conspiring with the devil in joining in battle and destruction of his strength."[13]

The devil's role in Job's story is one of usefulness, and Chrysostom explains how the devil is indeed useful to human beings. The devil is responsible for the attacks on Job, and the attacks are a test, giving Job the opportunity to display his virtue, even to strengthen his virtue. Chrysostom writes,

> Do not be distressed that he [the devil] was thrown from heaven to earth, but give thanks to God that he gave you a need for vigilance, that he gave you a horrible and difficult teacher. Do you want me to show you the benefit of the devil? . . . Not that the devil is the cause of good things, but God's loving-kindness uses the evil one properly.[14]

The devil is part of Chrysostom's theodicy as a temptation to do evil, and evil originates neither with God nor with the devil but with humans and with human choice. The devil's (God-controlled) presence on earth is for the purpose of encouraging humans to be vigilant and of giving them opportunities to resist evil. Thus, the devil allows humans the opportunity to be virtuous. This utility of demons is a theme that will carry throughout Chrysostom's demonology, but first a description of Chrysostom's demonology is in order.

ORIGIN OF DEMONS

Chrysostom does not often speculate about the origin of the devil and his demons. In *De diabolo tentatore*, there is only one passage that addresses the devil's origin, and that only tangentially:

> Let the devil be free to be exceedingly wicked, not wicked by nature [*physis*, φύσις], but by choice [*proairesis*] and mindset [*gnōmē*, γνώμη]. For that the devil is not wicked [*ponēros*, πονηρός] by nature learn from his name. . . . He is called wicked, but his wickedness is not from his *physis*, but from his

---

cattle unless he has received authority?" and "Do you see also the devil bridled?" (*Comm. in Iob* 1.16 [SC 346bis, 126]).

[13]Chrysostom, *Comm. in Iob* 19.1 (SC 348bis, 38).

[14]Chrysostom, *Comm. in Iob* 1.9 (SC 346bis, 110).

proairesis. . . . For he was not that way at the beginning, but afterwards he became thus; so that he is called apostate [*apostatēs*, ἀποστάτης]. Why is he said to be wicked then? Although many men are wicked, he alone is called this as the most prominent. Why is he so called? Because though in no way wronged by us, having no grudge whether small or great, when he saw humankind having been honored, he straightway [*eutheōs*, εὐθέως] envied him his good.[15]

Chrysostom wants his congregation to understand that the devil is evil not by nature but by his own choice. The details of this change from good to apostate are less important than the fact of it for Chrysostom's larger purposes. The biggest hint of the cause of Satan's fall in this passage is mention of the devil's immediate envy of humanity: "Satan envied [*ebaskēnen*, ἐβάσκηνεν] [Adam] his good." The statement about envy is, however, only indirectly linked to Satan's change into wickedness, for envy is given as the reason he is most prominent of the wicked, not as the reason for the beginning of his wickedness. Although it seems here that for Chrysostom the cause of Satan's fall is his envy of Adam, not unlike the claims of *Life of Adam and Eve*, mentioned in chapter one, more passages from Chrysostom's works will show that this picture is incomplete.[16]

In his *De poenitentia homiliae*, also written early in his career, Chrysostom preaches, "The devil was good at first, but he fell because of laziness and despair into such wickedness that he could not rise again. That he was good, listen to what Scripture says: 'I saw Satan fall like lightning from heaven.' This comparison to lightning shows the radiance of his way of life before his fall, and the suddenness of his fall."[17] Though Luke 10:18 is cited

---

[15]Chrysostom, *De diab. tent.* 1.2 (SC 560bis, 128-32).

[16]Irenaeus makes a similar argument in *Haer.* 5.24. Irenaeus writes, "Just as if any one, being an apostate, and seizing in a hostile manner another man's territory, should harass the inhabitants of it, in order that he might claim for himself the glory of a king among those ignorant of his apostasy and robbery; so likewise also the devil . . . becoming envious of man, was rendered an apostate from the divine law: for envy is a thing foreign to God." English from *ANF* 1:553.

[17]Chrysostom, *De poen. hom.* 1.2 (PG 49.279). The fall due to "laziness and despair" is significant because it is the disposition against which Chrysostom frequently warns his own congregants as leading to the gravest sins. Regarding the "could not recover," Chrysostom says that laziness casts down, but despair keeps one there. His positive examples are Paul, the thief on the cross, and the publican (of the Pharisee and publican parable). Each of these people had fallen into wickedness but did not become discouraged and so rose up. Judas, however, became discouraged after his fall and did not rise again. In this way Chrysostom protects the notion of choice. It is not that people fall beyond recovery but that if they choose despair as well, they cannot recover. They must make an effort.

for the original goodness of the devil, Chrysostom does not explain how he knows the cause of the fall to be "laziness and despair." In fact, this section of the sermon is a warning to his congregation against laziness, which he says causes falls that can cast a person out of heaven. The devil is his prime example. In a homily on John where the warning to his audience is against pride, Chrysostom will argue that pride was the cause of the devil's fall.[18] Chrysostom's inconsistency on the particular vice that causes the devil's fall demonstrates his willingness to use the devil in whatever way is most beneficial to his congregation at the time, in service of whichever virtue he is impressing on his audience.

A passage from Chrysostom's *Homiliae in Genesim*, written around the same time as *De diabolo tentatore*, is his most extensive discussion of the devil's origin, and it is prompted simply by his coming to Genesis 6 in the homiletical series.[19] Because it provides more depth to Chrysostom's understanding of the devil's origin, it bears quoting at length:

> It is necessary to make a great inquiry of this passage [Gen 6:2] and refute the fictions of all those who speak thoughtlessly. . . . Why, then? Now they [angels] fell, and was this the cause of their fall? In fact, Scripture teaches us otherwise, that before the creation of the first formed [human being] both the devil and those with him, who thought more highly of themselves than they were worth, were brought down from that worthiness, just as a sage has said: 'Through the devil's envy death entered the world' [Wis 2:24]. For tell me, if he had not fallen before the creation of the human being, how, remaining in his worthiness, could he have envied the human being? For what kind of logic would it be for an angel to envy a human being, the incorporeal one having such great honor to envy one who wears a body? But since he was brought down from the highest glory into the furthest dishonor, and being incorporeal himself, he saw the created human being deemed worthy of great honor in

---

[18]"For just as the devil fell because of pride, so also the one who is operated on by him is anointed into pride" (Chrysostom, *In 2 Thess. hom.* 1.1 [PG 62.470]).

[19]Both are considered to have been preached early in Chrysostom's career as priest in Antioch. The *Homiliae 1-67 in Genesim* are debated but generally accepted as having been preached between 386 and 389, with most recent scholarship arguing for 389. *De diabolo tentatore* was likely preached in either 386 or 388. See Adina Peleanu's introduction to *Homélies sur l'impuissance du diable*, SC 560 (Paris: Cerf, 2013), 13; Robert C. Hill's introduction to *Homilies on Genesis 1-17*, FC 74 (Washington, DC: Catholic University of America Press, 1986), 5-6; and J. N. D. Kelly, *Golden Mouth: The Story of John Chrysostom—Ascetic, Preacher, Bishop* (London: Duckworth, 1995), 89.

his body because of the loving kindness of the Creator, he was carried into envy. . . . Therefore it is clear to all that long ago the devil and all his company fell from that glory and became dishonored. Is it not a particular kind of folly to say that angels came down to have intercourse with women, and that their incorporeal nature was led into intercourse with corporeal creatures? . . . For it is not for such an incorporeal creature to ever experience desire.[20]

Chrysostom's primary argument in this passage is to refute those who propound the interpretation that Genesis 6:2 is about angels descending from heaven to engage in intercourse with human women, the interpretation offered by 1 Enoch, which some of the early fathers, most notably Justin Martyr, followed.[21] Chrysostom gives two reasons for his refutation. The first reason the watchers myth cannot be correct is that the devil and his demons fell *before* the creation of human beings.[22] Chrysostom here assumes this and then emphasizes to his congregation that this is obvious because the devil envied human beings even though he was incorporeal. An uncorrupted incorporeal being would not envy a corporeal being since incorporeality is the superior state. That the devil in his incorporeality still envied the corporeal proves the devil must have fallen at some time prior to this envy. Behind Chrysostom's belief that the devil's envy is proof of the devil's earlier fall is Wisdom 2:24, which says it was the devil's envy that brought death into the world.

Scripture is not, however, Chrysostom's only source for rejection of the watchers myth. The second reason Chrysostom gives for rejection is that demons are incorporeal, and incorporeal beings are incapable of lusting after corporeal women. Angelic beings do not feel desire. Chrysostom does cite Matthew 22:30 ("In the resurrection they neither marry nor are given in marriage, but are like the angels of God"[23]) to support his claim—or as the impetus of his understanding[24]—that angels could not be united with women at all,

---

[20]Chrysostom, *In Gen. hom.* 22.2 (PG 53.187-88).

[21]Justin Martyr, *First Apology* 5.

[22]Chrysostom also makes an argument that those who believe the watchers myth interpret the "sons of God" in Gen 6:2 as angels, but they are incorrect because nowhere in Scripture are angels referred to as "sons of God." That term is reserved for human beings and even the collective Israel. Angels are referred to as messengers and ministers. His texts are Ps 104:4, 82:6; Is 1:2; Ex 4:22 (*In Gen. hom.* 22.2).

[23]According to Chrysostom's translation.

[24]In this case it is not possible to know which resource or thought was the impetus for the other.

but he does not cite a text as evidence for his assertion that incorporeal beings do not experience the onset of desire. Chrysostom assumes it. Moreover, he assumes this knowledge of his congregation. To believe the things Chrysostom is refuting is "the fullness of folly" and "to take this into consideration is entirely absurd."[25] The rhetorical questions Chrysostom employs not only indicate his own position but also show that the congregation ought to know the answers as well. It is a logical argument based on common knowledge.

The level of specificity of *De diabolo tentatore* passage differs greatly from that of the *Homiliae in Genesim* passage. *De diabolo tentatore* is vague and lacking in description of the devil's fall, whereas *Homiliae in Genesim* is more specific, refuting the watchers myth and giving reasons for doing so. He is prompted to such speculation by the verse under examination, Genesis 6:2, as well as by Wisdom 2, Genesis 3, and various interpretations he takes to be incorrect. The *De diabolo tentatore* excerpt is concerned only to explain that the devil is evil not by nature but by choice. Any hint of the devil's origin comes only in service of this point. In the two homilies Chrysostom preached explicitly about demons, he is unconcerned with demonic origins and concerned instead with whether Satan's wickedness is intrinsic or by his own choice. This suggests that the perspective of *De diabolo tentatore* specifically and of Chrysostom's demonology generally is psychological. The devil's origin is less important than that he exists and that his wickedness is a result of his choice.

There are other comments scattered throughout Chrysostom's corpus that indicate his understanding of demonic origins remained largely consistent, even as he is inconsistent regarding the vice he ascribes to Satan. That is, whether the devil fell because of laziness, pride, or some other vice against which Chrysostom warns his congregation, the devil's fall is always his own choice. A few years after *De diabolo tentatore* and the *Homiliae in Genesim*, Chrysostom preaches in his *Homilies on John* (c. 391), "The devil would have been cast down and become the devil, not having been the devil before, if he had not been sick with this sickness [pride]. It threw him out of that freedom of speech, it sent him into hell, it became the cause of all evils for him."[26] Here again there is a time when the devil was not evil and

---

[25]Chrysostom, *In Gen. hom.* 22.2 (PG 53.188).
[26]Chrysostom, *In Ioh. hom.* 16.4 (PG 59.106). Pride as the cause of the devil's fall is a popular fourth-century assertion. For a small sample, see Gregory of Nazianzus, *Carm.* 1.1.7.68:

a time when the devil was cast down from a good position. This statement also adds a new element to Chrysostom's earlier discussion of demonic origins. Here Chrysostom claims that the devil not only fell out of heaven but also was thrown into hell. Since Chrysostom also speaks of the devil and his demons as working in the earth, in fact even having dominion on the earth, hell must be the devil's home and the earth his workplace. Other homilies, especially the Matthean homilies (c. 390), talk of the devil's final end in hell, but in the passage from *Homilies on John*, Chrysostom says that the devil was sent to hell by his pride. It is also possible to interpret this statement to mean that the devil's pride caused his fall, which will, in the end, result in hell for him.

Except for a passing reference to the devil "and all his company" in the passage from *Homiliae in Genesim*, Chrysostom does not speak about the origin of demons themselves, only of Satan's origin. However, in that passage he says that "long ago the devil and all his company fell from that glory and became dishonored."[27] Whether they fell because they followed Satan, thus falling simultaneously with him, or at some later time at the devil's instigation is unclear. Chrysostom is not concerned to speculate for his congregation about such details.[28]

"arrogance destroyed him [Satan]"; Augustine, *Trin.* 4.10: "The devil through pride led man through pride to death"; and Jerome, Letter 12: "Pride is opposed to humility, and through it Satan lost his eminence as an archangel."

[27]Chrysostom, *In Gen. hom.* 22.3 (PG 53.189).

[28]Chrysostom's silence regarding the fall of demons is not unusual. Except for Evagrius Ponticus, none of Chrysostom's contemporaries discuss this fall. Evagrius follows and develops Origen's fall narrative further, arguing for a fall of νοοῖ. As in Origen's account, Evagrius maintains that the level of fall determined the kind of being the νοῦς became (see Evagrius Ponticus, *The Praktikos & Chapters on Prayer*, trans. John Eudes Bamberger, Cistercian Studies 4 [Spencer, MA: Cistercian, 1970], 45, 59). The Cappadocians, however, refer to the devil's fall but not the angels' fall. Given that Chrysostom also separates—rather than conflates—demons and passions, we know he does not follow Evagrius fully in demonology. It is possible that Chrysostom refrained from speculating about the demons' origins as a way of avoiding being labeled an Origenist since the Origenist controversies were beginning during his career. It is more likely, however, that Chrysostom did not think the matter pressing. Chrysostom has shown a tendency—even a calculated aim—to provide his congregation the knowledge, exhortation, rebuke, etc. that they need and often explains that he is talking about a topic because it is a particular concern to the audience. He does this in both homilies of *De diab. tent.* as well as *De proph. obsc.* 3, which suggests that he regarded demonic origins as of less import than other aspects of demonology. Moreover, Chrysostom's later support of the Long Brothers, or Tall Brothers, as they are also called, suggests that he was less concerned with being labeled an Origenist than with being a faithful priest and bishop. For an account of the Long Brothers episode, see J. N. D. Kelly, *Golden Mouth*, 191-202.

NATURE

Chrysostom makes even fewer comments regarding the nature or composition of demons than he does about their origin. From the origin narratives Chrysostom employs, it is clear that demons and angels are ontologically the same; the only difference is the way in which they exercised their *proairesis*, their own choice, which resulted in a moral difference. Chrysostom emphasizes the devil's (and his demons') original goodness. In a discussion on whether evil is created or uncreated, Chrysostom writes, "Nothing is created evil by nature."[29] Though this is a parenthetical comment in this homily, it is an important point, and one Chrysostom makes often. In this instance, Chrysostom is arguing against those who believe that evil is uncreated and therefore equal to God, and Chrysostom contends that this is blasphemy. God alone is uncreated. Evil things become and are evil only by choice. Chrysostom writes in a similar discussion in his *In Mattheum homiliae* 59.3, "'From where do evils come?' one may say. From willing and not willing. . . . For evil is nothing other than this: disobedience to God."[30] One implication of this is that if nothing is evil by nature, then neither is the devil. If nothing is uncreated, then neither is the devil.

This discussion shows that according to Chrysostom, the devil and his demons all have *proairesis*, the faculty to which moral responsibility is applied. Moreover, the devil's abuse of his *proairesis* caused his fall.[31] This emphasis, as in the first passage quoted from *De diabolo tentatore*, implies that if not even the devil, who is the most evil being and beyond redemption, was created evil but became so by choice, then human beings, who are not as evil as the devil and who are offered redemption, are also not evil by nature but by choice. From his belief that even the devil is a creature inferior to God, Chrysostom reasons that there is no evil in the world that is beyond God's power.

What exactly demons—or even angels—are ontologically is something Chrysostom does not discuss. As with other writers, much of what we know

---

[29]Chrysostom, *In Act. apost. hom.* 2.4 (PG 60.31).

[30]Chrysostom, *In Matt. hom.* 59.3 (PG 58.576).

[31]Chrysostom does not comment specifically on whether demons also have προαίρεσις, but it is reasonable to assume he believes they do. Since he insists God did not create anything evil, and since he further insists that the devil has προαίρεσις, and given his emphasis on choosing evil, it is logical to assume Chrysostom extends προαίρεσις to demons as well.

about demons' natures can only be surmised from their origin narratives. Therefore, for Chrysostom, that demons are fallen angels means that they are incorporeal; that they are incorporeal means they cannot feel corporeal desire; and that they cannot feel corporeal desire means that they cannot have fallen through lust for human women. That they fell at all implies a freedom to choose since demons are creatures and God creates nothing evil.

What little Chrysostom does offer makes it clear that demons are spiritual beings. Chrysostom writes, "The demon is bodiless; he goes around everywhere."[32] The demons' incorporeality is what makes the idea of their lusting after human (corporeal) women absurd: "For what kind of logic would it be for an angel to envy a human being, the incorporeal one having such great honor to envy one who wears a body?"[33] This statement further assumes that demons, because they have no body, are ontologically superior to human beings. Of course, because they are incurably evil, they are ethically inferior to humans. A being's composition does not dictate its moral stature. The devil might be bodiless, but he is still wicked because of his choice.

DEMONIC ACTIVITY

What Chrysostom is most concerned about, far more than demons' origins and natures, is that his congregation have a detailed understanding of demonic activities. His audience must be aware of the ways in which demons interact with the world and especially the ways they interact with human beings, a concern prompted both by the congregation's misunderstandings about demons as well as by Chrysostom's general concern for the virtue and salvation of his people. Chrysostom states the importance of the question plainly in *De diabolo tentatore* 1:

> The Devil is wicked. I know it myself and it is admitted by everyone, but carefully pay attention to the things about to be spoken now. For they are not things that just happen to be, but those about which many words often come about in many places, about which there is many a fight and battle.[34]

---

[32]Chrysostom, *In 1 Thess. hom.* 3.6 (PG 62.414). Chrysostom likely preached his homilies on 1 Thessalonians around 402, in Constantinople, just a year before his first banishment from the city.

[33]Chrysostom, *In Gen. hom.* 22.2 (PG 53.188).

[34]Chrysostom, *De diab. tent.* 1.2 (SC 560bis, 132).

For some of Chrysostom's parishioners, the power they attributed to demons meant that demons, not God, ruled the world: "As bright as the sun is, the providence of God is clearer. But still some dare to say that demons manage our affairs."[35]

According to Chrysostom, demons have made themselves evil, and without proper knowledge and vigilance on a human's part, demons can lead human beings to become evil as well. At the outset of *De diabolo tentatore* Chrysostom explains his reason for preaching this series: "[The devil] is hateful and an enemy, and it is a great security to know clearly the ways of the enemy."[36] Chrysostom phrases his intent in gladiatorial terms. This is Chrysostom's motivation: to prepare the congregation for the devil's attempts so they can defend themselves. Such defense is an easy enough task, Chrysostom thinks, if they know exactly where the enemy is going to throw his spear. In this spirit, then, Chrysostom describes demons' primary activities.

The devil and his demons have one goal above all: to prevent a person's salvation. Chrysostom opens one of his sermons on the Gospel of John, "Mighty and violent, the devil presses in, besieging our salvation on every side."[37] Chrysostom emphasizes the enormity of the devil's aim when he discusses the armor of God (Eph 6:10-17), explaining why the congregation should take such care to defend themselves: "See how the power of the enemy rouses us and sobers us, knowing that the danger is of great things and the victory for the sake of great rewards."[38] Chrysostom has just said, "It is not so that they may gain something by conquering, but so that they may rob us."[39] Destruction itself is the demons' sole aim, not some gain on their part. Moreover, Chrysostom wants his congregation to understand that it is not some little destruction, some head cold or starvation or poverty; it is the worst kind of destruction. When Satan tempts a person to distraction by the theater, it is an attack not merely against the person's health or reputation but against her very salvation. Satan "is eager to throw us out of heaven."[40]

---

[35]Chrysostom, *De proph. obsc.* 3.6 (PG 49.253).
[36]Chrysostom, *De diab. tent.* 1.1 (SC 56obis, 122).
[37]Chrysostom, *In Ioh. hom.* 23.1 (PG 59.137).
[38]Chrysostom, *In Eph. hom.* 22.3 (PG 62.159).
[39]Chrysostom, *In Eph. hom.* 22.3 (PG 62.159).
[40]Chrysostom, *In Eph. hom.* 22.3 (PG 62.159).

Two aspects of this statement are interesting. First, the whole sentence, capped by this final, pointed clause, tells the listeners that they need to take the devil's threat more seriously than they have thus far. It is the very loss of heaven the audience faces, not the proverbial slap on the wrist from the grandfatherly God. This suggests that though there are many in the congregation who fear the devil because he is powerful, even to the extent of governing the world, there are others who do not consider demons seriously enough. Given the size of Chrysostom's average audience, it is likely people with both notions were present. On the other hand, maybe Chrysostom is preaching to those who fear the demons' governance but do not realize that his governance is a more serious matter than mere poverty or starvation. Second, for a person to be cast *out* of heaven, she must already be *in* heaven. Chrysostom seems to think that Christians already live in heaven or, as he often phrases it, "as if in heaven."[41] Whether God, in his saving work, placed the Christian in heaven at baptism or from birth or whether the Christian's virtue put him there is a matter for a later chapter, but in any case heaven is the Christian's to lose.

In his pursuit of humanity's destruction the devil uses many schemes, and his arsenal is extensive. Chrysostom describes the devil as attacking humans and describes humans as locked in a constant struggle with demons. The attacks may come either by word or by deed. In *De diabolo tentatore* Chrysostom offers Adam and Job as examples of the two types of attack, word and deed. Chrysostom also uses Adam and Eve as the negative example for dealing with the devil and Job the positive.[42] Chrysostom writes,

> [The devil] attacked Adam with mere words, but Job even with deeds. For the one he stripped of all his wealth and robbed of his children. But from this man he did not take away anything either little or great. But rather let us examine the very words and the method of the attack.[43]

---

[41]For example, see Chrysostom, *Comp. reg. et mon.* 3; *In Matt. hom.* 48.3, 68, 69, 82; *In 1 Tim. hom.* 14; *De stat.* 17. The goal of Christians is to live as if in heaven, and the monks Chrysostom champions exemplify this way of life.

[42]For more on this frequent contrast between Adam/Eve and Job, see my essay: Samantha L. Miller, "The Exemplary Role of Adam and Eve in John Chrysostom's Virtue-Building Program," in *John Chrysostom and Severian of Gabala: Homilists, Exegetes and Theologians*, ed. J. Leemans, G. Roskam, and J. Segers, 121-35 (Leuven: Peeters, 2019).

[43]Chrysostom, *De diab. tent.* 2.3 (SC 560bis, 178-80).

Chrysostom continues to retell the story of Genesis 3 with commentary. Regarding the serpent's question to Eve, Chrysostom says, "See the wickedness of the devil. He said that which was not spoken, in order that he might learn what was spoken."[44] Also, "exciting the woman with mere words and puffing her up with empty hopes, he thus deceived her."[45] The devil's attack on Eve was by word alone. Deception is one of the devil's principal schemes. In particular, the devil will make wicked and sinful things, such as Eve's fruit, look like good things. More than this, the devil claimed that what God had told Eve about the fruit was wrong. It would not cause her death. This is Chrysostom's negative example of dealing with the devil: Eve should have recognized the devil's words as a deception and refused to be deceived, just as the congregants ought to be vigilant, recognize the devil's deceptions, and refuse to be fooled.

Job is Chrysostom's choice of counterexample to Adam and Eve, his primary exemplar of virtue when discussing human interaction with demons. In *De diabolo tentatore* 2.3, Chrysostom notes that the devil wasted no words on Job but rather attacked him with deeds. Chrysostom writes, "To Job, after the destruction of his wealth, after the loss of his children, after being stripped of all of his things, her [Job's wife's] machinations were added."[46] In *De prophetiarum obscuritate* 3.6, he says, "Consider Job's herds of cattle, the flocks of sheep, how in one crucial moment he annihilated all; consider the pitiable death of his children, the blow he bore to his body."[47] When that apparently was not enough, Satan, through the words of Job's wife, tempted Job to "curse God, and die" (Job 2:9). Job, however, endured his suffering and the devil's attacks and refused to curse God, in contrast to Eve's action in the face of temptation.[48]

---

[44]Chrysostom, *De diab. tent.* 2.3 (SC 560bis, 178-80). Chrysostom claims the serpent's words and action as Satan's deception, but he does not suggest that the serpent was possessed. Chrysostom says the serpent "was a mere serpent" (*De diab. tent.* 2.4), suggesting that Chrysostom thought the serpent to be a form the devil took in that instance, though he is not clear enough to allow a decisive conclusion.

[45]Chrysostom, *De diab. tent.* 2.4 (SC 560bis, 184).

[46]Chrysostom, *De diab. tent.* 2.4 (SC 560bis, 186).

[47]Chrysostom, *De proph. obsc.* 3.6 (PG 49.253-54).

[48]In *Comm. in Iob* 2.9, Chrysostom says that the devil had Eve in mind when he used Job's wife to tempt him to curse. Words alone brought down Eve; perhaps they would also vanquish Job when the deed of causing suffering could not (SC 346bis, 174). He also draws this contrast in *De diab. tent.* 2.4.

Temptation is without question the devil's primary work. The devil can tempt a person to any number of sins, from lust to laziness to overactivity to attending the races instead of worship on Sunday morning.[49] Chrysostom speaks in many places and in varied ways about the snares of the devil, but rarely in any detail: "This is the plan of the wicked demon so as to trip you up by little things";[50] "the devil is in the habit of threatening us in every way, but especially through our tongues and mouths";[51] "such is the devil's deception; his tricks are not put out in the open."[52] Even stripping humans of wealth or afflicting them with illness or famine is an attempt to tempt them to lose faith and thus their salvation. Most of Chrysostom's many statements about demonic activity speak of generic "wiles" and "snares," or the aim of the devil to cause a person harm.

One of the most detailed descriptions of the devil's attacks comes from Chrysostom's homilies on Ephesians, which brings insight into his understanding of the nature of demonic plots:

> To use "wiles," is to deceive and to take by artifice or contrivance; something that happens by cunning, by words, by deeds, and by tricks, by those who lead us astray. I mean something like this: the devil never places sins before us clearly; he does not speak of idolatry, but he shows it off in another way, using "wiles," that is to say, making his discourse believable, using disguises.[53]

Deception is the tool the devil uses to bring about temptations. He will not present a sin as the ugly thing it is but will put it in a tuxedo and make it dance so that it is enticing, seductive, and desirable to a person, even distracting enough so that she will not realize it is a sin until it is too late. This implies that the devil makes suggestions to a person. Chrysostom's primary examples are Adam and Eve and Job, where Satan's action is clearly defined, and when he describes the devil's using "words, deeds, and tricks" against humans, Chrysostom does not explain the details of these attacks. How does a human hear the devil's words? In his mind? In her soul? Is it a general

---

[49]Chrysostom, *In Gen. hom.* 61 (PG 54.525-532), on Joseph with Potiphar's wife (lust); *In Ioh. hom.* 7.2 (PG 59.65-66) (laziness and overactivity) and *Cat.* 6 (SC 50bis, 215-28) (attending races).

[50]Chrysostom, *Cat.* 1.40 (SC 50bis, 129).

[51]Chrysostom, *Illum. cat.* 1.17 (SC 366bis, 146).

[52]Chrysostom, *In Gal. comm.* 1.5 (PG 61.621).

[53]Chrysostom, *In Eph. hom.* 22.3 (PG 62.158). This statement is prompted by Eph 6:11: "Put on the whole armor of God, so that you may be able to stand against the wiles of the devil."

impression? As with the monks, is it a suggestion of thought indistin-
guishable from one's own thought?[54] How precisely demons "dress up" sins
and tempt humans Chrysostom leaves vague. It is most important to him
that his congregation know that demons do tempt and deceive by both
words and deeds. It is even more important that the audience know one
ought to be able to recognize temptation and deception and resist them.
However great the devil's attempts to injure humanity, he is often unsuc-
cessful because God has put a limit on his power, and these limits are Chrysostom's chief concern.

DEMONIC LIMITS

The devil and his demons may not force human beings or use violence
against them to achieve their ends. Chrysostom notes, "[The devil] does not
overpower by strength, nor by tyranny, nor through compulsion, nor
through force. Since if this were the case, he would have destroyed everyone."[55]
The argument is logical. If the devil's aim is to destroy humanity and keep
human beings from the salvation God has for them, and if the devil is utterly
evil, then the devil will pursue this goal with every tool available to him.
Furthermore, if the devil's power were limitless, there would be no question
of humanity's destruction; it would be fact. Since humanity is still flourishing, there must be some hindrance to the devil's plan. The devil and his
demons must not be able to destroy by force or violence. This is an empirical
argument. Chrysostom takes the fears, assumptions, and excuses of his
congregation—that demons would want to be cause of all ills, sins, and
harms to human beings—and extends them to their logical conclusion to
show that the congregation's understanding is incorrect.

Chrysostom's argument is not only logical, however. Job is the primary
scriptural example of the devil's limitations. Chrysostom highlights the necessity of the devil's asking and receiving permission from God to harm Job.
The devil was not able to destroy Job's herds and flocks without first gaining
God's permission.[56] Moreover, Job is an example of the devil's defeat at the

---

[54]In one of his earliest works, his letter *Ad Theodorum lapsum*, Chrysostom does speak about the
devil plaguing a person with "thoughts of despair" (*Ad. Theod.* 1.2; SC 117bis, 86).

[55]Chrysostom, *De diab. tent.* 1.1 (SC 560bis, 122).

[56]Chrysostom, *De diab. tent.* 1.1 (SC 560bis, 122).

hands of a human being. Job never curses God, however great the temptation becomes. Thus, Job is Chrysostom's example of an athlete of virtue who overcomes the devil. If Job, a human being, could defeat the devil, then there is a limit to the devil's power.[57]

For all that Chrysostom praises Job and holds him up as a shining example of resistance for his congregation to emulate, Job also complicates Chrysostom's argument. In the story of Job's misfortunes, Job's herds *and children* are killed. The devil kills them. Chrysostom, in retelling the narrative, uses the word "annihilate" (*katanaliskō*, καταναλίσκω). Most reasonable human beings would consider this to be an example of the devil's power, but Chrysostom insists that the devil is powerless. The devil must ask permission of God before he is allowed to cause death, and this is Chrysostom's proof that God has placed limits on the devil's power. This permission is the key to understanding Chrysostom's view of Satan's power. It is not that Satan is incapable of causing physical harm—he is plainly capable—but that Satan is incapable of causing physical harm simply by his own choice, whenever he wants. Chrysostom finds this reassuring. God has limited the devil's power, even if God allows him to be in fact capable of great destruction.[58]

The other way Chrysostom explains what he means by the devil's powerlessness is that the devil is powerless to cause *true* harm. Chrysostom distinguishes between apparent harm—disease, famine, even death—and true harm—sin. The devil was powerless against Job because the devil was powerless to cause Job to sin. Therefore, for all the suffering he caused, the devil did not cause any true injury. This distinction between true and apparent harm is central to Chrysostom's theodicy. It is what allows him to separate suffering from evil and therefore the devil's actions from the human being's. Differentiating between true and apparent evil is what drives Chrysostom to insist that his congregation resist the devil. A person can resist the devil; it is within her power.

---

[57]Chrysostom, *De diab. tent.* 1.1 (SC 560bis, 122); 2.4-5 (SC 560bis, 186-92).

[58]One might wonder whether his congregation found this as reassuring as Chrysostom intended them to. Chrysostom trusts that God's character prohibits destruction on a whim, but Chrysostom also believes that God allows punishment and even suffering for pedagogical purposes. Even as Chrysostom gives his congregation a new way to understand suffering, the devil remains a being who can destroy physically.

In his *In Iohannen hom.* 9, Chrysostom offers a method for successfully resisting the devil:

> If he considers his own nature and the multitude of his sins, and the greatness
> of the tortures in that place [the next world], the extraordinary apparent ra-
> diance of the things here, but are just like cattle food and die more readily
> than the flowers of spring—if we continually move these thoughts within
> ourselves and keep remembering those who lived most virtuously, the devil
> will not easily be able to overcome us, though he make a thousand attempts,
> nor will he be able to begin to prevail over us.[59]

People can thwart the devil's attempts at destruction, which implies that the devil's powers are not only finite but limited enough that human beings can resist them. Thus, the devil's powers are limited to the realm of apparent evil.

Chrysostom does not say that a person must pray and wait on God to fight the devil but that she can stand against him herself. Here the emphasis is entirely on the human. Indeed, it even sounds vaguely Platonic. A person is supposed to value the goods properly: eternal life is better than eternal punishment and eternal joy than temporary joy. As with Plato, the imma-terial is by definition better than the material. By valuing these things rightly and judging events accordingly, one will choose the correct course of action, and it is on the basis of one's choice that God rewards or punishes.

Though this passage makes no mention of Christ's action, in other hom-ilies it is clear that Chrysostom believes Christ to have played a significant role in the Christian's struggle against the devil. In his *Catecheses ad illumi-nandos*, Chrysostom preaches that the devil will be frightened of a Christian who has come from the Eucharistic table and will flee from him because at the table he has fed on Christ.[60] There is something about the Christian—not as a human being but specifically as a Christian—that the devil fears. A few paragraphs before this Chrysostom explained what Christ does in our struggle with the devil: "In our struggle with the devil, Christ does not stand impartial but is wholly on our side. . . . He bound the devil with unbreakable chains in order to bind him hand and foot for the struggle."[61] Even in the *In Iohannem hom.*, Chrysostom explains the devil's destruction by Christ. The

---

[59]Chrysostom, *In Ioh. hom.* 9.2 (PG 59.72-73).
[60]Chrysostom, *Cat.* 3.12 (SC 50bis, 158).
[61]Chrysostom, *Cat.* 3.9 (SC 50bis, 156).

devil, Chrysostom argues, had the power and the right to destroy all people because they had sinned.[62] The devil reached beyond his bounds, however, and tried to destroy Christ as well. This reaching is the reason for the devil's own destruction: "The devil will have justice demanded of him for what he did to us, for what he undertook to do to Christ."[63]

Chrysostom is clear that Christ has overcome the devil. One must, then, understand Chrysostom's emphasis on the ability and method for human resistance in *In Iohannem hom.* 9 within the context of Christ's prior action. It is Chrysostom's directions for resistance now, after Christ has struck the first blow. That Chrysostom spends so much time instructing his audience about how to resist the devil implies that Christians both can and must still resist. *Catecheses ad illuminandos* 3 makes it clear that the struggle against the devil is not over; Christ bound him, but we must still fight because, in spite of his chains, the devil still fights. A person knows she can successfully resist the devil's wiles because Christ has put the devil in chains, and in the coming chapters we will see that a person must resist because it is part of what God requires for salvation.

Demon Possession

Before continuing, a note on demon possession is necessary. Chrysostom acknowledges the reality of demon possession, and this makes more difficult questions of *proairesis* and responsibility. For all that demons cannot force or tyrannize, they can, apparently, possess a person. Perhaps the most notable discussion of possession Chrysostom offers is in his letter to a young man apparently possessed by a demon, *Ad Stagirium*.[64] The letter addresses the monk Stagerios, who because of his possession has fallen into despair and is ashamed. Chrysostom repeatedly urges Stagerios to take heart. Because it is outside the realm of his moral responsibility, possession is not something to be ashamed of. The trials he was facing were opportunities to grow in virtue and faith, and thus providential. At the very least, God has permitted these trials; at most, they are a punishment for sin in order to reconcile Stagerios

---

[62]By "destroy" (ἀναιρέω), Chrysostom means "put to death."

[63]Chrysostom, *In Ioh. hom.* 67.3 (PG 59.373).

[64]J. N. D. Kelly writes that Stagerios's affliction was most likely epilepsy given the description of the seizures in the letter, but people of the time assumed this was demon possession. See Kelly, *Golden Mouth*, 43-44.

to God.[65] Those who should be ashamed are those who engage in sins of all kinds, not those possessed.[66] Admittedly, this makes Chrysostom sound callous, but it is in keeping with his understanding of demonic activity. Suffering is suffering but not true evil. Here we do see Chrysostom allow demons to compel—that is the understanding of possession—but in that compulsion the human no longer has responsibility and instead is to be pitied. Stagerios does not need to be ashamed of his action because he was not responsible. Further, even this possession happens with God's permission. Though the demons are able to compel in this instance, they do so only within God's providence, not of their own volition. Demons are still limited. Finally, we see in this letter that Chrysostom's primary concern is for Stagerios's virtue rather than the demons themselves or even explaining demon possession.

Beyond *Ad Stagirium*, Chrysostom speaks of possession only infrequently, and even in his discussion of Jesus' exorcisms in the Gospels, he often focuses on issues other than the possession. For instance, the healing of the Gerasene demoniac is for Chrysostom primarily a rebuttal of the claim that demons are the souls of the dead, though Chrysostom does make a side comment about the "hidden meaning" that "swinish sort of men are especially susceptible to the works of demons."[67] Other points that receive brief mention in the comments on this pericope include the demonstration of God's providence, the demons' sin, and the crazed nature of sinners, especially the covetous, which resembles that of demoniacs.

Chrysostom also, on occasion, mentions the presence of demoniacs in his audience and tells his congregants that the demoniacs ought to be pitied and prayed for. For instance, he asks, "Is the sight of [the demoniacs] alone not enough to astound you and lead you to sympathy? Is your brother in chains, and you're indifferent? And what kind of excuse will you have, tell me, being so unsympathetic, so inhuman, and so savage?"[68] Demoniacs are to be pitied as those who are ill or captive, unable to control themselves.[69] It is for their

---

[65]Chrysostom, *Ad Stag.* 3.14 (PG 47.491-94).

[66]Chrysostom, *Ad Stag.* 2.2-3 (PG 47.447-49).

[67]Chrysostom, *In Matt. hom.* 29.2-5 (PG 57.352-57). Quotation at 29.4 (PG 57.356).

[68]Chrysostom, *De incompr. hom.* 4.37 (SC 28bis, 256). For other examples, see *De incompr. hom.* 3.42, 4.31-41 (SC 28 bis, 224, 252-60); *In Gen. hom.* 29.5 (PG 53.267); and *De res. dom.* 1-2 (PG 50.434-35).

[69]For an excellent discussion on the relationship between demoniacs, the mentally ill, and sinners in Chrysostom's rhetoric, see Claire Elayne Salem, "Sanity, Insanity, and Man's Being as Understood by St. John Chrysostom" (PhD diss., Durham University, 2010). Salem argues that

lack of control that they are to be pitied, but it is also their lack of control that removes responsibility from them for their actions. No choice, no responsibility. This is clear when Chrysostom states that demoniacs are not punished (with an eternal punishment), but those who come to Eucharist unworthily are "handed over to unceasing punishment."[70] According to Chrysostom, one is punished only for things one chooses; punishment implies responsibility. If a demoniac is not punished, neither is he responsible.

Though Chrysostom makes it clear that demoniacs are not in control of their own actions, he suggests that possession only occurs when one allows it:

> Are you not afraid, while conversing with yourself, while being indifferent, while thinking little of your brother, that some demon may not leap out of him, and, discovering your soul unoccupied and swept clean, enter it with much fearlessness, since he has found a house without a door?[71]

Chrysostom is using the allusion to Jesus' caution here to say that the sinner, by his sin, has prepared his soul for the demon to take possession of it. Sin made the soul an inviting house for a demon.[72] Even when someone is

---

Chrysostom has in mind a spectrum of what it is to be human. She frames this spectrum as one of sanity—with the upper limit being the monks ("preeminently sane") and the lower limit the self-centered person at war with God and neighbor and focused only on temporal things (insane) (pp. 5-6). As a way of exploring this spectrum, Salem focuses on Chrysostom's rhetorical treatment of the demon-possessed and the mentally ill. She concludes that Chrysostom saw both groups as those to be pitied because of their lack of self-control, but sinners are to be pitied even more because they sin of their own choice. We will see in chaps. 4 and 5 the significance of responsibility, reward, and punishment in Chrysostom's accounts of virtue and salvation. Salem gives only a cursory treatment to the question of whether a demoniac can be responsible for the initial possession, a possibility suggested by the *De incompr. hom.* 4 passage quoted below. What Salem does note is Chrysostom's use of μανία to describe the mentally ill, the demon-possessed, and sinners. Wendy Mayer notes this broad use of μανία and draws out the differences among the kinds of mania in Wendy Mayer, "Mania and Madness in the Works of John Chrysostom: A Snapshot from Late Antiquity," in *The Concept of Madness from Homer to Byzantium: Manifestations and Aspects of Mental Illness and Disorder*, ed. Hélène Perdicoyianni-Paléologou (Amsterdam: Hakkert, 2016). She concludes that both mental illness and possession are "purely physiological and involuntary" madness, whereas sin is a "volitional madness" (p. 360). These two categories, Mayer argues, are of primary significance for Chrysostom.

[70]Chrysostom, *In Matt. hom.* 82.6 (PG 58.745).

[71]Chrysostom, *De incompr. hom.* 4.37 (SC 28bis, 256). The "unoccupied and swept clean" is a reference to Lk 11:24-26.

[72]See also, "It is . . . necessary to be awake and sober and to wall off his attack everywhere. For if he gets hold of some small starting point, he prepares a wide entrance for himself and gradually introduces his whole power. If, then, our salvation matters to us, let us not yield to his attack in a small thing in order that we may check beforehand the great ones" (Chrysostom, *In Ioh. hom.* 23.1 [PG 59.137]).

possessed by a demon, when a demon compels action from a human being, the human is responsible for the possession in the first place. This leaves the matter of responsibility in the case of demon possession ambiguous, and Chrysostom does not say enough in his corpus to allow a conclusion regarding how much responsibility a demoniac has for her sin. Because the issue of possession and responsibility is unclear in Chrysostom, I bracket that discussion from the rest of this study and leave it for future research.[73]

THE REALITY OF DEMONS

Before discussing the uses to which Chrysostom puts demonic rhetoric I need to note that demons are not mere rhetorical devices for Chrysostom but real spiritual beings. It was common belief in the late fourth century that the world was populated not only with visible beings but with invisible ones as well. Chrysostom never refutes this assumption; it is where he begins. In his *De prophetiarum obscuritate* 3, traditionally titled *That Demons Do Not Govern the World*, the problem is not that the congregation believes demons to exist but that they believe demons to be governing the world. Similarly, in the two homilies *De diabolo tentatore*, Chrysostom speaks about the powers the demons have (and do not have), but not about their existence. It would be strange if Chrysostom had not believed in demons and never mentioned this to his congregation. His constant attempts to correct errant beliefs in his audience suggest that if Chrysostom had not believed in the devil as a real being, he would have tried to convince his congregation of it.

Chrysostom's belief in demons was not merely psychological, as may be the modern expectation. Demons are external to human beings in Chrysostom's thought. They can tempt a person, deceive her, even suggest thoughts to a person's mind, but these are all attacks on a person from outside her. The passions are something that afflict a person from within, and demons and passions are not the same for Chrysostom.[74] Evagrius described passions as demons, such as the demon of anger or the demon of sloth, but Chrysostom is not doing this. Chrysostom sometimes speaks of passions

---

[73]This study, therefore, is a one of Chrysostom's demonology, anthropology, and soteriology for unpossessed Christians.
[74]I explain Chrysostom's understanding of the passions in chap. 5 below.

without mentioning the devil or his demons.[75] Passions are the desires humans have that, left unchecked, can lead to sin. Demons are also not simply a way to explain certain illnesses or the inclination to sin. Chrysostom dismisses both of these ideas in *De diabolo tentatore* by arguing that demons are spiritual beings external to human beings who tempt, deceive, and sometimes cause natural disasters or illnesses, all in an attempt to destroy humanity. They are not mere psychological creations or another name for our sinful desires. This conviction was a shared cultural assumption, and there is no reason to think Chrysostom did not share it.[76] I make this note about the reality of demons for Chrysostom because much of this discussion will emphasize demons' rhetorical usefulness for Chrysostom, and it is important that one not take rhetorical usefulness to preclude existential reality.

DEMONS IN CHRYSOSTOM'S SPEECH

Except for monastic authors, Chrysostom discusses demons more often than his contemporaries and predecessors. When he does, there are two broad reasons for his demonic rhetoric. Often Chrysostom's comments about demons arise either because the passage he is expounding mentions demons or because mention of demons will help his argument to be useful

---

[75]Chrysostom, *In Ioh. hom.* 74.3: "Let us quench lust; let us kill anger; let us destroy envy. . . . Cut out from your heart excesses and foreign things. . . . Diseased and wicked desires usually block up the entrance of God's word. . . . Let us destroy, then, our evil desires" (PG 59.403).

[76]Ludlow's article about the Cappadocians' demonologies argues that the Cappadocians believed demons to be real and not mere rhetorical devices, even as they did at times use demons for a given rhetorical purpose or effect. She claims that belief in demons was not limited to the laity or the "uneducated" or lower classes, but the intellectual elites believed in the existence of demons as well, a point that transfers to Chrysostom, an intellectual and near contemporary (Morwenna Ludlow, "Demons, Evil and Liminality in Cappadocian Theology," *JECS* 20, no. 2 [2012]: 182). Peter Brown also argues that belief in demons was not restricted to any one group of people but was a "fact of life" in late antiquity: Peter Brown, *The Cult of the Saints: Its Rise and Function in Latin Christianity* (Chicago: University of Chicago Press, 1981), 114-15. Brown indicates the externality of demons as well: "They were invoked to explain sudden and incongruous misfortunes, deviations from normative behaviour such as riots, plagues and inappropriate love-affairs" (Peter Brown, *The World of Late Antiquity: From Marcus Aurelius to Muhammad* [London: Thames & Hudson, 1971], 54). So too David Brakke, who is concerned with monastic demonology and wishes to show that monks were not all from illiterate, uneducated classes: "Demonology . . . is an activity of literate, educated persons, who often use demons to address pressing intellectual problems," and demons are not "remnants of a pagan past that uneducated monks could not leave behind but adapted to their new Christian worldview" (David Brakke, *Demons and the Making of the Monk: Spiritual Combat in Early Christianity* [Cambridge, MA: Harvard University Press, 2006], 9-11).

in some way. Examples of the first instance include Chrysostom's discussion of Ephesians 6, which speaks of the armor of God used to stand against the devil's wiles; in his *Commentarius in Iob*, a discussion of Satan's role in Job 1–2; and accounts of exorcisms in the Gospels. When Scripture talks about demons, Chrysostom treats the demons as part of his exposition.

The second reason Chrysostom talks about demons, their usefulness for his argument, is the focus of this chapter. On the one hand, it is not surprising that Chrysostom talks about demons when they can be useful. Chrysostom is a trained orator, and he uses many rhetorical tools to shape his homilies and arguments. His goal is to provide useful words to his audience. Even in the cases of demons in Scripture mentioned above Chrysostom aims at usefulness because he understands that Scripture has mentioned demons for this reason.[77] Job would not have mentioned Satan unless Christians could learn something from his role in Job's suffering. In the homily on Genesis 6:2, where Chrysostom discusses the origin of demons at greater length than anywhere else, he writes thus not only because he wishes his congregation to know where demons come from but also because they have been told erroneous things about the devil's origin and he wants them to have correct information.

In other places, though, Chrysostom might choose to mention the devil or demons because they help his argument to a goal, such as in a homily on Jeremiah 10:23, where Chrysostom says that the devil pressures people to "give a distorted account of the contents of the Scriptures" and in his attempt to blaspheme adds words to Scripture and suggests poor readings.[78] False readings of Scripture come from the devil and therefore should be ignored.

There is one goal above all others for which Chrysostom aims when he preaches about demons: encouraging his congregants to be virtuous. In this goal, there are two primary ways Chrysostom preaches about demons, and

---

[77]Chrysostom believes that everything in Scripture is present for a reason, and that reason should be sought out and explained. He writes, "Consider the precision of Scripture, how it is simply not possible to find a chance syllable laying there neglected" (*In Gen. hom.* 23.2 [PG 53.198]). For Chrysostom, there is no wasted syllable; it stands to reason that syllables about the devil fall under the same principle. For more about Chrysostom's understanding of Scripture's precision, see Robert C. Hill, "*Akribeia*: A Principle of Chrysostom's Exegesis," *Colloquium* 14 (1981): 32-36; and Hill, "On Looking Again at *sunkatabasis*," *Prudentia* 13 (1981): 3-11.

[78]Chrysostom, *Dom., non est in hom.* 2 (PG 56.157-58; Robert C. Hill, trans., *Old Testament Homilies* [Brookline, MA: Holy Cross Orthodox Press, 2003], 2:10-12).

these two ways are the focus of this chapter. First, Chrysostom preaches reactively. His listeners experience various forms of suffering and question the origin of it. They look around, see the chaos and suffering in the world, and attribute all of this to demons. Their neighbors—pagan, Jewish, and Christian alike—use amulets and other magical items to ward off the evil demons. Some of those neighbors call on the demons, whom they perceive as benign spirits, to work for them or to protect them. There is a background buzz of fear, and Chrysostom preaches into this buzz. He tries to respond to his congregants' fears and assures them that demons are powerless to cause any true harm.

The other side of Chrysostom's preaching about demons begins in the same place. He tells his audience that demons are powerless to cause them true injury. True injury is sin, and however much his audience believes demons can cause them to sin, or however much they blame demons for their sins, the demons cannot cause sin. Each person is responsible for his own sin, uncoerced by any outside influence. The demons' inability to cause sin is not for their lack of effort, however. They make every attempt to draw people into sin and thus destroy them, making them unworthy of the kingdom of God. Though this part of Chrysostom's rhetoric is partly a response to these beliefs, it is also an attempt to prepare the congregation. Chrysostom knows the devil's tricks, knows how hard he fights to lead Christians to sin, so Chrysostom preaches about those tricks. In this way he prepares his congregation that they might not be deceived; he prepares them to fight for their virtue and their salvation.

Don't Fear the Reaper: Reactive Rhetoric

Chrysostom's reactive demonological speech is primarily an attempt to eradicate the fear of demons from his congregants, which is Chrysostom's immediate goal in *De diabolo tentatore*, *De prophetiarum obscuritate hom.* 3, and the *Catecheses ad illuminandos*. Chrysostom understands that fear of demonic powers plagues his congregation, but he is insistent that his audience be afraid neither of the devil nor of his demons. This is surprising given Chrysostom's predilection for inspiring fear in his audience in other contexts, for example, through vivid images of the horrors of hell. In a letter to his friend Theodore, Chrysostom writes,

That [fire of hell], which seizes, burns completely, and it never ceases once that person has been grabbed by that which burns through everything. Therefore it is also called unquenchable. For even those who have sinned need to put on immortality, not for honor, but to have a constant supply of material for punishment; and how terrible this is, speech could never be strong enough to explain.[79]

Chrysostom's aim is to put the fear of hell in his friend so that he might avoid behaviors, sins, which would lead to his suffering such torment. He does the same with his congregation in statements such as this:

The kingdom urges the good, and hell frightens usefully. For God threatens hell, not in order to throw into hell, but in order that he may set free from hell. If he wanted to punish, he would not threaten ahead of time that we might safely flee the things he threatens. He threatens punishment so that we might flee the experience of punishment. He frightens with words so that he will not punish with actions.[80]

Chrysostom believes his preaching is following the example God has set in Scripture. God threatens with hell so that people will not have to experience hell. The threat is a tool to frighten people into virtuous living.

But Chrysostom tells his congregation not to fear the devil or his demons. Insistence on not fearing demons is not exclusive to Chrysostom, but it is worth noting both because of Chrysostom's practice of motivating by fear and because Chrysostom's denial of the fear of demons highlights, and is a result of, his emphasis on human *proairesis*. After recounting the story of Job, Chrysostom preaches, "Therefore do not fear the devil, even if he has no body."[81] Most people understood incorporeal beings to be ontologically superior, and their invisibility likely added some uncertainty about where they were or whom they were attacking at any given moment, not to mention that it is hard to know how to defend against invisible beings, since swords are unlikely to be effective. Chrysostom, however, offers an explicit imperative against fearing the devil. The rationale is what he has just said in the homily: the description of Satan's asking God's permission to afflict Job. This is the reason one must not fear: Satan is subordinate to God. God's character,

---

[79]Chrysostom, *Ad Theod.* 1.10 (SC 117bis, 128).
[80]Chrysostom, *De eleem.* 7.7 (PG 49.336).
[81]Chrysostom, *De diab. tent.* 1.4 (SC 560bis, 142).

order, and rule are the foundations for a Christian's confidence against the devil and his demons. Therefore, the Christian ought to have no fear of demons. God is governing the world, and the devil is subordinate to God. That God is governing the world rather than demons is the theme of *De prophetiarum obscuritate* 3, and both homilies of *De diabolo tentatore* are concerned with the limits of the devil's power.

Chrysostom's *Catecheses ad illuminandos* also have a strong emphasis on not fearing the devil. When he describes the renunciation of Satan in the baptismal liturgy, Chrysostom explains that a catechumen's answer means, "I am bold, and I rebel, for I have a strong refuge. This made me superior to the demon, even though before this I was trembling and afraid."[82] Speaking of the catechumenate as a training school for wrestlers, he says, "Let us learn in this time [the devil's] grips, where his strength comes from, and how he can easily threaten us abusively so that, when the contest comes, we will not be caught off guard nor be thrown into confusion."[83] Chrysostom wants his congregation to have the proper object of fear, and his rhetoric is aimed at a correction of this object. Instead of fear mongering, Chrysostom's demonological discourse is empowering and encouraging. The congregation is able to win out over the devil.

KNOW THY ENEMY: PREPARATORY SPEECH

What begins as reactive preaching becomes preparatory. As he rids his congregation of their fear of demons, Chrysostom makes it clear what demons can and cannot do, as well as what they are trying to do. In this way, Chrysostom's speech about demons aims to strengthen his audience against the deceptions of the devil, giving his audience the knowledge they need to avoid being deceived and to resist the devil. In *De diabolo tentatore*, Chrysostom's motivation is to explain the "ways of the enemy,"[84] suggesting not a reaction but a preemptive strike. He is teaching his congregation what they need to know in order to take up the correct posture against the enemy, who is the devil, the enemy of our salvation. Chrysostom tells his congregation that they need not fear physical harm or poverty from demons, but they

---

[82]Chrysostom, *Cat. ult. ad bapt.* 3.6, (SC 366bis, 232).
[83]Chrysostom, *Illum. cat.* 1.16 (SC 366bis, 144).
[84]Chrysostom, *De diab. tent.* 1.1 (SC 560bis, 122).

should fear losing their salvation. The stakes are higher than they thought. And in his constant attempts to bring his people to salvation, Chrysostom finds demons particularly useful.

Chrysostom writes, "The devil, if you would understand, is even useful to us—if we use him correctly—and he helps us and we gain great things, not ordinary things. And this we demonstrated from Job."[85] Again, Job is the exemplar of virtue in the face of the devil's work, showing the congregation that, employed properly, the devil can be "useful" (*chrēsimos*, χρήσιμος) to them. If the congregation has a proper understanding of who the devil is and what his goal is, the congregation may "use" (*chraō*, χράω) the devil, or their knowledge of the devil, to gain advantages over him and benefits for themselves. The clause "if we use him correctly" is significant. Chrysostom's aim is to teach his congregation the proper way to use the devil so that they may gain great benefit, salvation itself.

Chrysostom's other example of using the devil for one's own profit is Paul, who writes to the Corinthians to hand over the fornicator to the devil so that the flesh may be destroyed but the soul saved (1 Cor 5:5). Chrysostom tells his congregation to take from the devil whatever chastisement comes, for this will rid a person of his impurities and earthly desires, making it possible for the soul to be saved. The devil is only allowed to punish as much as God allows, so the devil cannot destroy a person completely. As an extreme example of the profitability of the devil, Chrysostom writes, "Behold even the devil has become a cause of salvation, but not because of his own disposition, but because of the skill of the Apostle."[86] It is possible, therefore, for the devil even to be an aid to salvation, if one is skillful enough to use him rightly.

Prior to this point in the homily, Chrysostom has been expounding the reasons why God allows the devil still to roam the earth and wreak havoc. People can only win crowns if they can exhibit their power, so if there is no adversary against whom to struggle, the righteous person cannot win a crown.[87] This is another way to use the devil. To struggle against the devil is to become stronger, better able to resist, to forge one's character out of stronger

---

[85]Chrysostom, *De diab. tent.* 1.4 (SC 560bis, 140).
[86]Chrysostom, *De diab. tent.* 1.4 (SC 560bis, 140).
[87]Chrysostom, *De diab. tent.* 1.1-2 (SC 560bis, 126). "Winning a crown" is one of Chrysostom's descriptions of salvation.

steel. Chrysostom seems to believe this is an intrinsic benefit of struggling. His illustration is that of a wrestler. Even if the wrestler's antagonist has been taken away at the last minute, the wrestler who has prepared well, who has done all his exercises, is better for his practice, whether in the end there is an antagonist or not.[88]

One of Chrysostom's frequent rhetorical uses of demons is his practice of juxtaposing Christ and the devil in order to make his congregation's choice clear. Christ's goodness makes the devil's wickedness appear more wicked, and the devil's vileness makes Christ's goodness appear more pure. When juxtaposed for rhetorical effect, they provide a stark contrast. Many times Chrysostom offers his congregation two ways: they can follow Christ, or they can follow the devil. Each is traveling to his home, and the disciple chooses one to follow to his destination. Often when Chrysostom speaks of demons, he holds them as the alternative to following Christ. There is no gray area for Chrysostom: a person is always following either Christ or the devil.

Jesus' portrait of the sheep and the goats (Mt 25:31-46) drives much of Chrysostom's rhetoric about demons and their relation to a person's virtue. For instance, in *Homiliae in Genesim* 17, Chrysostom says, "Do you see the unquenchable fire prepared for [the devil], and, for us, unless we are lazy, the kingdom? Then let us consider these things and take charge of our lives. Let us flee evil and never be victim to the devil's machinations."[89] Chrysostom notes the claim of Matthew 25:41 that hell was prepared for "the devil and his angels," and the claim of Matthew 25:34 that the kingdom was prepared for humanity "from the foundation of the world." Doing evil and falling prey to the devil's wiles leads to the devil's home, in contrast to the kingdom God has prepared for us. In a reflection of the scriptural passage, Chrysostom offers no third way. There are but two options, and the way in

---

[88]Chrysostom, *De diab. tent.* 1.1-2 (SC 560bis, 126). This is similar to the Stoic understanding of evil. Exemplified well in Seneca's *On Providence*, which claims that things people refer to as evil—any kind of adversity—are not truly evil but only apparently so. Seneca argues that nothing evil can befall a good man and that adversities are only ever training. Similar to Chrysostom's reason for God's keeping Satan around, Seneca writes, "Without an adversary, prowess shrivels. We see how great and how efficient it really is, only when it shows by endurance what it is capable of. Be assured that good men ought to act likewise; they should not shrink from hardships and difficulties, nor complain against fate; they should take in good part whatever happens, and should turn it to good" (Seneca, *On Providence* 1.4; LCL 214:8-9).

[89]Chrysostom, *In Gen. hom.* 17.6 (PG 53.141).

which Chrysostom describes the evil option makes clear that there is only one true choice for the faithful Christian.

Chrysostom states the choice another way: "To Christ, who promises countless good things, no one pays any attention. But to the devil, who promises nothing of the kind but sends them on to Gehenna, all give way."[90] In statements like these the choice is meant to be plain: blessings or hell. What right-minded individual would choose hell? By setting the choice so starkly, Chrysostom implicitly encourages his congregation to choose virtue, to choose Christ. In his *Catacheses ad illuminandos*, the catechumens have made their choice. Chrysostom explains to them what their renunciation of Satan and choice for baptism and for Christ means. They have become willing slaves, pledging themselves to Christ, who won them from the devil, to whom they had formerly been enslaved.[91] At every step, however, they were and are slaves of someone. Christ and the devil are juxtaposed for effect. Chrysostom's binary rhetoric makes it clear to his audience that if they are not doing good, they are doing evil, and if they are not following Christ, they are following the devil. Describing sin as willingly following the devil makes virtue a more appealing decision.

I admit that this sounds as though Chrysostom is only making the devil the "face" of bad choices, and Christ the "face" of good choices, but Chrysostom means something stronger by his contrast. The juxtaposition is meant to highlight the Christian's choice: both that a choice exists and that it should be easy to make. A person can choose to do evil, thereby allying herself with the devil, or she can choose to do good, thereby allying herself with Christ. Christ and the devil are not mere faces or mere exemplars but real beings to whom a person pledges allegiance, and each of them is attempting to lead a person either to heaven or to hell. This is not simply a "Christ as exemplar" model; as noted above, Chrysostom understands Christ to have defeated the devil already, making the choice against the devil possible.

DEMONOLOGICAL DISCOURSE USED TO MOTIVATE VIRTUE

Strengthening his congregation and encouraging them to be virtuous is Chrysostom's central enterprise throughout his corpus. In his *De sacerdotio*,

---

[90]Chrysostom, *In Eph. hom.* 4.1 (PG 62.31).
[91]Chrysostom, *Cat.* 2.14-21 (SC 50bis, 141-45).

Chrysostom tells his audience that the role of a priest is to "train [Christ's body, the church] to great health and extraordinary beauty, looking everywhere lest somewhere a spot or a wrinkle or some other such disgrace ruin that appearance or even that attractiveness. For what else than the pure and blessed head to which it is subjected is worthy, according to human power, to display it?"[92] What defines worthiness for Chrysostom is virtue. Therefore, the priest's job is to bring about the virtue of his congregation, which is ultimately a concern for the salvation of his congregation.[93]

In pursuit of this virtue-building program, Chrysostom employs many varied techniques. Prominent methods in his homiletic toolbox are the "carrot and stick," rebuke and imitation. The carrot/stick method is one for which Chrysostom is well known. As noted above, Chrysostom threatens his audience with hell for wrongdoing in hope of scaring them into doing good. On the other side of that is language meant to entice toward the kingdom. Chrysostom is also not afraid to rebuke his congregation for sin that he knows about. The most famous example is his rhetoric against Empress Eudoxia, which got him exiled, but he was never shy about telling people that they needed to stop attending the theater instead of worship, that they were selfish and were not giving enough alms, or that they were too preoccupied with earthly beauty. Chastising the audience is an important part of building virtue, for it is hard to improve what one does not realize one is doing wrong. Chrysostom also encourages the imitation of the saints. Chrysostom not only upholds Job as an example of virtue; he does the same with many other biblical saints, Paul foremost among them. Additionally, Chrysostom urges his audience to observe the monks outside Antioch as those who live like

---

[92]Chrysostom, *De sac.* 4.2 (SC 272bis, 248). Jaclyn Maxwell has noted this goal of inspiring the audience to live virtuously: "Chrysostom envisioned a more intensely Christianized world, where the laity would be just as religious at home, at work, and in the streets as they were in the church. . . . If people could develop Christian habits, then a virtuous life would come naturally." Jaclyn L. Maxwell, *Christianization and Communication in Late Antiquity: John Chrysostom and His Congregation in Antioch* (Cambridge: Cambridge University Press, 2006), 21.

[93]There is, however, also a present (as opposed to future) dimension. Margaret Mitchell argues that Chrysostom is aiming at a Christian πολιτεία now: "He understands the Sermon on the Mount as the foundational speech—now become the charter document—of Christian *politeia* that constitutes the life of all Christians, who are called to a philosophical life lived always within an eschatological horizon" (Margaret M. Mitchell, "John Chrysostom," in *The Sermon on the Mount Through the Centuries*, ed. Jeffrey P. Greenman, Timothy Larsen, and Stephen R. Spencer [Grand Rapids: Brazos, 2007], 22-23). Chrysostom believes the earthly Christian community is meant to reflect the heavenly one.

angels on earth and to imitate these monks in the cities. Chrysostom has a catalog of virtue-building rhetorical techniques, and he uses whichever rhetoric he believes will bring about a desired action from his congregation. Among these, speech about demons is prominent and usually linked to the reward and punishment of kingdom/hell language. Moreover, when Chrysostom speaks about demons, it is most often for this virtue-building purpose.

The stated goal of *De diabolo tentatore* reads, "We do this, not because our talk about the devil is sweet to us, but because the instruction about him is an assurance for us. He is hateful and an enemy, and it is a great assurance to know clearly the way of your enemy."[94] Chrysostom goes on to say that the devil cannot force or use violence, for if he could, he would have destroyed all people already. The destruction of humanity, human beings' eternal death and torment in hell, is the devil's goal. In order to avoid their own destruction, Chrysostom wants his audience to know the devil's tactics so that they may be able to outsmart or otherwise overcome their enemy, and in doing so not only survive but even, through the cultivation of virtue, be found worthy of entrance to the kingdom of heaven.

Another example of this rhetorical aim comes from the *Ad illuminandos catechesis* 2, where Chrysostom argues that not even the devil can harm the soul of the faithful Christian, and nothing can hinder a Christian's virtue:

> I want you to know this more than everything: that no one is able to harm the soul of the faithful Christian, not even the devil himself. Not only is this a wonderful thing, that God made us unconquerable by all plots, but that he equipped us for the goal of the work of virtue, and nothing hinders us if we are willing. . . . For neither poverty, nor sickness, nor bodily disability, nor slavery, nor any other such thing can ever be an impediment to virtue.[95]

Poverty, weakness, disability, and slavery are all things Chrysostom has argued in *De diabolo tentatore* that demons are not necessarily responsible for, in contrast to his audience's beliefs. Therefore, on the one hand, if the devil did not cause these ills, the devil cannot have hindered a person's virtue. On the other hand, even if the devil did cause them with God's permission, Chrysostom argues, these things, and thus the devil himself, are

---

[94]Chrysostom, *De diab. tent.* 1.1 (SC 560bis, 122).
[95]Chrysostom, *Illum. cat.* 2.3 (PG 49.235).

still no hindrance to a person's pursuit of virtue. As noted, Chrysostom distinguishes between true and apparent harm, and all external sufferings like poverty and slavery are only apparent harm.[96] Injury to virtue is true harm, which is where Chrysostom's primary concern lies and where Chrysostom says the devil has no power.

CONCLUSION

Though Chrysostom frequently speaks of the devil and his demons, very little of this discourse is with regard to the demons' origins or nature. Chrysostom explains when necessary that demons are angels who fell before the creation of the world. They are incorporeal, spiritual beings, ontologically superior yet morally inferior to human beings, and all possessing a *proairesis*. The poor exercise of this faculty resulted in their fall. Of far more interest to Chrysostom are the ways demons interact with human beings. The devil's goal is to thwart humanity's salvation, and he and his demons resort to temptation, deception, and all manner of wiles to provoke humans to sin. Chrysostom acknowledges these ploys but tells his congregants that they are no excuse. The devil is powerless to cause any one of them to sin. Sin and virtue are the human's choice. Chrysostom preaches about demons in order to spur his audience on to virtue. In this way Chrysostom finds demons useful.

The mechanics of this approach, Chrysostom's use of demons to encourage virtue, are located in his theological anthropology. How Chrysostom understands the human being is the foundation of his concept of virtue, and key to his understanding of the human being is the term *proairesis*. This faculty is that which Chrysostom urges his congregation to remember in the light of the devil's attacks and that which the devil and his demons are unable to coerce. By exercising their *proaireseis* well, human beings can and should be virtuous. In order to understand these mechanics, it is necessary to explore the Greco-Roman history of *proaisesis* as a term as well as the Stoic ideas of virtue that influenced Chrysostom.

---

[96]This is not to say that Chrysostom has no concern for his congregants' sufferings. He can be gentle and pastoral, as is particularly seen in his *Letter to a Young Widow* (*Ad vid. iun.*) and his letters to Olympias (*ep. ad. Olymp.*). Moreover, he himself suffered ill health most of his life and then two banishments so he does not make this distinction between true and apparent harm from some sort of safe distance. When he speaks of demons, however, his concern is to show that they can do no real harm.

3

Greco-Roman Accounts of *Proairesis* and Virtue

CHRYSOSTOM'S PHILOSOPHICAL SOURCES

The question of Chrysostom's philosophical sources is a difficult one. Both his classical rhetorical training and his homilies and treatises themselves indicate that he has knowledge of philosophy, but whom exactly he knows, what concepts exactly he is choosing to use, and what is merely common knowledge or images "in the water" of his culture are far more difficult matters to ascertain. On occasion, Chrysostom cites philosophers: Zeno, Socrates, Diagoras, Pythagoras, Aristotle, and above all Plato, whom he mentions thirty times in his corpus.[1] In this way we know that Chrysostom was familiar with classical philosophy. Further, many of his moral statements, as we will see, sound very much like Stoic teachings, but since he does not credit Stoic authors, and since these ideas would have been common among the intellectuals of Chrysostom's day, it is impossible to know with certainty whether he is using an idea because he read it in a Stoic author's work or a *florilegium* and found it useful or whether he is only drawing on a common Christian wisdom that was itself borrowed from Stoic thinkers.

Many of these quotations reflect Chrysostom's primary use for philosophy, and for Plato in particular: as a foil for Paul or for Christ. According to Chrysostom and many of his predecessors, including Origen and the

---

[1]Chrysostom, *Adv. Iud.* 5.3 (PG 48.886); *In 1 Cor. hom.* 7.7 (PG 61.63); and *In Rom. hom.* 3.2 (PG 60.414). The count of thirty references to Plato is from Chrysostomus Baur, *John Chrysostom and His Time*, trans. M. Gonzaga (Westminster, MD: Newman, 1959), 1:306.

Cappadocians, the philosophers were intelligent, respectable teachers from whom Christians can learn, but their knowledge was incomplete. Christ has the full knowledge. Christ is the true philosopher and Christianity the true *philosophia* (φιλοσοφία). Chrysostom has a tendency to pit Paul against Plato in a battle of philosophy in order to show Paul's supremacy, often using Plato as a metonym for all Greek philosophy. This victory is intended to be a victory of the "unlearned" Paul against the highest-educated philosophers, symbolic of the gospel's victory over all philosophy.[2] Chrysostom writes, "Do you not see that Paul defeated the whole world and that he was more powerful than Plato and all the others?"[3] This is a common theme for Chrysostom. He states elsewhere,

> This "barbarian" [John the Evangelist], then, by the writing of his gospel seized the whole world. With his body he occupied the middle of Asia, where of old all those of Greek company used to philosophize, and there he is frightening to the demons. . . . He blotted out and destroyed all the teachings of the Greeks, while his teachings become brighter every day. From the time of both he and the other fishermen on, the teachings of Pythagoras have fallen silent, as well as those of Plato.[4]

Often Chrysostom aims to demonstrate that the ability to sound educated does not necessarily mean that a person is in possession of the truth and that the "unlearned" Christians are truly wiser than the "learned" pagan philosophers.[5]

As with many of his predecessors, notably Basil in his *Letter to Young Men*, Chrysostom did not think Greek philosophers entirely useless because they were superseded by Christ. Instead, Chrysostom used philosophy as it aided his argument and pointed to Christ the true philosopher and Christianity as the true *philosophia*. There are places where Chrysostom quotes from Plato's *Apology, Republic, Crito,* and *Timaeus,* among others.[6] Aside from

---

[2]Mitchell explores this theme in Margaret M. Mitchell, *The Heavenly Trumpet: John Chrysostom and the Art of Pauline Interpretation* (Tübingen: Mohr Siebeck, 2000), 74-75.
[3]Chrysostom, *In Tit. hom.* 2.2 (PG 62.673).
[4]Chrysostom, *In Ioh. hom.* 2.2 (PG 59.31).
[5]He thinks not that education unimportant but that it needs to be the right education and used toward proper ends (living a Christian life).
[6]Those listed are the most frequently cited, according to P. Ubaldi, "Di due citazioni di Platone in Giovanni Crisostomo," *Rivista di filologia e di istruzione classica* 28, no. 1 (1900): 69-75. In Chrysostom, see *Adv. opp. vit. mon.* 2.4 (PG 47.336); 3.11 (PG 47.367-68); and *In Ioh. hom.* 2.3 (PG 59.33) for a sampling.

these specific quotations, there are also places where Chrysostom alludes to Platonic ideas without a direct quotation, as when he uses the image of the soul as charioteer and horses: "Therefore, indeed, having trained these two faculties of the soul, ἐπιθυμία [epithymia] and θυμός [thymos], and having put them under the yoke of reason just like obedient horses, let us establish the mind as charioteer, in order that we may 'receive the prize of our high calling' [Phil 3:14]; which God grant that we may all attain, through Jesus Christ our Lord."[7] In another instance, Chrysostom uses the image to describe the damage sin does to the soul: "It is your own soul that you cut, that you wounded: you threw your charioteer down from his horses, you prepared to drag him on his back and you did just that!"[8] Chrysostom uses the Platonic image, but whether he gets it from the *Phaedrus* or whether it is commonplace enough in the rhetorical world that it is a "stock image" of sorts is impossible to know.[9]

Another example of Chrysostom's borrowing from Plato is in *Quod nemo laeditur nisi a seipso*, an important treatise for understanding Chrysostom's anthropology and account of virtue. Chrysostom appears to borrow his first argument from the tenth book of Plato's *Republic*: though Plato's argument is for the immortality of the soul, Chrysostom uses the same beginning steps to prove that the only one who can harm a person is the person himself.[10] First, Chrysostom discusses the definitions of good and evil, maintaining that things that are evil destroy whereas good things preserve and benefit, just as Plato writes (*Republic* 608e; Chrysostom, *Quod*

---

[7]Chrysostom, *In Eph. hom.* 17.3 (PG 62.120-21). For other examples, see *In Gen. hom.* 22.3 (PG 53.189); *In 1 Cor. hom.* 37.3 (PG 61.320); *In Tit. hom.* 5.2 (PG 62.689); and *In Rom. hom.* 14.2 (PG 60.525), where Chrysostom describes the Holy Spirit as the charioteer of the Christian soul. For an insightful discussion of Chrysostom's use of *Phaedrus* imagery, see Constantinos Bosinis, "Two Platonic Images in the Rhetoric of John Chrysostom: 'the Wings of Love' and 'the Charioteer of the Soul,'" in *Studia Patristica: Orientalia, Clement, Origen, Athanasius, the Cappadocians, Chrysostom*, ed. F. Young, M. Edwards, and P. Parvis, vol. 41 (Leuven: Peeters, 2006), 433-38.

[8]Chrysostom, *In Act. apost. hom.* 15.5 (PG 60.126).

[9]Chrysostom also uses the image of a winged soul that is lifted by love to heavenly realms. Though the image originates in the *Phaedrus*, the winged soul is common in Chrysostom's time, a favorite of the Cappadocians (see Nazianzus, *Epig.* 33; Nazianzus, *Or.* 2.22; Nyssa, *In cant. cant.* 5), making it even harder to know where Chrysostom gets it. For a discussion of this image in Chrysostom, see Bosinis, "Two Platonic Images," 433-36. An excellent catalog of Chrysostom's references and allusions to Greek philosophers is found in P. R. Coleman-Norton, "St. Chrysostom and the Greek Philosophers," *Classical Philology* 25, no. 4 (1930): 305-17.

[10]See the introduction to Chrysostom, *Quod nem. laed.* in the *NPNF* for a detailed comparison, including a translation of the relevant passage from *Republic* (*NPNF* ¹, 9:269-70).

nem. laed. 2). Next, Plato claims that everything has its own vice, something that corrupts the thing alone, such as disease for the body, blight for corn, or rust for iron (*Republic* 609a). Chrysostom, too, argues that everything has its particular evil, which he defines more clearly as something destructive of a thing's virtue, using the same three examples as Plato (Chrysostom, *Quod nem. laed.* 2).[11]

The next step in Plato's logic is that only an object's vice is able to harm that object: good things and neutral things cannot destroy; only the evil inherent to a thing can destroy (*Republic* 609b). Here Plato will go on to argue for the immortality of the soul. Plato seeks to demonstrate that the soul's particular evil cannot destroy the soul, only mar it (*Republic* 609b-c). He begins his search with the admission that what harms the soul is "injustice, licentiousness, cowardice, and ignorance" (*Republic* 609b).[12] Having established that these things can harm but not completely destroy the soul, Plato argues that nothing else could destroy the soul either (*Republic* 609d-610a). Therefore, Plato concludes, since neither the soul's own particular vice, nor anything else, can destroy a soul, the soul must be immortal (*Republic* 610e-611a). Chrysostom begins in a similar way, looking for the vice peculiar to human beings. Arguing against those who would claim poverty, disease, loss of property, or even death are the evils that corrupt a person's virtue, Chrysostom claims that none of these can harm a person's virtue, that a person herself is the only one capable of corroding her virtue (*Quod nem. laed.* 2). Since vice attacks the virtue of a thing, Chrysostom begins this section by defining the virtue of a human being. Through an examination of Job's story, Chrysostom concludes that a person's virtue does not lie in his wealth, health, or any other external thing since Job was considered virtuous after the loss of all these (*Quod nem. laed.* 3). Chrysostom also inserts a secondary argument here, claiming that no being is able to harm a person's virtue either, just as Plato argues that nothing but a thing's particular vice can harm it. In the example of Job, the devil is unable to injure him; in the examples of Abel and Joseph, it is brothers who cannot harm (*Quod nem. laed.* 3-4). Chrysostom argues that it is not the one who suffers, but the one

---

[11] Though Chrysostom uses Plato's examples, and adds many more of his own, there are no significant lexical echoes between the two authors. The echoes are in logic only.

[12] ἀδικία τε καὶ ἀκολασία καὶ δειλία καὶ ἀμαθία.

who causes suffering, whose virtue is injured, and that injury comes from within (*Quod nem. laed.* 5). Thus Chrysostom follows Plato as far as concluding that only the soul's particular vice can harm the soul, but where Plato goes on to argue for the immortality of the soul, Chrysostom moves to emphasizing the agency of the person herself in damaging her virtue.

In most places, rather than use Plato's concept of the tripartite soul, Chrysostom uses the more generic dualism of body and soul, which is more Stoic in nature.[13] Certainly the argument that no one can harm a person except himself, as well as his instructions to Olympias to remember that "insults, accusations, confiscation, exile, a sharpened sword, the sea, the warring of the whole world . . . are temporary and perishable, and happen in a mortal body without harming the vigilant soul" are redolent of Stoic influence.[14] A case can also be made for Aristotelian elements in Chrysostom's account of the soul. Aristotle argues that the soul moves the body like a person plays an instrument or uses a tool, and Chrysostom employs this same analogy in his *In epistulam ad Romanos hom.* 13.[15] Aristotle writes, "Each craft must employ its own tools, and each soul its own body."[16] Chrysostom has a similar opinion, writing in *In epistulam ad Romanos hom.* 13.2,

---

[13]The only explicit reference to the tripartite soul in Chrysostom is in *Inan. glor. et ed. lib.* 65: "The seat and habitation of spirit, we are told, are the breast and the heart within the breast; of the appetitive part of the soul, the liver; of the reasoning part, the brain" (SC 188bis, 162). English from M. L. W. Laistner, *Christianity and Pagan Culture in the Later Roman Empire; Together with an English Translation of John Chrysostom's Address on Vainglory and the Right Way for Parents to Bring Up Their Children*, James W. Richard Lectures in History for 1950–1951 (Ithaca, NY: Cornell University Press, 1951), 112. Chrysostom goes on to explain what each part does and how to train children to use the parts properly.

[14]Chrysostom, *ep. ad Olymp.* 7.1 (SC 106).

[15]Raymond Laird also argues for the centrality of γνώμη to both Aristotle's and Chrysostom's understandings of soul, citing *Nicomachean Ethics (Eth. nic.)* 6.11 as an instance when Aristotle names γνώμη alongside νοῦς, φρόνησις, and σύνεσις as a δύναμις of the soul, as well as a ἕξις: Εἰσὶ δὲ πᾶσαι αἱ ἕξεις εὐλόγως εἰς ταὐτὸ τείνουσαι· λέγομεν γὰρ γνώμην καὶ σύνεσιν καὶ φρόνησιν καὶ νοῦν ἐπὶ τοὺς αὐτοὺς ἐπιφέροντες γνώμην ἔχειν καὶ νοῦν ἤδη, καὶ φρονίμους καὶ συνετούς. πᾶσαι γὰρ αἱ δυνάμεις αὗται τῶν ἐσχάτων εἰσὶ καὶ τῶν καθ᾽ ἕκαστον. See Raymond Laird, *Mindset, Moral Choice and Sin in the Anthropology of John Chrysostom* (Strathfield, NSW: St. Pauls, 2012), 174. However, this is Laird's only cited instance of γνώμη in Aristotle, and Aristotle does not use the term at all in *De anima*. It may play some role in Aristotle's account, but this instance is not enough to suggest that Chrysostom is thoroughly Aristotelian. If anything, the body-as-instrument metaphor is better evidence, and that would have been a commonplace image by Chrysostom's time.

[16]Aristotle, *De anima* I.3.407b26-27: δεῖ γὰρ τὴν μὲν τέχνην χρῆσθαι τοῖς ὀργάνοις, τὴν δὲ ψυχὴν τῷ σώματι. The previous paragraph states, "The soul causes the body's movement" (ἡ ψυχὴ μᾶλλον ἐκείνῳ) (*De anima* I.3.407b10).

"As a lyre is [subject] to the lyre player and a ship to the pilot, so the body is subject to the soul."[17] Wendy Mayer provides a helpful summary when she concludes, "John's [Chrysostom's] conception of the soul is probably best described as eclectic."[18]

Chrysostom's emphasis in discussing the soul is, like his discussion of demons, not for the sake of speculation but for the practical edification of his audience. This is true of most treatises on the soul, which are similarly for edification of the audience. The difference in content is reflected in the difference of audience. In Chrysostom's case, the homilies focus on the relationship between the soul and body in the working of virtue and vice, or where responsibility for sin or virtue lies, since this is what he believes his audience needs. Plato, then, is useful for explaining that sin is a result of not allowing reason to bridle one's passions[19] and for arguing that harm to virtue comes only from a person herself.[20] Aristotle is useful for understanding *proairesis*, and Stoicism is useful for distinguishing true harm from apparent harm. Chrysostom uses what will fortify his argument and does not discuss the rest.

For all of this complexity, however, Chrysostom's account of virtue appears to rely far more on Stoic concepts than on Platonic ones. This is more difficult to demonstrate in part because more of the sources are fragmentary, and Stoicism as a school comprises a range of ideas and authors. Nonetheless, Chrysostom's anthropology has significant similarities to Stoic accounts of virtue and vice, particularly his use of exemplars, his emphasis on detachment from earthly things, and his attention to human freedom and *proairesis* in the classification of virtue and vice. Chrysostom does not mention Stoic authors by name the way he does Plato, but ideas and vocabulary are similar in places, as though they are a background that gives Chrysostom's ideas more texture and depth. Here I examine the Stoic concept of virtue, how a person might become virtuous, and what role freedom plays in this account in order to provide context for the discussion of Chrysostom's own account of virtue, which draws on Stoic concepts.

---

[17]Chrysostom, *In Rom. hom.* 13.2 (PG 60.509).

[18]Wendy Mayer, "The Persistence in Late Antiquity of Medico-Philosophical Psychic Therapy," *Journal of Late Antiquity* 8 (2015): 345, n. 37.

[19]See note 7 above.

[20]Chrysostom, *Quod nem. laed.* 2-6 (SC 103bis, 62-95).

STOIC ACCOUNTS OF VIRTUE

Put simply, virtue according to the Stoics is living in harmony with Nature, or with the will of God. This is one commonality that spans various Stoic authors and eras. Nature, the will of God, is perfect reason and the order of the universe. Moreover, this reason is the same as that which human beings possess and, indeed, which makes them human and allows them to perceive the reason and order of the universe. Therefore, virtue is recognition of this order and acquiescence to it. Seneca's famous quip, "I do not obey God; rather, I agree with Him," can be understood as the epitome of this view.[21] There is also room, however, for a definition of virtue as a consistency of character. A virtuous person is one who will always act in accordance with nature.

Diogenes records a statement from Chrysippus (280–207 BCE) that offers a similar definition of virtue:

> Living virtuously is equivalent to living in accordance with experience of the actual course of nature, as Chrysippus says in the first book of his *De finibus*; for our individual natures are parts of the nature of the whole universe. And this is why the end may be defined as life in accordance with nature, or, in other words, in accordance with our own human nature as well as that of the universe, a life in which we refrain from every action forbidden by the law common to all things, that is to say, the right reason which pervades all things, and is identical with this Zeus, lord and ruler of all that is. And this very thing constitutes the virtue of the happy man and the smooth current of life, when all actions promote the harmony of the spirit dwelling in the individual man with the will of him who orders the universe.[22]

The touchstone of virtue is harmony, the harmony of the individual's spirit with the will of Zeus, who orders the universe. When this harmony is achieved, a person is both virtuous and happy, and a person's actions affect this harmony. This paragraph also assumes that a person has access to the right reason of the universe and is able to know precisely what actions are in line with the will of Zeus. Because human nature is part of the nature of

---

[21]Seneca, *Ep.* 96.2. English from Richard M. Gummere, trans., *Epistles*, vol. 3, epistles 93-124, LCL 77 (Cambridge, MA: Harvard University Press, 1996), 104-5.

[22]Diogenes, *Lives* 7.88. Quotations are from Diogenes Laertius, *Lives of Eminent Philosophers*, trans. R. D. Hicks, vol. 2, LCL 185 (New York: Putnam's Sons, 1925), 194-97.

the universe, humans know the order by which they are to live as well as the actions forbidden to them. For Stoics, virtue is simple: perform the actions that line up with the will of God, the order of nature.

Yet a related question immediately arises, that of moral responsibility. If Stoics have a determinist understanding of the universe, and if virtue is living in accordance with Nature, which everyone should know how to do, then how can a person ever be responsible for his or her actions? How can a person be praised or blamed? This is a question of particular relevance to this study, since Chrysostom's argument for human freedom is founded on reward and punishment.

STOICISM AND MORAL RESPONSIBILITY

The key to any Stoic's claim that a person can be responsible for his or her actions is to say that even within the determined order of the universe, there is some aspect of human action that is within our power (*eph hēmin*, ἐφ᾽ ἡμῖν). The debate concerns how to delineate and define what particularly *is* in a human being's power. Chrysippus (280–207 BCE) and Epictetus (55–135 CE) are the Stoic philosophers whose ideas are most examined in relation to this question. Though I examine both Chrysippus and Epictetus, I will focus on Epictetus because his understanding of things that are *eph hēmin* and the centrality of *proairesis* to his ethical theory will most help understanding Chrysostom's own account of virtue.

Those scholars who want to understand Chrysippus as offering a possibility for moral responsibility within the context of Stoic determinism attempt to explain the theory by redefining freedom. Rather than freedom as the "ability to do otherwise," freedom is understood as the autonomy of the agent.[23] Susanne Bobzien argues that Chrysippus claims fate works through

---

[23]This is Bobzien's phrasing of the issue (*Determinism and Freedom in Stoic Philosophy*, 235), and other scholars discuss a similar idea. For instance, Dobbins argues, "According to Epictetus, freedom is secured by limiting oneself to τὰ προαιρετικά, or what he otherwise calls τὰ ἐφ᾽ ἡμῖν" (Epictetus, *Discourses and Selected Writings*, trans. Robert Dobbin, new ed., Penguin Classics [London: Penguin, 2008], 128). Frede defines freedom in Stoicism on the basis of what the agent is able to do without coercion, rather than what he is able to choose: "Freedom is the ability to act on one's own initiative, as opposed to being compelled to act the way one does, running after some things and avoiding others, because one has enslaved oneself to them." Michael Frede, *A Free Will: Origins of the Notion in Ancient Thought*, ed. A. A. Long (Berkeley: University of California Press, 2011), 68.

human beings, through their dispositions and beliefs, and in this way, since the human is still the agent of his action and fate is not forcing him but working through his character, he can be held responsible for his actions.[24] This is true of Epictetus's account as well. Both philosophers insist that fate does not act as some kind of external force compelling the agent to act in a given way. Gellius, one of the recorders of Chrysippus's ideas, titles one section of his *Attic Nights*, "How Chrysippus also maintained the power and inevitable nature of fate, but at the same time declared that we had control over our plans and decisions," and quotes Chrysippus's response to the question of the compatibility of determinism, freedom, and responsibility.[25] Chrysippus replies, "The order, the law, and the inevitable quality of fate set in motion the various classes of things and the beginnings of causes, but the carrying out of our designs and thoughts, and even our actions, are regulated by each individual's own will [*voluntas*] and the characteristics of his mind."[26] Both Epictetus and Chrysippus define freedom as the absence of compulsion, or the absence of the necessary, and both claim that humans have this freedom even within a framework of determinism.

The free soul the Stoics believed in was a unified soul. The soul has different powers, but it is not composed of parts as in Plato's account.[27] In this

---

[24]Bobzien, *Determinism and Freedom in Stoic Philosophy*, 250.

[25]Aulus Gellius, *Noct. att.* 7.2.1. Quotations from Aulus Gellius, *Attic Nights*, trans. John C. Rolfe, vol. 2, bks. 6-13, LCL 196 (Cambridge, MA: Harvard University Press, 1927), 94-95.

[26]Gellius, *Noct. att.* 7.2.1 (LCL 196:98-99). Gould points out that part of Chrysippus's commitment to moral responsibility is his understanding that wicked people must suffer punishment for their crimes. Such punishment, however, requires agency. Therefore, the crimes cannot be the work of fate alone. Chrysippus assigned this responsibility to the moment of assent; the same will be true of Epictetus. Josiah B. Gould, *The Philosophy of Chrysippus* (Leiden: Brill, 1970), 149.

[27]The soul is said to be composed of eight "parts" (μέρη), but Stoic authors do not mean conflicting parts as does Plato. For Stoics, the soul is unified, and the "parts" are perhaps understood better as "'functions' or 'powers' of the soul" (Gould, *Philosophy of Chrysippus*, 129). Aetius offers a helpful summary: "The Stoics say that the commanding-faculty is the soul's highest part, which produces impressions, assents, perceptions and impulses. They also call it the reasoning faculty. From the commanding-faculty there are seven parts of the soul which grow out and stretch out into the body like the tentacles of an octopus. Five of these are the senses, sight, smell, hearing, taste and touch. . . . Of the remainder, one is called seed, and this is breath extending from the commanding-faculty to the genitals. The other . . . which they also call utterance, is breath extending from the commanding-faculty to the pharynx, tongue and appropriate organs" (Aetius, 4.21.1-4; A. A. Long and D. N. Sedley, eds., *The Hellenistic Philosophers* [Cambridge: Cambridge University Press, 1987], 1:315-16). This commanding-faculty is the part of central concern for ethics since it is the part where impressions and assents are located. A good overview of the composition of the soul and scholarship on this composition is found in Inwood, *Ethics and Human Action*, 29-41.

understanding of a unified soul, Stoics held to a theory of human action wherein an impression or appearance (*phantasma*, φάντασμα) occurs to the mind, the person must assent (*synkatathesis*, συγκατάθεσις) to the impression, and then an impulse (*hormē*, ὁρμή) toward action occurs, causing the person to act on the impression.[28] Assent is the aspect that is under human control. The mind can choose either to give or to withhold assent to a given impression, and it is this aspect to which responsibility can be attached. Assent separates humans from animals.[29] Assenting is, in Epictetus's phrase, "up to us" (*eph hēmin*).[30]

That there are things that are *eph hēmin* is the key to understanding the Stoic account of virtue and responsibility. It is also central to understanding Chrysostom's account of virtue and responsibility. Among the philosophers, very few authors used the term *proairesis* at all, and only Aristotle and Epictetus used it with any frequency or import.[31] Epictetus does not speak directly of fate, but insists that the gods have given humans a realm of things in their own power, which cannot be compelled by any external forces. He writes, "What has He [god] given me for my own and subject to my authority [*autexousion*, αὐτεξούσιον], and what has He left for Himself? Everything within the sphere of the moral purpose [*ta proairetika*, τὰ προαιρετικὰ] He has given me, subjected them to my control, unhampered and unhindered."[32] The gods themselves have decreed that humans be freed

---

[28]This broad outline of human action can be found described in Inwood, *Ethics and Human Action*, 42-101; Gould, *Philosophy of Chrysippus*, 33, 53-60; and Frede, *Free Will*, 35-44.

[29]Impulse is what separates animals from plants: "Animals have the additional faculty of impulse" (Diogenes, *Lives* 7.85). "A rational animal, however, in addition to its impressionistic nature, has reason which passes judgement on impressions, rejecting some of these and accepting others, in order that the animal may be guided accordingly" (Origen, *Princ.* 3.1.3, endorsing Stoic ideas). Both quotations are from Long and Sedley, *Hellenistic Philosophers*, 1:346 and 313, respectively.

[30]For a sampling of Epictetus's use of this phrase, see *Diatr.* 1.1, 6, 18, 19, 22, 29; 2.2, 5, 13; 3.3, 24; 4.7, 10. How Epictetus intends the phrase is unpacked below.

[31]Robert Dobbin reports that the term is entirely absent from Xenophon, Lysias, Andocides, Isaeus, and Dinarchus, appears only once in Plato's works, four times in Isocrates's works, and three times each in Aeschines's and Hyperides's corpuses. Demosthenes does use the term about twenty times, but this is still minuscule in comparison to both Aristotle and Epictetus. Even then, Epictetus is the one who uses the term such that it becomes a central aspect of his ethical theory; for Aristotle it is not central but only one aspect. Robert Dobbin, "Προαίρεσις in Epictetus," *Ancient Philosophy* 11, no. 1 (1991): 111.

[32]Epictetus, *Diatr.* 4.1. Translation is from Epictetus, *Discourses, Books 3-4; Fragments; the Encheiridion*, trans. W. A. Oldfather, LCL 218 (New York: Putnam's Sons, 1928), 276-79.

from compulsion, and this absence of compulsion is what allows for moral responsibility. Therefore, responsibility resides in the fact that a person is the agent of her actions and is able to act free of external constraint; freedom is the basis of responsibility. Since she is the one who acts, she is responsible. Epictetus writes, "the nature of the good as well as of the evil lies in a use of the impressions of the senses [*en chrēsei phantasiōn*, ἐν χρήσει φαντασιῶν], but the things which lie outside the province of the moral purpose admit neither the nature of the evil, nor the nature of the good."[33] In the Stoic account, this use of appearances, this assent, is the key moment of action and the locus of moral responsibility.

Epictetus discusses assent in different words but means that a person can be held responsible not for the appearance of impressions but for what a person does with those impressions. He writes, "That which is best of all and supreme over all is the only thing which the gods have placed in our power, the right use of appearances; but all other things they have not placed in our power."[34] In this statement Epictetus claims that the only thing human beings have control over is the right use of the appearances they receive. They cannot control external circumstances or the appearance of impressions, but they may control what they do with the appearances. For Epictetus, a person decides whether she will act on the impression. In one place he defines this as the "faculty of choice and refusal, of desire and aversion, or, in a word, the faculty which makes use of external impressions."[35]

A second, subtler, claim Epictetus makes is that only the human being has control over his use of appearances. The gods have given each human being this power, and they have given it to each individual human being alone, not to any other human. Since it is in her power, no other being may force her to use her appearances in a particular manner. The use of appearances is hers alone. Epictetus says this elsewhere also: "It is not possible that that which is by nature free should be disturbed or thwarted by anything but itself. But it is a man's own judgements that disturb him." "Who is there left, then, for me to fear? The man who is master of what? The things that are under my

---

[33]Epictetus, *Diatr.* 2.1. Translation is from Epictetus, *Discourses, Books 1-2*, trans. W. A. Oldfather, LCL 131 (Cambridge, MA: Harvard University Press, 1925), 211-12.
[34]Epictetus, *Diatr.* 1.1 (LCL 131:11).
[35]Epictetus, *Diatr.* 1.1 (LCL 131:11). According to Epictetus this faculty comes directly from the gods as a part of themselves they gave to humanity.

control? But there is no such man."[36] This understanding that a person is alone able to use his appearances is the basis for Epictetus's claim that humans are responsible for their actions.

The way to become virtuous for Epictetus is to learn how to use one's appearances correctly. A person can learn to distinguish between what is and what is not within her power. So Epictetus writes,

> What, then, does it mean to be getting an education? It means to be learning how to apply the natural preconceptions to particular cases, each to the other in conformity with nature, and, further, to make the distinction, that some things are under our control while others are not under our control. Under our control are moral purpose and all the acts of moral purpose; but not under our control are the body, the parts of the body, possessions, parents, brothers, children, country—in a word, all that with which we associate.[37]

That a person can learn to use his appearances correctly also suggests that humans are not inherently able to make these distinctions, which explains why there are so few sages. Though much of the Stoic theory of action and discussion of virtue can make it sound as though humans know what is the rational, right course of action and thus virtue is easy, Epictetus makes it clear that humans are not born with this knowledge. They must be educated in the correct use of their appearances in order to be virtuous.

In perhaps the strongest statement about what is required for a person to be virtuous, Epictetus writes,

> What is by its very nature capable of hindering [*ti empodizein pephyken*, τί ἐμποδίζειν πέφυκεν] the προαίρεσις [*proairesis*]? Nothing that lies outside its sphere [*aproaireton ouden*, ἀπροαίρετον οὐδέν], but only itself [*proairesis*] when perverted. For this reason moral purpose [*proairesis*] becomes the only vice, or the only virtue.[38]

What constitutes vice or virtue is not the act performed but the *proairesis*, the use of appearances, which is in a person's power. No external circumstance, no god, no fate, can compel a person's *proairesis*; it is free. Since it is free, it is the seat of virtue and vice, which are mental, consisting solely in

---

[36]Epictetus, *Diatr.* 1.19, 29 (LCL 131:128-29, 184-85).
[37]Epictetus, *Diatr.* 1.22 (LCL 131:142-43).
[38]Epictetus, *Diatr.* 2.23 (LCL 131:400-403).

how one uses or responds to one's appearances. The *proairesis* is the locus of human freedom and thus moral responsibility.

PROAIRESIS IN ARISTOTLE AND EPICTETUS

Before moving to look at the importance of *proairesis* in Epictetus's works, it is necessary to take a moment to examine Aristotle's use of the term since Aristotle is prior to Epictetus and is often assumed to be one of the foundational sources on which Stoic thought developed. Aristotle's most in-depth analysis of *proairesis* occurs in *Nicomachean Ethics* (*Eth. nic.*) 3.2-3, where he first says that *proairesis* is "intimately connected with virtue" and affords "a surer test of character than do our actions."[39] He then further distinguishes *proairesis* from desire, passion, wish, or some kind of opinion before suggesting, "Perhaps we may define it [*proairesis*] as voluntary action preceded by deliberation, since choice involves reasoning and some process of thought. Indeed previous deliberation seems to be implied by the very term προαίρετον [*proairesis*], which denotes something chosen before other things."[40] This definition makes *proairesis* distinct from deliberation, another important aspect of Aristotle's ethics, but connects *proairesis* to deliberation by requiring deliberation prior to *proairesis*. He further clarifies his thinking: "As then the object of *proairesis* is something within our power [*eph hēmin*] which after deliberation we desire, *proairesis* will be a deliberate desire of things in our power [*eph hēmin*]; for we first deliberate, then select, and finally fix our desire according to the result of our deliberation."[41] Dobbin simplifies this definition to "reasoned desire."[42]

Aristotle's definition also highlights the choice aspect of *proairesis*. *Proairesis* is the reasoned choice of one action over another in a given situation, and it is this ability to choose that makes moral responsibility for actions, and thus virtue, possible. The other point to note is that *proairesis* is concerned only with things in our power (*eph hēmin*), a theme Epictetus will

---

[39] Aristotle, *Eth. nic.* 3.2.1 (LCL 73:128-29). Translations of the *Eth. nic.* are from Aristotle, *Nicomachean Ethics*, trans. H. Rackham, LCL 73 (Cambridge, MA: Harvard University Press, 1968), 128-29.

[40] Aristotle, *Eth. nic.* 3.2.17 (LCL 73:132-33).

[41] Aristotle, *Eth. nic.* 3.3.19 (LCL 73:140-41).

[42] Dobbin, "Προαίρεσις in Epictetus," 114.

emphasize as well. Aristotle writes, "It is manifest that προαίρεσις [*pro-airesis*] is not opinion either, nor something that one simply thinks; for we saw that a thing chosen is something in one's own power, but we have opinions as to many things that do not depend on us."[43] A bit later he asserts, "It is clear that προαίρεσις [*proairesis*] is deliberative appetition of things within one's power."[44] Virtue concerns only the things over which we have control. So according to Aristotle's definition, *proairesis*, as the choice of action concerning what is within a person's power, is at the center of virtue. It is the locus of moral responsibility.

I use the phrase "moral responsibility" to refer to that which is required for praise or blame to be assigned to a person for a given action. I further mean that one is responsible for an action—that is, he could be praised or blamed for an action—because that person is himself the cause of that action, not someone or something else.[45] The autonomy of the agent is key here, and thus, too, the phrase *eph hēmin*. If an action is *eph hēmin* it is not up to someone else, but to us alone. Therefore, those for whom an action is *eph hēmin* are the ones causally responsible for the action and the ones to whom praise or blame can be assigned. Aristotle writes, "A man is the origin of his actions, and . . . the province of deliberation is to discover actions within one's own power to perform."[46] He also contends, "Virtue also depends on ourselves. And so also does vice. . . . If it is in our power to do and to refrain from doing right and wrong, and if, as we saw, being good or bad is doing right or wrong, it consequently depends on us whether we are

---

[43]Aristotle, *Eth. eud.* 2.10.5 (LCL 285:288-89). Translation from Aristotle, *The Athenian Constitution: The Eudemian Ethics; On Virtues and Vices*, trans. H. Rackham, LCL 283 (Cambridge, MA: Harvard University Press, 1952), 288-89.

[44]Aristotle, *Eth. eud.* 2.10.17 (LCL 285:294-95).

[45]Bobzien provides a helpful and complex discussion of what is meant by "moral responsibility" and how responsibility relates to determinism in her *Determinism and Freedom in Stoic Philosophy*, at 276-90. She suggests there are two primary understandings of "moral responsibility," the first of which is the autonomy-based model explained here. The second is "the freedom to do otherwise." According to this second conception, a person is responsible for an action and could incur praise or blame when he could have done something other than he did but did not. This second type is often related to feelings of guilt or regret. I focus on the first understanding here because it is that reflected in Aristotle and Epictetus. Among the Stoics, moral responsibility is a question, as we saw, that arises out of the commitment to determinism. Chrysostom, similarly, will be concerned with moral responsibility so as to ward off the possibility that someone— whether God, the devil, or some other factor—other than the agent is the cause of an action because Chrysostom is concerned that praise or blame be assigned correctly.

[46]Aristotle, *Eth. nic.* 3.3.15 (LCL 73:138-39).

virtuous or vicious."[47] Moral responsibility is the condition of humanity that allows for actions to be labeled virtue or vice.

Epictetus's use of *proairesis* is also highly specific and also the central aspect of his account of virtue, though he is not so kind as to offer an explicit definition. Epictetus is the foremost Stoic to use the term, and he uses *proairesis* to mean a rational decision and something very like will, though void of any notion of willpower, even as it is often translated into English as "will."[48] It also appears primarily in discussions of the things that are "up to us" (*eph hēmin*). Epictetus seems to claim for *proairesis* a position as a faculty or power (*dynamis*) of the soul, but without suggesting it is its own part of the soul, since the soul is single and unified in Epictetus's Stoic thinking. The *proairesis* is a person's using his appearances. It is, further, the faculty that tells a person whether a thing can be evil or good since only what is within the control of the *proairesis* can be either: "The impressions of our senses . . . put interrogations to us. So-and-so's son is dead. Answer, 'That lies outside the sphere of the προαίρεσις [*proairesis*], it is not an evil.'"[49] The action of this *proairesis* faculty would seem to be immediately prior to the moment of assent. A person decides how she will use her appearances, which ones she will accept as true and right to act on; then she may assent or not, which leads to the impulse and the action. Yet that scheme divides the process too neatly. In fact, *process* is too neat a word. *Proairesis* is part of assent. In this sense, the *proairesis* is a rational decision, not a faculty distinct from reason, as though a person reasons first and then desires to do something based on her reasoning.[50] Instead, *proairesis* itself involves an act of reasoning; it is pervasive: "It is reason that analyzes and perfects all else."[51] Still, *proairesis* is the central aspect of assent, and assent is the central aspect of determining virtue or vice, which makes *proairesis* an integral part of moral responsibility and virtue.

One other important aspect of Epictetus's understanding of *proairesis* is that the *proairesis* is the part of the person identifiable with the self.[52] He

---

[47] Aristotle, *Eth. nic.* 3.5.2-4 (LCL 73:143-45).

[48] This is in contrast to translations of Aristotle's works, which prefer "choice."

[49] Epictetus, *Diatr.* 3.8 (LCL 218:60-61).

[50] Richard Sorabji, "Epictetus on *proairesis* and Self," in *The Philosophy of Epictetus*, ed. Theodore Scaltsas and Andrew S. Mason (Oxford: Oxford University Press, 2007), 87.

[51] Epictetus, *Diatr.* 1.17 (LCL 131:112-13).

[52] Sorabji raises two important issues with the simple equation of the προαίρεσις with the self in Epictetus's works in "Epictetus on *proairesis* and Self." The first issue is how a person can be his

makes statements such as "'I will fetter you.' What is that you say, man? Fetter me? My leg you will fetter, but my προαίρεσις [*proairesis*] not even Zeus himself has power to overcome."[53] "[News] that someone is speaking ill of you. Very well, what is that to you? [News] that your father is making certain preparations. Against whom? Surely not against your προαίρεσις [*proairesis*], is it? Why, how can he? But against your paltry body, against your paltry possessions you are safe."[54] Epictetus has here claimed that the part of a person that is central is the *proairesis*. It is the part known to others as "you." Whereas modern readers think of "you" or the "self" as the unified soul and body, Epictetus (and other Stoics) do not have this understanding. A. A. Long refers to the *proairesis* as "the bearer of personal identity."[55] Even more strongly, Epictetus writes, "Because *you* are not flesh, nor hair, but *proairesis*."[56] Elsewhere he makes a similar statement: "Are you a piece of crockery, then? No, but you are *proairesis*."[57] The way a person uses his appearances or impressions is the only thing a person can control, and so it is the aspect of a person that can be identified with that person.

One final aspect of *proairesis* implied in these assurances of Epictetus is that it is a faculty so intrinsic to the self that nothing can harm it but itself. Epictetus writes, "For nothing outside the sphere of the *proairesis* can hamper or injure the *proairesis*; it alone can hamper or injure itself."[58] "Nothing else can overcome *proairesis*, but it overcomes itself."[59] The corollary to this is that the *proairesis* is what determines moral responsibility, as noted in the previous section, when Epictetus writes that the *proairesis* alone is vice or virtue.[60] Since it is what a person has power over, and since only the person himself, no outside force, has power over it, it is the locus of responsibility, what allows for praise or blame. This is the significant

προαίρεσις if he can also destroy his προαίρεσις. The second issue is that Epictetus sometimes implies more than one "self," which means that "you are your προαίρεσις" needs to be clarified. Sorabji does not resolve these issues (Sorabji, "Epictetus on *proairesis* and the Self," 87).
[53]Epictetus, *Diatr.* 1.1 (LCL 131:12-13).
[54]Epictetus, *Diatr.* 3.18 (LCL 218:112-13).
[55]A. A. Long, "Representation and the Self in Stoicism," in *Psychology*, ed. Stephen Everson (Cambridge: Cambridge University Press, 1991), 112.
[56]Epictetus, *Diatr.* 3.1 (LCL 218:18-19); emphasis added.
[57]Epictetus, *Diatr.* 4.5 (LCL 218:334-35).
[58]Epictetus, *Diatr.* 3.19 (LCL 218:114-15).
[59]Epictetus, *Diatr.* 1.29 (LCL 131:188-89).
[60]Epictetus, *Diatr.* 2.23.

commonality in both Aristotle's and Epictetus's thinking, which is important to remember when dealing with Chrysostom's thinking, as Chrysostom also argues for the inability of anything to hinder a person's *proairesis* and thus the inability of anything to hinder virtue.

CONCLUSION

Trained by Libanius in a classical rhetorical education, Chrysostom was familiar with Greek philosophy. Like his predecessors and contemporaries in the church, Chrysostom's theology could not but be influenced by his philosophical training. He often uses the philosophers as mere foils to demonstrate the superiority of Christ, but he also shows distinct influence from Stoicism in his anthropology and account of virtue.

Stoics believed that enacting virtue is up to each individual. Though impressions and thoughts occur to everyone, each person must assent to an impression in order to act on it, and that assent is purely within the control of the individual. For this reason, the moment of assent is the moment of moral responsibility. Both Aristotle and Epictetus explain that every person has a *proairesis*. The faculty of choice to assent or not to assent cannot be compelled by any outside force or actor, only by the person herself. If an act is compelled, be it good or evil, the one compelled is not responsible. If, however, the act is chosen freely, then the person is responsible for her choice. A person's *proairesis* determines virtue or vice. Understanding this Stoic account provides depth and nuance to Chrysostom's own account of virtue, which is also centered on each person's *proairesis*.

4

Chrysostom's Anthropology

WHEN SPEAKING TO HIS CONGREGATION ABOUT DEMONS, the point Chrysostom emphasizes most is that the devil's power is limited and unable to harm a person's virtue. This statement has two implications for the congregation. First, the congregants ought not fear demons as they do because demons cannot cause any true harm. The congregation fears demons because it believes demons can hurt them with unemployment, disease, or death, but Chrysostom maintains that those things do not constitute true harm. True harm is harm to the soul, and that harm is sin, or injury to virtue. Therefore, second, since demons are limited and unable to harm a person's virtue, human beings are responsible for their own state of virtue. This understanding removes an excuse for sin, emboldens the audience with the real possibility of victory over the devil, and allows Chrysostom to exhort them to vigilant effort to defeat the devil by developing their virtue. The question at hand now is what Chrysostom means by virtue.

PROAIRESIS AND GNŌMĒ

In speaking of demonic interaction with human beings, Chrysostom's key term is *proairesis*. Chrysostom uses the term much like Aristotle and Epictetus do, making *proairesis* the seat of morality. In one instance, speaking about the parable of the sheep and goats and the reason each group went to a different end, Chrysostom puts the matter starkly, stating that *proairesis* is the cause:

How were their ends not the same? Because the προαίρεσις [*proairesis*] did not allow it; for this alone made the difference. For this reason one group entered Gehenna and the other entered the kingdom. But if the devil were the cause of their sins, they would not be destined to be punished because someone else sinned and forced them. Do you see here both those who sin and those who live righteously? . . . Do you see again that the προαίρεσις [*proairesis*] is the cause of the end, not the devil?[1]

Proairesis "alone made the difference"; it is the locus of moral responsibility, that which makes both praise and blame possible. Chrysostom tells his congregation, "Recognize the cause of the sin, and you will find that it was no one other than yourself who sinned. Everywhere there is need of a good *proairesis*."[2] *Proairesis* alone is the cause of sin.

In the final homily of *De diabolo tentatore*, when Chrysostom speaks to his congregation about those who had been attending the theater instead of worship, he emphasizes *proairesis* as the cause:

The day before yesterday we got going our message about the devil, out of our love for you. But others the day before yesterday, while such matters were getting going here, were sitting in the theater and watching the Devil's show. . . . They ate the Devil's garbage: you were fed on spiritual juices. . . . Did the Devil trick them? How did he not trick you? You and they are the same humans; I mean, with regard to your nature. You have the same soul as they do, you have the same natural desires. How then were you and they not in the same place? Because you and they do not have the same προαίρεσις [*proairesis*].[3]

Chrysostom reframes the choice so that it is not merely about attending the theater or worship, but a choice between Satan or Christ in order to urge his audience against specific sins. Put so starkly, how could they but follow Christ? The sermon continues to say that the choice to attend worship is the strongest proof that "in every case, the *proairesis* is lord."[4]

---

[1]Chrysostom, *De diab. tent.* 2.3 (SC 560bis, 174).
[2]Chrysostom, *De diab. tent.* 2.2 (SC 560bis, 168). Chrysostom says this in response to those who claim the devil is the cause of their sin, a problem in his congregation: "[The devil] eagerly wishes to carry off the cause of our sins for himself in order that we, being maintained by these hopes, and beginning every form of evil, may increase our own punishment, meeting with no forgiveness from having placed the cause on him" (*De diab. tent.* 1.5 [SC 560bis, 144]).
[3]Chrysostom, *De diab. tent.* 2.1 (SC 560bis, 154-56).
[4]Chrysostom, *De diab. tent.* 2.1 (SC 560bis, 154-56).

In *Mindset, Moral Choice and Sin in the Anthropology of John Chrysostom,* Raymond Laird argues that those scholars who have found the key to Chrysostom's anthropology in *proairesis*—in particular, Nowak, Hall, and Traktellis—have missed something vital.[5] Laird argues that *gnōmē* is in fact the key term for Chrysostom, and that "mindset," as he translates it, is the final locus of moral responsibility. For Laird, *gnōmē* controls *proaireseis*.[6] Laird argues that this passage from Chrysostom's *In epistulam ad Romanos Rom. hom.* 13, on Romans 7:19-20, indicates the relationship between *proairesis* and *gnōmē*:

> Do you see how Paul acquits both the οὐσία [*ousia*] of the soul and the οὐσία [*ousia*] of the flesh and transfers the blame entirely to the evil action? For if he did not wish to do it, the soul is freed from blame. If he himself did not accomplish it, the body is also acquitted. And the entire blame belongs to the πονήρα προαίρεσις [*ponēra proairesis*]. For the οὐσία [*ousia*] of the soul and the οὐσία [*ousia*] of the body are not the same as the οὐσία [*ousia*] of the προαίρεσις [*proairesis*]. The first two οὐσίαι [*ousiai*] are ἔργα [*erga*] of God; the third οὐσία [*ousia*] is a κίνησις [*kinēsis*] that comes from ourselves and is directed toward whatever object to which we may wish to lead it. Βούλησις [*Boulēsis*] is a natural thing and comes from God. But such a use of the will belongs to us and comes from our own γνώμη [*gnōmē*].[7]

According to Laird, this passage defines *proairesis* as "a form of chosen desire that has its source in the γνώμη [*gnōmē*]."[8] Laird also notes a statement where Chrysostom speaks of "the προαίρεσις [*proairesis*] of our γνώμη [*gnōmē*]" as the origin of virtue and vice, and the phrasing does suggest that the *proairesis* is some kind of function or movement of the *gnōmē*.[9] This is

---

[5]See DemetriusTrakatellis, "Man Fallen and Restored, in the Teaching of St. John Chrysostom," *Sobornost* 4, no. 10 [1964]: 573; Demetrius Trakatellis, "Being Transformed: Chrysostom's Exegesis of the Epistle to the Romans," *GOTR* 36 [1991]: 216; Edward Nowak, *Le chrétien devant la souffrance: Étude sur la pensée de Jean Chrysostome* (Paris: Beauchesne, 1973), 57-69; Christopher A. Hall, "John Chrysostom's 'On Providence': A Translation and Theological Interpretation" [PhD diss., Drew University, 1991], 16-47; and Adina Peleanu, ed. *Homélies sur l'impuissance du diable*, SC 560 (Paris: Cerf, 2013), 34.

[6]Raymond Laird, *Mindset, Moral Choice and Sin in the Anthropology of John Chrysostom* (Strathfield, NSW: St Pauls, 2012), 2.

[7]Chrysostom, *In Rom. hom.* 13.2 (PG 60.510). English from Panayiotis Papageorgiou, trans., *Homilies on Romans* (Brookline, MA: Holy Cross Orthodox Press, 2013), 255.

[8]Laird, *Mindset, Moral Choice and Sin*, 107.

[9]Chrysostom, *In Gen. hom.* 31.6 (PG 53.290): Εἶδες πῶς οὐκ ἐν τῇ φύσει, ἀλλ' ἐν τῇ προαιρέσει τῆς γνώμης τῆς ἡμετέρας κεῖται καὶ τὰ τῆς ἀρετῆς, καὶ τὰ τῆς κακίας;

the only section where Laird discusses the relationship between *proairesis* and *gnōmē*; the rest of the book is an argument for the *gnōmē* as the locus of moral responsibility in Chrysostom's anthropology.[10]

Laird's work adds important nuance to the articulation of Chrysostom's anthropology, but it does not alter my argument here. Even if the *gnōmē* is the source of the *proairesis*, they together serve as the locus of moral responsibility, for if *proairesis* is the expression of the *gnōmē*, they are still bound together. In the above example, virtue and vice originate in the "the προαίρεσις [*proairesis*] of our γνώμη [*gnōmē*]," which suggests that though the *proairesis* is a sort of faculty or power of the *gnōmē*, it is where one defines virtue or vice. It could be said that a virtuous person's *gnōmē* is her orientation toward eternal things, her scorn for temporal realities, which is the disposition or "mindset" Chrysostom sees as a key indicator of a virtuous person. From this orientation, a person exercises her *proairesis* and chooses virtue or vice. Moreover, even if the *gnōmē* is somehow "behind" the *proairesis*, Chrysostom does speak of the *proairesis* as a factor determining one's virtue or vice. In the quotation about the sheep and the goats laid out above, Chrysostom says they do not go to the same end because the *proairesis* of each is different. *Gnōmē* does not appear in this instance.[11] Thus, whether *gnōmē* leads the *proairesis* or not, the *proairesis* is here the determining factor in where a person spends eternity. In some sense, each one chooses his end by *proairesis*.

Functionally, Chrysostom uses *proairesis* and *gnōmē* more or less synonymously. It does not appear that he has any system for using one over the other, and often in his homilies he uses both together as synonyms. Since Chrysostom is so fond of precision, his lack of concern is telling. Such a lack of precision would be arbitrary or haphazard if he understood a significant

---

[10]In fact, Laird offers only four quotations as evidence. The two not here quoted are from *In Gen. hom.*18.5 (PG 53.155) and *In Gen. hom.* 18.4 (PG 53.154). The first, ἀλλ' ἡ διαφορὰ τῆς γνώμης λοιπὸν καὶ τῆς προαιρέσεως ἡ ῥᾳθυμία τοῦ μὲν εὐπρόσδεκτον ἐποίησε τὴν προσαγωγήν, τοῦ δὲ ἀπόβλητον, uses προαίρεσις and γνώμη more synonymously than Laird allows. The second, ὅτι διαφορὰν προσώπων οὐκ οἶδεν ὁ Δεσπότης ὁ ἡμέτερος, ἀλλὰ ἐκ προαιρέσεως ἐξετάζων τὴν γνώμην στεφανοῖ, refers to the crowning of the γνώμη. Laird notes that later in the same homily it is the προαίρεσις that is crowned and the γνώμη applauded, but does not allow that this could be a synonymous usage. The only two passages that are convincing, then, are those quoted in my text above.

[11]In fact, as Laird notes, both terms appear far more on their own than together.

distinction between the terms.[12] As it is, his apparent arbitrariness indicates some degree of synonymous understanding. Both *proairesis* and *gnōmē* are terms for the part of the person that is responsible for sin and virtue.

For instance, Chrysostom speaks of the difference between good and evil men, saying, "Everywhere the προαίρεσις [*proairesis*] is the cause, everywhere the γνώμη [*gnōmē*] is lord."[13] The structure of the sentence—word placement identical in both phrases—suggests apposition. Chrysostom is preaching, reaching the height of the sermon, and his language becomes more poetic. If parallel, since both describe the reason one person is injured when the other is not, *proairesis* and *gnōmē* are, if not synonyms, then only shades different in meaning. Functionally, however, they are identical here. Both designate that which is responsible for the difference between good and evil human beings, just as in the example of the sheep and goats. In *In epistulam ad Romanos hom.* 13.7, Chrysostom applies the same logic and vocabulary to *gnōmē* alone: "If you give your soul and body to the better thing, you become among that better part. And again, if you give them to what is worse, you are brought down, sharing in destruction there. This is not because of the nature [*physis*, φύσις] of the soul and of the flesh, but because of the *gnōmē*."[14] Chrysostom uses *kyria* (κυρία) as a predicate of *proairesis* as well. In the very next homily, Chrysostom preaches that the difference between those who had attended the theater and those who worshiped the previous day is each person's *proairesis*. They are all human beings and so all share the same nature. The only difference, Chrysostom argues, is *proairesis*. He says, "In everything, the προαίρεσις [*proairesis*] is κυρία [*kyria*]."[15] This is essentially the same statement he made above, suggesting that *proairesis* and *gnōmē*, at the very least, perform the same function in Chrysostom's anthropology and preaching.

---

[12]On the other hand, Chrysostom is preaching, and it is dangerous to assign too much weight to any word choice since in preaching he may have grabbed the closest word, or his scribe was less than careful in his transcription. Yet the frequency of these words in Chrysostom's corpus indicates their importance, and he may have been intentional about them. He may have had definitions in mind. It is impossible to be certain, but it is unlikely Chrysostom would be careless, so I will argue for significance in Chrysostom's using both words similarly.

[13]Chrysostom, *De diab. tent.* 1.4 (SC 560bis, 140).

[14]Chrysostom, *In Rom. hom.* 13.7 (PG 60.518).

[15]Chrysostom, *De diab. tent.* 2.1 (SC 560bis, 158).

In Chrysostom's discussion of the origin of evil in *In Matthaeum hom.* 59, he preaches, "Then where does this change [from wickedness to the virtuous life] come from? Is it not clear that it is from the γνώμης καὶ προαιρέσεως [*gnōmēs kai proaireseōs*]?"[16] Here the use is either synonymous or implying that *proairesis* and *gnōmē* are two different faculties that together result in action or change. The use of *kai* to connect *proairesis* and *gnōmē* is not uncommon in Chrysostom's work. In *De diabolo tentatore*, Chrysostom says that the devil has both *proairesis* and *gnōmē* and that those are the source of his wickedness: "He [the devil] is wicked because of τὴν γνώμην καὶ τὴν προαίρεσιν [*tēn gnōmēn kai tēn proairesin*]."[17] Again the *kai* could mean that *gnōmē* and *proairesis* are synonymous, but it is also possible that they are two different faculties in the devil's possession.[18] In this example, however, the previous sentence speaks of the devil's having a wicked *proairesis* alone. One final example of this use together is from Chrysostom's *In epistulam ad Romanos hom.* 12, where the *hē rhaithymos proairesis* (ἡ ῥᾴθυμος προαίρεσις) and the *hē diephtharmenē gnōmē* (ἡ διεφθαρμένη γνώμη) are listed with *epi to cheiron hormē* (ἐπὶ τὸ χεῖρον ὁρμὴ) and *autē ē praxis* (αὐτὴ ἡ πρᾶξις) as the cause of all evils.[19] Given the format of the list, *proairesis* and *gnōmē* seem to have at least a nuanced difference, one perhaps explained by Laird's analysis.

When Chrysostom contrasts *physis* with both *gnōmē* and *proairesis* in different places, *gnōmē* and *proairesis* function the same way in each instance. Both are set against necessity; both are the faculty to which Chrysostom ascribes moral responsibility after he says that evil is not part of human nature. He preaches, "Good and evil are not according to φύσις [*physis*], but are of γνώμη [*gnōmē*] and of προαίρεσις [*proairesis*] alone."[20] In a discussion of human sin in *In Matthaeum hom.* 59, Chrysostom says, "Therefore when you accuse, you show that the sin is not of the φύσις [*physis*]

---

[16]Chrysostom, *In Matt. hom.* 59.3 (PG 58.577).

[17]Chrysostom, *De diab. tent.* 2.2 (SC 560bis, 164).

[18]A further possibility is that this phrase is a hendiadys, two different words working together to describe one complex idea. For discussion of this form of grammar, see Herbert Weir Smyth, *Greek Grammar*, ed. Gordon M. Messing, rev. ed. (Cambridge, MA: Harvard University Press, 1956), 3025. In this case, the idea being described is "that in the human being which is responsible for morality."

[19]Chrysostom, *In Rom. hom.* 12.6 (PG 60.502).

[20]Chrysostom, *In Rom. hom.* 19.5 (PG 60.591).

but of the προαίρεσις [*proairesis*]. For if we testify that everything is of φύσις [*physis*] in the things that we do not accuse, it is clear that in those things we do censure, we show that the offense is of the προαίρεσις [*proairesis*]."[21] In the next paragraph he juxtaposes *gnōmē* with *physis* instead: "For if these things do not require any γνώμη [*gnōmē*], but are of φύσις [*physis*], how are [some good], the others [bad]?"[22] Both because punishment and blame fall on humans for their wickedness and because not all humans are wicked, wickedness cannot be an intrinsic property of human nature. There must be some other responsible faculty, and both *proairesis* and *gnōmē* are mentioned as filling this role.

One further distinction is clear from the passage from *In epistulam ad Romanos hom.* 13 quoted above, where *proairesis* is contrasted with the *ousia* of the soul and body. Chrysostom seems to say that the soul is also not responsible for evil, in contrast to what he says elsewhere in this same homily, where the soul rather than the body is morally accountable. Chrysostom is clear here, though, that the *ousia* of the soul is not responsible. Since it is clear that the soul is responsible for the body and that virtue is located in the soul, there must be some aspect of the soul that is responsible for evil. It is likely that by the soul's *ousia* Chrysostom means something similar to his statements about human nature not being evil. The soul in itself is not evil; that is, it is not evil by nature, intrinsically. This is because the soul is a work of God, just like the body, and therefore cannot be intrinsically evil, for then God would have both made something evil (an impossibility) and blamed the soul for something it had no control over (an injustice, which is an impossibility for God). Therefore, the soul as soul is not responsible for evil, but the *proairesis* is responsible. It is a dimension of a human being that is free and makes a person self-determining.

Understanding Human Nature from Creation

In order to demonstrate that a person is free and self-determining, Chrysostom frequently contrasts *proairesis* with *physis*. If a person acts a certain way by nature, then he has no choice in the matter, and he is therefore not self-determining. Chrysostom considers the nature of a thing to be a necessity

---

[21]Chrysostom, *In Matt. hom.* 59.2 (PG 58.576).
[22]Chrysostom, *In Matt. hom.* 59.2 (PG 58.576).

or compulsion, something a person cannot change. Choice is the opposite of necessity. Before exploring this contrast and the way it serves as evidence for humanity's self-determination, we must first understand what Chrysostom means by *physis*. What is the nature Chrysostom contrasts with *proairesis*?

An example of this contrast is from the quotation noted above from *De diabolo tentatore* 2 about those who chose the theater instead of worship: "Did the devil trick them? How did he not trick you? You and they are the same humans; I mean, with regard to your nature [*physis*]. You have the same soul [*psychēs*, ψυχῆς] as they do, you have the same natural [*physis*] desires. How then were you and they not in the same place? Because you and they do not have the same προαίρεσις [*proairesis*]."[23] Chrysostom preaches something similar a few paragraphs later in a discussion of the parable of the sheep and goats: "Both these and those [those separated as sheep and goats] are humans. Why then are those sheep but these goats? In order that you may learn not a difference in their nature [*physis*], but the difference in their προαίρεσις [*proairesis*]."[24] From these quotations it appears that, at least in the context of contrast with *proairesis*, Chrysostom uses *physis* to refer to that which is common to all things of a kind. In this case, it is the set of things that are common to human beings.

In the first of these quotations, Chrysostom says that both the theatergoers and the churchgoers are human beings with the same souls and desires "as regards *physis*." What are the things common to human beings? The desires they have? Presumably these desires would include the desires to eat and drink, to be dry and warm, and so on. That is, humans have common desires for sustaining life. In a passage on Lenten fasting, Chrysostom remarks that Christ fasted forty days, the same number as humans, to show that he shares human nature and not only the appearance of human nature.[25] It is the desire, or necessity, of eating that proves Christ's human *physis*.

Because Chrysostom refers specifically to the "same souls" in the previous quotation, however, it is likely he also means desires of another kind, those that relate to the soul. An example from *Homiliae in Genesim* 1 may help here. Speaking of Daniel's encounter in the lion's den, he preaches,

---

[23]Chrysostom, *De diab. tent.* 2.1 (SC 560bis, 154-56).
[24]Chrysostom, *De diab. tent.* 2.3 (SC 560bis, 172).
[25]Chrysostom, *In Gen. hom.* 1.3 (PG 53.24).

"Daniel . . . fasted for many days and was deemed worthy of that marvelous vision which even bridled the anger of the lions and changed them into the gentlest sheep, not changing their nature [*physis*] but by changing their *pro-airesis* while keeping their ferocity."[26] Here again the contrast is between *physis* and *proairesis*, though this time in animals other than humans. Chrysostom implies that the nature of lions is to be fierce and furious, that is, that a trait common to all lions is ferocity. *Physis*, then, is that which is intrinsic to a thing.

The question is what traits, what desires, what parts of the soul, are intrinsic to human beings. Chrysostom often upholds the saints as those to emulate, and when he does so, he sometimes tells the audience that they are able to have the virtue of the saints because they have the same nature as the saints. The congregants are not to excuse themselves by saying something along the lines of, "They are saints, and I am not, so I cannot have that virtue."[27] Paul is Chrysostom's example in this homily of a saint who shares our nature, "subject to the same passions and being in such times of difficulty."[28] Passions and difficulty in life are part of the common *physis* of human beings. So is reason: "There is reason in your soul, and the fear of God, and many other aids from other places. Therefore do not speak excuses or pretences. For it is possible, if you wish, to be gentle and mild and reasonable."[29] Though he does not use the term *physis* here, Chrysostom is speaking in general about all humans as opposed to all animals. He assumes reason is common to humans, which makes it part of human *physis*.

Chrysostom does not provide a list of things that compose human *physis*, but from the way that he contrasts it with *proairesis*, it is clear that, at least in that context, he means the set of things common and intrinsic to human beings. What Chrysostom does do, in several places, is explain what kinds of things are common. In particular, as with most of his predecessors,[30] Chrysostom finds his understanding of humanity in the creation account:

---

[26]Chrysostom, *In Gen. hom.* 1.3 (PG 53.24).

[27]The heading for Chrysostom, *In Gen. hom.* 11, is "That it is necessary that great consideration be made of virtue and to imitate the saints, who, being of the same nature [φύσις] as us, act virtuously with precision; and that laziness on our part will have no defense" (PG 53.90).

[28]Chrysostom, *In Gen. hom.* 11.5 (PG 53.96).

[29]Chrysostom, *In Gen. hom.* 9.3 (PG 53.78).

[30]Irenaeus, *Against Heresies* 4; Athanasius, *On the Incarnation*; and Gregory of Nyssa, *On the Making of Man*, to name a few examples.

"Do not speak to me about fallen, dishonored, condemned humanity. But if you wish to learn what sort of body God formed for us from the beginning, let us go to Paradise and see the human that was created at the beginning."[31] What is common to all is that which God created. In that homily from *De statuis* that I have just quoted, Chrysostom describes the body God gave Adam: "That body was not corruptible and mortal. . . . Labor did not trouble it, nor sweat ruin it. Concerns did not plot against it; nor sorrows besiege it."[32] In his *Homiliae in Genesim*, Chrysostom describes the same thing, adding that Adam and Eve lived an angelic life before the fall: "Just like some angel, this is how the human passed his time on earth, wearing a body, but happening to be free of bodily needs; and just like a king arranged in his purple robe and a crown, so he reveled in living in freedom and great affluence in paradise."[33] He also says they "lived on earth as if in heaven."[34] By this Chrysostom means that Adam and Eve had no concern for bodily things. They had bodies, but they "did not feel the limitations of their bodies."[35]

It is also from the Genesis creation account that Chrysostom understands humans to have been created with the knowledge to distinguish good from evil. This is the reason the soul has a "greater wisdom" than the body; it was designed for virtue. When preaching to his catechumens, Chrysostom asks, "Do you see how the faith in Christ and the return to virtue are called a new creation?"[36] Their baptism is a "return" (*epanodos*, ἐπάνοδος) to virtue, which suggests that at one time people were virtuous. So baptism must be a return to some other time or state of humanity, their prelapsarian existence. Before the fall, according to Chrysostom, Adam and Eve were indeed choosing virtue, as is implied by Chrysostom's statements regarding Adam and Eve's angelic life noted above. That is the state to which Chrysostom urges his catechumens to return. Christ's work makes it possible for them to be virtuous again. Chrysostom does believe that humans were created with the knowledge of good and evil, preaching in his *In epistulam ad Romanos hom.* 13 that the ability to distinguish good and evil is innate to

---

[31]Chrysostom, *De stat.* 11.2 (PG 49.121).
[32]Chrysostom, *De stat.* 11.2 (PG 49.121).
[33]Chrysostom, *In Gen. hom.* 13.3 (PG 53.109).
[34]Chrysostom, *In Gen. hom.* 16.1 (PG 53.126).
[35]Chrysostom, *In Gen. hom.* 16.1 (PG 53.126).
[36]Chrysostom, *Cat.* 4.16 (SC 50bis, 191).

humans. He asks, "Do you see how [Paul] explains that the knowledge of good things and of things that are not [good] has been put down in us as a foundation from the beginning?"[37] According to Chrysostom, this ability is demonstrated in Adam's naming of the animals. That God asks Adam to name them and that Adam gets them all correct show with what great wisdom (*sophia*, σοφία) God has endowed Adam. If he had the kind of wisdom to name the animals properly, his wisdom was so great that it must have included the ability to know right from wrong.[38]

The problem came when Adam sinned.[39] After explaining the body Adam had in *De statuis hom.* 11, Chrysostom explains that when Adam sinned, God decided "chastening him through these acts, made him corruptible and mortal and bound him with many necessities."[40] Mortality is now common to humans, which suggests that it was not before.[41] The reason for the change is that Adam deemed "a deceiving demon more worthy of credit than God who cared for him," and, with this demon's prompting, Adam believed he could be like a god. According to Chrysostom, God wanted to "eradicate this idea" and thus made the human body subject to suffering and disease "to persuade him by this that he should never imagine or dream such a thing."[42] What God changes about the nature of humans is their immortality and awareness of the body, not, as we will see, their freedom or self-determination.

Along with an awareness of the body, Chrysostom discusses in *In epistulam ad Romanos hom.* 11 how the passions entered human beings when Adam sinned. Chrysostom writes,

> Before the coming of Christ, our body was easily overcome by sin. For after Adam's sin brought death, a great swarm of passions entered into man. And

---

[37]Chrysostom, *In Rom. hom.* 13.2 (PG 60.510).

[38]Chrysostom, *In Gen. hom.* 14.5 (PG 53.117).

[39]When describing this wisdom, Chrysostom says the reason God made sure we knew Adam was given this intelligence was so we would also know his sin did not come out of ignorance. Had he transgressed God's commandment out of ignorance, there could have been no punishment. Since he had wisdom, however, the sin was due to sloth and thus Adam is responsible (*In Gen. hom.* 14.5).

[40]Chrysostom, *De stat.* 11.2 (PG 49.121).

[41]It is significant that Chrysostom argues for God's changing of nature, for we will see that it is essential to his arguments about self-determination that nature does not change. Here nature only changes because God, who created it in the first place, changes (or re-creates) it.

[42]Chrysostom, *De stat.* 11.2 (PG 49.121).

for this reason he was not very nimble in the race for virtue. Neither was the Spirit yet present to help, nor was baptism, which could deaden these passions. Man was like a resistant and ill-bridled horse that ran but often went astray.[43]

The faculty of wisdom was not corrupted by the fall of Adam; the soul still knows good from evil, but in the fall the body became incorrigible. A prime example of this is Paul's anguish in Romans 7, trying to understand why he does what he hates. About that passage Chrysostom writes, "Do you see that your understanding has not been corrupted but preserves its own noble character in its action?"[44] Paul still understands right from wrong, even if he does not always do right. Though knowledge was not corrupted, the soul was now not strong enough to control the body that pulled against the reins, as argued in the quotation above.

Christ, however, made the body obedient to those reins again. Christ's incarnation, death, and resurrection restored the soul's control over the body. In the *Catecheses ad illuminandos*, Chrysostom makes a similar point using different language. In the first homily following the baptisms, Chrysostom tells his congregants about the change that has taken place in the new Christians, saying,

> Did you see how a new creation has really happened? For the grace of God, having entered the souls, remolded and re-formed them and, and made them different from what they were, not changing their οὐσία [*ousia*] but making over [*metaskeuasasa*, μετασκευάσασα] their προαίρεσις [*proairesis*], not allowing the court of the mind's eyes to have the opposite assumption about the deeds anymore, but . . . made them see precisely the ugly deformity of evil and virtue's shining beauty.[45]

The important feature here is that since God did not change human beings' understanding of good and evil when he made them mortal, they are still responsible for their actions, and even more so because Christ enabled their obedience again. Chrysostom says here it is the grace of God that transforms the *proairesis*.[46]

---

[43]Chrysostom, *In Rom. hom.* 11.3 (PG 60.487-88; Papageorgiou, *Homilies on Romans*, 207).
[44]Chrysostom, *In Rom. hom.* 13.2 (PG 60.509).
[45]Chrysostom, *Cat.* 4.14 (SC 50bis, 190).
[46]Chrysostom does not elaborate on the mechanics of this change. He says only that God's grace, in the event of baptism, works a change in people, which explains how "he who yesterday and

Since humans experienced the fall and no longer live in the same state as Adam, Adam's original way of life is now for Chrysostom the orientation toward which Christians strive. According to Chrysostom, Adam shows humanity the life God intended for human beings, that angelic life that has no thought or concern for bodily things: "Consider . . . how [Adam and Eve] were superior to all bodily matters, how they lived on earth as if they were in heaven, and though happening to be in a body they were not subject to bodily concerns. For they did not need shelter or habitation, clothing or anything of that kind."[47] In *De statuis hom.* 11, Chrysostom says that God made humans mortal and subject to suffering, aware of their bodies, which suggests that God has changed the things that were common to humans: immortality to mortality, impassible to passible, and with no thought for their bodies to an awareness of them. Therefore, humans cannot of their own accord regain the prelapsarian nature, but Chrysostom does encourage the audience to strive for the same orientation, or mindset, of the prelapsarian Adam. They ought to live as Adam lived, that is, as an angel on earth. In *In epistulam Romanos hom.* 13, Chrysostom describes the angelic life this way:

> The one who lives rightly will not even be in the body. Since it was surely clear to everyone that the spiritual one was not in sin, Paul sets out the greater fact that a person is spiritual not only in the matter of sin, but, from now on, also in the matter of flesh. Becoming an angel here already, and going up to heaven, he simply carried his body around with him from then on.[48]

Chrysostom tells the catechumens that the baptized live this angelic life, preaching, "Should this person [the newly baptized] continue to walk on the earth, he will have an attitude as though he passes his time in heaven . . . no longer fearing the plots of the evil demon."[49] Shortly after this in the same homily, Chrysostom tells his congregation that their "return to virtue" is the new creation to which Paul refers.[50] Chrysostom's contemporary exemplars of the spiritual man are the monks outside Antioch. He urges his

---

the day before rested in luxury and gluttony suddenly embraces self-control and a life of simplicity" (*Cat.* 4.13, SC 50bis, 190). Chrysostom is more concerned to explain *that* a "new creation" happens in baptism than *how* the new creation takes place.
[47]Chrysostom, *In Gen. hom.* 16.1 (PG 53.126).
[48]Chrysostom, *In Rom. hom.* 13.7 (PG 60.517-18).
[49]Chrysostom, *Cat.* 4.5 (SC 50bis, 185).
[50]Chrysostom, *Cat.* 4.16 (SC 50bis, 191).

congregation to emulate them, and for them he claims lives lived in the same paradisiacal state as Adam had before the fall.[51] In his *Comparatio regis et monachi*, Chrysostom says that the monk needs little sleep and so he spends the night "living with the angels, talking with God, enjoying the good things of heaven."[52] In *Adversus oppugnatores vitae monasticae,* Chrysostom says that the monks' way of life is a heavenly way of life and that "they are in a state in no way inferior to the angels."[53] The paradisiacal life of virtue, of concern only with heavenly realities, is possible for Christians, and monks are Chrysostom's prime examples.

One other thing common to human beings is the presence of the *proairesis* or *gnōmē*. Every human being has this, and it is this, though part of the nature of human beings, that is free and morally responsible, and so that which causes difference among humans. It is each person's exercise of his *proairesis* that is different, not intrinsic, and *eph hēmin*. This is the root of the contrast with *physis*.

BODY AND SOUL RELATIONSHIP

The ideal state toward which Christians strive, for Chrysostom, is that which Adam enjoyed before the fall and which monks enjoy now, a state where bodily limitations are not felt, or at least require only minimal attention. Chrysostom also places an emphasis on *proairesis* and *gnōmē* as the location of sin and virtue. These aspects of Chrysostom's thought raise the question of how the body and soul relate. Does virtue exist only in the soul, or does bodily action matter as well? Chrysostom writes in *Quod nemo laeditur nisi a seipso*, "Since the virtues of a person are not wealth, neither to be free, nor to live in our homeland, nor the other things that I have said, but right actions of the soul, when harm comes to these things, nothing is able to hinder human virtue."[54]

---

[51]"Their work, the same as what Adam's was at the beginning and before his sin, when he was clothed with the glory, and spoke openly with God, and lived in that place that was full of the greatest blessedness. For why are they in a worse state than he, when before his disobedience he was placed there to work the garden? Were there no concerns about life for him? Neither do these have any. Did he speak to God with a clean conscience? These do this also; or rather they have a greater freedom than he, inasmuch as they also enjoy a greater grace through the supply of the Spirit" (Chrysostom, *In Matt. hom.* 68.3 [PG 58.643-44]).

[52]Chrysostom, *Comp. reg. et mon.* 3 (PG 47.389).

[53]Chrysostom, *Adv. opp. vit. mon.* 3.11 (PG 47.366).

[54]Chrysostom, *Quod nem. laed.* 5 (SC 103bis, 82).

"Right actions of the soul" (*tēs psyxēs ta katorthōmata*, τῆς ψυχῆς τὰ κατορθώματα) is an intriguing phrase. People often think of virtue as actions performed by the body; one does or does not do virtuous acts: going to worship, giving to the poor, not causing physical harm to another. Chrysostom here suggests that virtue is about the actions of the soul, the choices, the exercise of *proairesis*, which is *eph hēmin*. What relation, then, is there between the body and the actions of the soul?

Chrysostom's *In epistulam ad Romanos hom.* 13 is useful for understanding this passage. There he preaches that the soul's duty with regard to the body is like the duty of a harpist toward a harp or of a helmsman toward a ship; the soul guides and operates the body.[55] He also refers to the body as "an exceptional work of God that is useful for us for virtue if we are vigilant."[56] Therefore, a right action of the soul would be manifested in a person's life as the soul directs the body to act, just as a ship's pilot moves the rudder that turns the ship. Right movement of soul also sounds similar to Stoic ideas of movement of soul. There is not an overlap in vocabulary regarding *hormē* (ὁρμή), but the concept is similar. I noted in the previous chapter that for Stoics there are movements of the soul that lead to action in the body.[57] For Epictetus, what determines virtue or vice is the use of impressions, and this is all in the soul. Intent is what matters since the completion of an intended act (raising one's arm, for instance) may be hindered by some outside force (a restraint). For Chrysostom, this intent is important, but the intent will, barring some restraint, manifest itself in action. The body does what the soul has decided, though the body may for some reason be prevented.

The above claim that the body is a work of God useful for virtue is part of a refutation of the claim that the body is inherently evil.[58] Chrysostom is saying that it is not evil; the soul plays the instrument of the body. In fact, the body, as a work of God, is good because everything God creates is good. Chrysostom finds support for this in Christ's own taking on of flesh as reported in Romans 8:3, among other places: "[Paul] said 'sinful' because he was also establishing 'in the likeness.' For Christ did not have sinful flesh,

---

[55]Chrysostom, *In Rom. hom.* 13.2 (PG 60.509).
[56]Chrysostom, *In Rom. hom.* 13.3 (PG 60.511).
[57]See above, "Stoicism and Moral Responsibility."
[58]Chrysostom, *In Rom. hom.* 13.3 (PG 60.511).

but flesh 'in the likeness' of our sinful flesh, except that Christ's flesh was sinless. But in nature Christ's flesh was the same as ours. Thus from this it is clear that the nature of the flesh is not evil."[59] Even when discussing the act of creation, Chrysostom argues that the body exists to serve the soul. So Chrysostom preaches that just as the animals were made before humans in order to be ready to serve humans when finally they were created, "The body is created before the soul, so that when the soul is produced according to God's ineffable wisdom, it will have its own energy to be displayed through the movement of its body."[60] This is because the soul has wisdom God did not grant the body: "The soul is wiser and is able to perceive what should be done and what should not be done. However, it lacks the strength to control the horse, that is, the body, as it wishes."[61] Later Chrysostom clarifies that Christians have the ability to control their bodies, saying, "The one who saved the soul [Christ] is the one who also made the flesh obedient to its rein."[62] Those baptized into the death and resurrection of Christ and so sharing his life have bodies that are obedient to the soul.

NATURE VERSUS CHOICE

The contrast between *physis* and *proairesis* or *gnōmē* is the most frequent way Chrysostom discusses human freedom, arguing that humans are evil not by nature but by choice.[63] The dichotomy between nature and choice

---

[59]Chrysostom, *In Rom. hom.* 13.5 (PG 60.514-15).
[60]Chrysostom, *In Gen. hom.* 13.3 (PG 53.108; FC 74:174).
[61]Chrysostom, *In Rom. hom.* 13.2 (PG 60.509). It is tempting to make this an echo of Plato's horse-and-chariot image, but Chrysostom here refers to the soul as a rider (or possibly charioteer; the text is unclear), and the body as the horse. Plato refers to the charioteer and two horses as the three parts of the souls (λογός, θυμός, and ἐπιθυμία). In the passage, Chrysostom has been using metaphors of music and instruments, pilots and ships, and this is the only mention of a horse until the mention of rein at the end of the homily (see next quotation). Chrysostom does use Plato's charioteer image elsewhere in his corpus, so he is aware of the metaphor, but in those instances the body is not part of the metaphor. See above, "Chrysostom's Philosophical Sources." Here it is more likely that Chrysostom sought another example of controlling something unwieldy, and horse came to mind. He does speak often about the horse races, after all.
[62]Chrysostom, *In Rom. hom.* 13.5 (PG 60.514).
[63]Chrysostom spends significantly less time saying that humans are virtuous not by nature but by choice. In fact, an occasional comment from Chrysostom may sound as though humans were created virtuous, such as, "It is clear that virtue is according to nature for us; we all, from our own resources, know our duties; and that it is not possible for us ever to flee into ignorance" (*In Matt. hom.* 23.5 [PG 57.314]). This statement could also be read as humans having been gifted with the ability to be virtuous and the knowledge to do so. At any rate, these comments are considerably rarer than Chrysostom's rhetoric about humans not being evil by nature.

appears over and over again in Chrysostom's homilies as he argues that not only are humans not evil by nature, but that *nothing* is evil by nature: "There is nothing that is evil by nature."[64] If something were evil by nature, that would imply it was created evil, and Chrysostom is adamant that God does not create evil. Rather than argue that God would not create something evil, however, Chrysostom argues that God created everything good. Scripture says that God created everything and pronounced it all "good" and "very good," so everything God creates is good in its very nature, even those things that appear not to be, such as thorns, scorpions, storms, and sea monsters. Chrysostom says that God looked at all of these things, "Not only light, but also darkness. . . . Not only human beings, but also poisonous reptiles. Not only fish, but also sea monsters. . . . Not only sun, moon, and stars, but also thunderbolts and hurricanes."[65] What is more, Chrysostom writes, "He declares [his judgment] about all things in general, saying, 'God saw everything which he made, and behold, it was very good.'"[66] When his audience suggests that a given experience is evil, Chrysostom responds that the thing is not truly evil but is in fact good, for God created everything good. By demonstrating that God created everything good, Chrysostom has disallowed the possibility that God created something evil.

Chrysostom also adds an empirical argument. Humans cannot be evil by nature because humans are not all equal in virtue and vice. If good or evil were part of their nature, then all would be either good or bad, since anything that is part of "human nature" is common to all humans. If people were bad by nature, good people would be an impossibility. Chrysostom preaches, "Did God create all people? . . . For if by nature all were evil, no one would be able to be good, but if good by nature, then no one could be bad. For if there were one nature of all people, they would need

Perhaps his audience did not assume people are virtuous by nature but, in looking around at the chaos and suffering in the world, did assume that evil was part of human nature.

[64]Chrysostom, *In Act. apost. hom.* 2.4 (PG 60.31): φύσει γὰρ οὐδὲν ἔστι κακὸν. This section of the homily is an argument against the Manichees, who claim that evil is uncreated. Chrysostom avers that arguing the uncreatedness of evil is blasphemy against God, and in a parenthetical comment he makes this statement about nothing's being evil by nature. That it is parenthetical here shows that Chrysostom assumes this to be true.

[65]Chrysostom, *Ad eos qui scand.* 4.2-3 (SC 79bis, 79).

[66]Chrysostom, *Ad eos qui scand.* 4.5 (SC 79bis, 79).

to all be one, whether they were to be this, or whether they were to be that."[67]

This would seem to be a contradiction. If God made all things and called them "good," and if God made human beings, then God made human beings good. Yet Chrysostom says that not all people are good (nor are all evil). Chrysostom further says that good and evil are not part of human nature because nature is what is common to all things of a set, and good and evil are not common to all humans. Yet again, God made all things good. Chrysostom resolves this in his discussions about the origin of evil. If some people are evil, and if God did not create them thus, this must come from somewhere. Chrysostom preaches that God did create humans good—and also free. In that freedom it is up to them to remain good; they may choose evil. Therefore humans were not created evil but chose it, which further implies that God created them with the ability to choose between good and evil.

This still does not fully resolve the contradiction. Chrysostom does not himself comment on this contradiction. The two strains of thought do not come together in Chrysostom's works. He either speaks of God's creating all things good as a refutation of the claim that God would create evil, or he speaks of the impossibility that good or evil is an aspect of human nature. In the context of these discussions about human *proairesis* and moral responsibility, Chrysostom's emphasis is on the latter; Chrysostom contrasts *proairesis* with *physis*.

Chrysostom further notes that nature is unchangeable, so that if goodness or wickedness were matters of nature, people would always be either good or bad without possibility of change. Chrysostom's belief in the immutability of nature is clear from his own statement: "The things of nature are not changed."[68] This belief is one that he assumes and from which he builds his argument rather than one he explains, which suggests that he has inherited this idea from elsewhere. Though it is impossible to ascribe with certainty a source for Chrysostom's claim, Aristotle's *Metaphysics* book five explains many of these ideas, and in *De fato* 27 Alexander of Aphrodisias makes an argument not unlike Chrysostom's.[69] It was not an uncommon idea in philosophy.

---

[67]Chrysostom, *In Matt. hom.* 59.2 (PG 58.576).

[68]Chrysostom, *In Matt. hom.* 59.2 (PG 58.576).

[69]Alexander argues that no one is virtuous by nature, even as the capacity for virtue comes from nature, because nature does not change.

There is one apparent contradiction here. Earlier I concluded that, according to Chrysostom, God made human nature mortal because of Adam's sin, which is a change in nature. However, human nature did not change of its own accord or by some inevitable process. It is most likely that Chrysostom means by the statement, "the things of nature are not changed," that they do not change apart from God's intervention. Given that God created all things, God is able to re-create or change any created thing.[70] Chrysostom does not himself address the issue, but it is reasonable to think that God's action could be the exception to the rule of immutable nature. If God is the only one able to change nature, and if God's only change to human nature, according to Chrysostom, is of mortality, then Chrysostom's argument that people are neither always good nor always bad and therefore neither goodness nor wickedness is a matter of nature remains true since God did not change that aspect of nature. Even in the fall, that Adam sinned in his prelapsarian body indicates that something other than Adam's nature is the locus of evil.[71]

Though nature cannot change, Chrysostom is committed to the possibility that humans can change. It is, in fact, central to how he speaks about conversion. Especially in his *Catecheses ad illuminandos*, Chrysostom tells his congregation that becoming a Christian requires a significant change of life. He exhorts them to be like Paul, who converted "from evil to virtue and . . . from error to truth."[72] Paul is Chrysostom's exemplar for the magnitude of the change of life required by conversion. Christians must cease doing evil and begin doing good. He also preaches,

> Have you ever been bad, and have you ever also been good? What I mean, is this: Did you at one time prevail over passion, and were you at another time conquered by passion? . . . Did you at one time plunder things that didn't belong to you; and after that, overcome by pity, did you give of yourself to someone in need? Then where did this change come from? Is it not clear that it is from the γνώμη [*gnōmē*], and the προαίρεσις [*proairesis*]?[73]

---

[70]In fact, it is possible to understand the change from immortality to mortality as an act of re-creation of sorts, in which case, since God does not create evil, the postlapsarian nature also is not evil.

[71]I will show below that this is similar to Methodius's theodicy, where he argues that nothing is evil by nature, which is part of his argument that evil finds its origin neither in God nor in the "leftover" (ὕλη) but in the creature's choice.

[72]Chrysostom, *Cat.* 4.12 (SC 50bis, 189).

[73]Chrysostom, *In Matt. hom.* 59.3 (PG 58.577).

That Chrysostom is certain about the necessity of changed ways of life for conversion implies that he believes it is possible for people to change to being virtuous when before they participated in evil, and this is why evil is not a matter of nature but of choice.

This is Chrysostom's overriding concern: without agency there can be no responsibility. As all the preceding arguments have assumed, *physis* in Chrysostom's characterization of human goodness and badness indicates that a person who is evil by nature cannot do otherwise than evil, which precludes punishment. Above we saw that an act must be free in order to be punishable and that Chrysostom understands punishments as evidence of human freedom. If evil or good were part of nature, a person would not be free to do evil or good, and thus punishment or praise would be unjust, something God is not. Chrysostom preaches, "They [fictitious adversaries] make other objections again, asking, 'And why did God make him [evil man] this way?' God did not make him this way. Far from it! Since if he had, he would not have punished him."[74] In his homily on the parable of the sheep and goats, Chrysostom says that the sheep are fruitful by nature, but the goats are unfruitful by nature. In contrast, he says, the humans whom Jesus has compared to sheep and goats are fruitful or not by choice rather than by nature, and this is the cause of their reward or punishment. So Chrysostom preaches, "The animals have from nature their unfruitfulness and fruitfulness, but these [people] have it from προαίρεσις [*proairesis*], on which account some are punished, and others crowned."[75] The quotation above from a discussion in homily 59 on Matthew 18:7 concerning the origin of evil also makes this point clear. Chrysostom's immediate goal in this passage is to protect God from accusations that God created humans evil, and his final goal is to remove any question of God's having had anything to do with the creation of evil at all. Since it is not God, it must be humans.

This is the project of *De diabolo tentatore*, where Chrysostom was concerned that his congregation know the devil was not created evil but good. Because of this, the devil's wickedness cannot belong to his nature but must belong to his choice. In those passages, Chrysostom argues that if not even the devil, that most wicked of creatures, is evil by nature, then neither can

[74]Chrysostom, *In Matt. hom.* 59.2 (PG 58.575).
[75]Chrysostom, *In Matt. hom.* 80.1 (PG 58.717).

human beings, who are less wicked, be evil by nature: "Although many men are wicked, he alone is called this as the most prominent. . . . What therefore could be worse than this wickedness?"[76] This argument serves Chrysostom's larger purpose in those homilies, which is to remove demons as an excuse for humans' sin. In the Matthean homily, Chrysostom's purpose is to correct those who would use God as an excuse for sin since God created human nature. The two enterprises are similar, and in both cases Chrysostom shifts the emphasis back to the human's responsibility for himself and his own choices.

HUMAN FREEDOM

When Chrysostom contrasts *physis* with *proairesis*, he allows the terms to act as synonyms of "necessity" (*anankē*, ἀνάγκη) and "freedom" (*eleutheria*, ἐλευθερία). For Chrysostom, *physis* is a matter of *anankē*; if something is part of a thing's or a person's nature, then it is compulsory. A person must do that which is in his nature. A person's *proairesis*, on the other hand, is *eleutheria*; there is no compulsion. The *proairesis* is self-determining (*autexousios*, αὐτεξούσιος), making human beings self-determining, and this self-determination and freedom are what allow for virtue and vice, praise and blame. We saw Chrysostom preach in *In Matthaeum hom.* 59 that God's punishment of human wickedness is evidence that God did not create humans wicked by nature.[77] He makes a similar statement about God's justice in a homily on Jeremiah 10:23: "What could be more unjust than punishing those who have no power over matters of moral action, and for people to suffer punishment whose way and life are not under their own authority?"[78] Furthermore, if there were no punishment, no praise nor blame, there would also be no grounds for calling a person virtuous or sinful. So using words fundamental to his account of freedom, Chrysostom tells his audience, "These things are not of necessity [*anankē*]. For if they were of necessity, he would not have said, 'Woe to the person through whom the stumbling comes.' For he only calls unhappy those who are evil from their προαίρεσις [*proairesis*]."[79]

---

[76]Chrysostom, *De diab. tent.* 1.2 (SC 560 bis, 130-32).
[77]Chrysostom, *In Matt. hom.* 59.2 (PG 58.575).
[78]Chrysostom, *Dom., non est in hom.* 5 (PG 56.160).
[79]Chrysostom, *In Matt. hom.* 59.3 (PG 58.577-78).

Ananke is one of the words Chrysostom uses frequently to discuss the ideas of compulsion and freedom. Anything that is *ananke* is not free and thus not something for which one can be responsible, so Chrysostom contrasts *ananke* with *autexousion, eleutheros,* and *proairesis,* which Chrysostom understands to be intrinsically free. Indeed, Chrysostom sets *proairesis* over against *ananke,* as when he says, "Let us make what is a matter of ἀνάγκη [*ananke*] a matter of our προαίρεσις [*proairesis*]."[80] He thus indicates the autonomous nature of one's *proairesis.* Chrysostom is discussing things that happen to a person, such as a loss of fortune or the death of a child. These external circumstances are matters of *ananke,* forced on a person. Chrysostom urges the congregation to focus on their reactions to such events, which are within a person's control, so he exhorts them to make things a matter of *proairesis.* Lack of compulsion is also how Platonists, Stoics, and Aristotle spoke about such issues. Virtue is a matter of voluntary action, at the center of which is *proairesis,* or reasoned desire. In his comments on Romans 7, Chrysostom uses this language again: "From this it is clear that Paul did not say 'not what I wish' because he was denying αὐτεξούσιον [*autexousion*], nor because he was bringing in some overpowering ἀνάγκην [*ananken*]. For if we sin because we are forced to do so, there would be no reason for the punishments that were inflicted in former times."[81]

In *Quod nemo laeditur nisi a seipso* Chrysostom emphasizes the inability of anyone or anything to harm a person except the person herself. The loss of virtue is the only true harm a person can undergo, and since the devil cannot rob a person of her virtue, since every person is responsible for maintaining her own virtue, true harm befalls only the person who brings it on herself. Again, the human cannot be forced. Chrysostom is explicit about this: "[The devil] does not conquer with force, nor with tyranny, nor by compelling."[82] He is also clear about the role of a person's *proairesis:* "In all circumstances, the προαίρεσις [*proairesis*] is the cause [of harm]."[83] A person can be deceived, but the responsibility for sin still lies with her, as in the case

---

[80]Chrysostom, *In Rom. hom.* 9.4 (PG 60.473; Papageorgiou, *Homilies on Romans,* 177).
[81]Chrysostom, *In Rom. hom.* 13.1 (PG 60.508; Papageorgiou, *Homilies on Romans,* 252).
[82]Chrysostom, *De diab. tent.* 1.1 (SC 560bis, 122).
[83]Chrysostom, *De diab. tent.* 1.4 (SC 560bis, 140).

of Eve, since her *proairesis* remains in her own control. Moreover, the devil tries everything in his power to destroy human beings, a point Chrysostom makes clear when discussing how he knows demons do not govern the affairs of the world. He says, "If God had entrusted the whole world to [the demons'] authority, they would have confounded and confused everything, and would have arranged things for us just like they did for the pigs," referring to the healing of the Gerasene demoniacs (Mt 8:28-34).[84] If the demons do all they can to destroy a human's salvation, but in every case responsibility for sin remains with the human who makes a choice, and if the *proairesis* is the locus of responsibility, then the thing the devil cannot coerce is the *proairesis*.

Not only is the devil not able to force, but God does not compel either. Chrysostom writes, "Since God loves humanity, beloved, and is beneficent, he creates and does all things so that we might shine with virtue. And since he desires for us to be well-esteemed, he might persuade us to this, but he does not constrain or compel anyone."[85] Instead, God will draw and attract, and, when necessary, threaten.[86] God "everywhere threw out coercion, and highlighted αὐθαίρετον καὶ αὐτεξούσιον [*authaireton kai autexousion*]."[87] In his *Catecheses ad illuminandos*, Chrysostom says something similar: God's very way of acting toward us reveals that humans are free, and the choice between good and evil is ours. Chrysostom preaches, "This is the greatest proof of his [God's] wisdom and unspeakable love: that he entrusts to us the care of what is greater to us—I mean the soul—teaching us through his actions that he made us αὐτεξούσιος [*autexousios*] and left our being up to us [*eph hēmin*] and in our γνώμη [*gnōmē*] both the choosing of virtue and the deserting to evil."[88] Especially in his *Catecheses ad illuminandos*, Chrysostom is fond of battle imagery. He believes there is a war raging all the time between God and the devil, between angels and demons, and humans must choose a side because they are caught in the crossfire on earth. There is neither a neutral stance nor a "no man's land." There is also, however, no conscription. All is choice.

---

[84]Chrysostom, *De proph. obsc.* 3.6 (PG 49.252).
[85]Chrysostom, *In Ioh. hom.* 10.1 (PG 59.73).
[86]Chrysostom, *In Ioh. hom.* 10.1 (PG 59.73).
[87]Chrysostom, *In Ioh. hom.* 10.3 (PG 59.76).
[88]Chrysostom, *Cat.* 8.22 (SC 50bis, 258-59).

WHAT IS VIRTUE?

Having explored the mechanics of virtue, let us now look at how Chrysostom describes for his congregation just what virtue is. A broad description of human virtue as Chrysostom understands it is living the way God calls a person to live. Or, more simply, virtue is obedience to God. This is, on the surface, not unlike the Stoic idea of living in accordance with God's will, except that the Stoic understanding of the character and person of God differs from that of Chrysostom, and this difference results in a difference of interpretation. The Stoics believe "the will of God" to be the order of nature, the way the world works. Therefore, living in harmony with this natural order is virtuous living. Stoics do not believe in a personal God who commands or makes specific requests of humans. Chrysostom does. For Chrysostom, virtue is not about "agreeing" with God and living in harmony with the natural order, but about obeying God and living the way God intends humans to live.[89] Chrysostom preaches, "Evil is nothing other than the disobedience of God."[90] As noted above, the origin of evil lies in the creature's choice. The converse of this is that good is found in obedience to God, and that obedience to God is a choice, a complex matter at the center of which is human freedom and responsibility.

In *Quod nemo laeditur nisi a seipso* Chrysostom discusses the nature of suffering, distinguishing between true and apparent harm. True harm is harm to the soul, to one's virtue, and Chrysostom therefore discusses the nature of virtue (*aretē*, ἀρετή), defining it as "precision in true doctrine, and the right way of life."[91] For Chrysostom there are two aspects of virtue; if a person is missing one of the two, she cannot be considered virtuous. Right thinking and right living are both imperative. Of the two, Chrysostom's preaching emphasis falls on the right-living component.

However, Chrysostom in no way neglects the importance of right thinking; a person must have correct content in his beliefs. For instance,

---

[89]This is the opposite of Seneca's often-quoted quip, "I do not obey God; rather, I agree with him" (*Ep.* 96.2). However, Chrysostom would have agreed with Cicero, who writes, "Anyone who speaks of the worst of evils in terms of pain has no business talking about virtue" (*Tusculan Disputations* 3.49; Marcus Tullius Cicero, *Cicero on the Emotions: Tusculan Disputations 3 and 4*, trans. Margaret Graver [Chicago: University of Chicago Press, 2002], 23).

[90]Chrysostom, *In Matt. hom.* 59.3 (PG 58.577).

[91]Chrysostom, *Quod nem. laed.* 3 (SC 103bis, 70).

early in his career, Chrysostom preached a series of homilies against the Anomeans, titled *De incomprehensibili dei natura,* in which he responded to the heretical Anomeans who had been attending his homilies and arguing with Chrysostom about the nature of God and human understanding of the Trinity.[92] Aside from what must have been extreme annoyance at such interruptions of his sermons, Chrysostom's concern was that these Anomeans were leading the faithful astray into heresy. It should be noted that Chrysostom was also concerned about the Anomeans themselves, whose dogmatic errors would lead *them* away from God. Chrysostom preaches, "I took these weapons, not in order to throw them at my enemies but in order to raise them up when they are lying down. For these weapons . . . do not inflict wounds but heal the sick."[93] He adds, "All my zeal and eagerness were not only to sew shut the mouths [of my Anomoean opponents] but also to teach more and more to your loving assembly."[94] Chrysostom's insistence that his congregation understand the inaccuracy of accounts that claim demons are angels who fell from lusting after human women is another example of his concern for right belief.[95] Everywhere Chrysostom desires his congregation to have correct knowledge.[96]

---

[92]*Anomean* is a general term of opprobium for the extremist branch of Arians, in other places known as heteroousians. Eunomians and Aetians followed particular anomean writers (Eunomius and Aetius); Chrysostom is addressing the extreme Arians broadly and without reference to any particular leader. Those against whom Chrysostom argues in these homilies believed it was possible to grasp fully the essence, or nature, of God, not only his works. Like the Cappadocians opposing the Eunomians, Chrysostom argued for the incomprehensibility of God's nature.

[93]Chrysostom, *De incompr. hom.* 1.39 (SC 28bis,132).

[94]Chrysostom, *De incompr. hom.* 4.1 (SC 28bis, 228). The past tense is a result of Chrysostom's recalling what led him to take up the issue of divine incomprehensibility. In the first quotation Chrysostom explains that it was when the Anomeans challenged him directly that he thought it necessary to engage them. The second quotation is from the first paragraph of a homily in which Chrysostom is recalling what he has accomplished in the previous homilies in the series.

[95]See discussion above, "Origin of Demons" in chapter 2. Another example comes from *In Gen. hom.* 8.3 (PG 53.71-72), where Chrysostom warns his congregation against heretics who would use the sentence, "Let us make human beings in our image" to "speak of the divine in human terms." He also uses this passage to declare the Jews' rejection of the Trinity to be heresy, reading "let us" as the Father speaking to the Son and Holy Spirit, per the common Christian reading of his time.

[96]The reason for this is that if a person misunderstands true doctrine—in the case of the Anomeans, the doctrine of the Trinity—then she has an incorrect understanding of God. This could lead to blasphemy, and it could also lead to poor actions. If a person misunderstands who God is, she might misunderstand that God does not compel a person to act, that each person has a

As important as good doctrine was to Chrysostom, though, most of Chrysostom's homiletical effort was spent not on instilling orthodox belief in his congregation but on encouraging his congregation to live in obedience to God. Chrysostom's sermons are full of exhortations to specific virtuous acts, for example, reading the Bible, being chaste, and his favorite, giving alms and caring for the poor, and against specific sins, for example, frequenting the theaters and horse races, especially in place of attending worship. These exhortations are the primary reason Chrysostom has been labeled "just" a moralist. The impression of his homilies is that he is more concerned with the morality and virtue of his congregation than anything else. Chrysostom is not shy about speaking of any sin he sees. In fact, his decision to note the sin of Empress Eudoxia was not an insignificant factor in his being exiled twice.[97] Often he lists things he considers to be virtues like "virginity, contempt for death, and all of the other sufferings."[98] It was, however, just as common for Chrysostom to exhort his audience to virtuous lives and good deeds generally and to allow the congregation to decide how that would translate into the exigencies of their lives, as when he preaches, "Let your virtue, your precise way of life, and the righteousness of your deeds rouse those who see you to praise the common Lord of us all."[99] In another place, he says, "I urge you . . . be zealous for virtue. The pleasure of evil is brief, but the pain [of punishment] is incessant. But the joy of virtue is timeless, and the work is temporary."[100]

Chrysostom further breaks virtue into the absence of evil and the accomplishment of good. Referring to Paul's statement in Romans 13:10, Chrysostom

---

choice, and thus exercise her προαίρεσις poorly. Chrysostom also seems in many places to argue that it is important to have right doctrine without telling his congregation why this is important. It simply is, as though having the correct content of doctrine is an essential aspect of being a Christian. We will see in chapter 5 that Chrysostom includes faith as part of the human's contribution to salvation.

[97]Eudoxia's sin, according to Chrysostom, was her inexcusable and conspicuous wealth (*In Col. hom.* 10.4 [PG 62.371]). For a description of Chrysostom's interactions with Eudoxia, see J. N. D. Kelly, *Golden Mouth: The Story of John Chrysostom—Ascetic, Preacher, Bishop* (London: Duckworth, 1995), 238-40. To be fair, Eudoxia recalled Chrysostom from his first exile because of a miscarriage she thought to be the result of God's anger. It is also important to note that various political situations and controversies, not only his accusations of her sin, played a role in Eudoxia's clashes with Chrysostom.

[98]Chrysostom, *In Rom. hom.* 13.7 (PG 60.517).

[99]Chrysostom, *Cat.* 4.21 (SC 50bis, 193).

[100]Chrysostom, *In Ioh. hom.* 36.2 (PG 59.206).

preaches that love "has both virtues, abstinence from evils (for it 'does no evil,' he says), and doing good deeds."[101] It is not enough to keep oneself from sin; one must actively pursue good.

HEAVENLY ORIENTATION

Another way to understand what Chrysostom means by the kind of virtue he urges his congregation to seek is to look at the exemplars he uses. There was a long tradition in the rhetorical world of using exemplars to portray specific virtues, and Chrysostom does this as well.[102] His examples, however, are primarily biblical rather than those drawn from Greco-Roman myths. Job is one of Chrysostom's chief exemplars, particularly so in discussions of demons, sin, and virtue. Since much of Chrysostom's discussion of demons and virtue is lodged within a narrative of theodicy, the choice to use Job makes sense. He is the paradigmatic sufferer, and the narrative offers everything he seeks in explaining why the world appears to be as evil as it is.[103] Chrysostom's use of Job as an exemplar often focuses on Job's resistance to the devil. Regardless of the disasters or temptations the devil tries in order to provoke Job to curse God, Job resists. Job never loses sight of God or God's goodness and thus defeats the devil. Furthermore, Chrysostom often juxtaposes Job with Adam and Eve. The latter are Chrysostom's negative example or antitype of a virtuous human, especially with regard to interactions with the devil. Chrysostom criticizes Eve for allowing herself to be deceived by the devil and scolds Adam for his failure to follow the commandment God gave him. After comparing the two stories, Chrysostom preaches,

---

[101]Chrysostom, *In Rom. hom.* 23.4 (PG 60.619).

[102]For pagan examples, see Virgil's *Aneid*, where Aeneas is the example of Roman virtue, and Seneca's *On Firmness* 2.2: "In Cato the immortal gods had given to us a truer exemplar of the wise man than earlier ages had in Ulysses and Hercules," and he goes on to explain why Cato is the truly wise man. For other Christian authors who appropriate this pagan rhetorical technique and use biblical exemplars, see 1 Clement 9–12; Methodius's *Symposium* 11; Athanasius's *Life of Antony*; and Gregory of Nyssa's *Life of Moses* and *Life of Macrina*. Having studied rhetoric under Libanius, Chrysostom would have been familiar with the technique. For a discussion in secondary literature about the use of exemplars in education and public life, see Clive Skidmore, *Practical Ethics for Roman Gentlemen: The Work of Valerius Maximus* (Exeter: University of Exeter Press, 1996), 3-21.

[103]It is also likely that in asking the questions of God's justice, Chrysostom receives answers from Job. However, Chrysostom does not find Job to provide only the ideas Chrysostom wants to present to his congregation. It is a fusion of exegesis and evidence.

Nowhere [for Adam] was there hard work or pain, neither depression nor concerns, nor accusations and abuse, nor the myriad evils which fell on Job. But all
the same, when nothing of this kind existed, he fell and was brought down. Is
it not clear that it was because of laziness? Therefore just as [Job], being pressed
on and weighed down by all these things, stood nobly and did not fall, is it not
clear that it is because of his vigilance of soul [nēpsin psychēs, νῆψιν ψυχῆς]?[104]

Continual resistance of the devil and obedience to God, a negative and a
positive aspect of the same action, are key components of virtue.

A paragon of resistance is Chrysostom's representation of Job in *De diabolo tentatore* and in most homilies in Chrysostom's corpus that mention
Job.[105] But in his *Commentarius in Iob*, the focus shifts slightly. The *Commentarius in Iob* is not primarily about Job's resistance to the devil, even as
that narrative takes up one-quarter of the commentary, but the commentary
is rather primarily about how to suffer. The focus is not on Job's innocence
but on Job's persistence in looking to eternal, rather than earthly, things and
on his seeing God's care and pedagogy in his suffering. Chrysostom writes,

Let us listen to his wise sentiments on the moment of the disaster: what he
advises in his sufferings and godly reflection. . . . He declares that God was
the one at war with him. But let us see the athlete's words. . . . Let us see how
he tore apart his enemy, firstly by worship; for having worshiped, he then
trusted his soul to say nothing harsh. His reasoning leapt up immediately to
God, and he no longer had eyes for the present.[106]

Further on, commenting on Job's reply to his friends, Chrysostom says, "I
know, [Job] says, that the ungodly are destroyed, but the righteous are not.
Do you see how nowhere he accuses God of injustice?"[107] Finally, he writes,
"I have a teacher [God] capable of proving that the blows, the things that
happened to me, are divine."[108]

Both of these emphases, looking to eternal things and seeing God's pedagogy in suffering, provide another key aspect of Chrysostom's understanding

---

[104]Chrysostom, *De diab. tent.* 2.4 (SC 56obis, 188).

[105]Chrysostom, *De diab. tent.* 2.1, 3.2; *Quod nem. laed.* 3-5; *In 1 Cor. hom.* 28.6, to name a few examples.

[106]Chrysostom, *Comm. in Iob* 1.23 (SC 346bis, 140-42).

[107]Chrysostom, *Comm. in Iob* 9.1 (SC 346bis, 300). Just after this Chrysostom writes in Job's voice,
"I know I suffer for my sins" (SC 346bis, 300). The story is not about Job's innocence but about
his suffering.

[108]Chrysostom, *Comm. in Iob* 19.13 (SC 348bis, 48).

of virtue: keeping one's mind on eternal things rather than on temporary, earthly things. This is the virtue of Shadrach, Meshach, and Abednego in the story of the fiery furnace in Daniel 3. Chrysostom tells his congregation that they refused to sin regardless of their external circumstances. They held fast to the truth of invisible realities and put no stock in the temporal. He preaches,

> What about the three children? Tell me, did the evils that came upon them ruin their virtue? . . . They did not consider the necessity [of their situation] nor the tyranny of the one who owned the state sufficient to defend themselves, but they devised and busied themselves with everything so as to flee sin, even though they were abandoned everywhere.[109]

Chrysostom's use of monks as paragons of virtue inculcates the same heavenly orientation praised in Job and Shadrach, Meshach, and Abednego, and Chrysostom urges his audience to emulate this lifestyle in the cities:

> However, if you did not know the dead through the Scriptures, you should have seen these living men. But is there no one to lead you? Come to me, and I will show you the dwellings of these holy ones; come and learn something useful from them. . . . For this reason they lived in solitude, that they might teach you to despise the clamor in the midst of the world.[110]

In both his *Comparatio regis et monachi* and his *Adversus oppugnatores vitae monasticae* Chrysostom argues that what makes the monk's way of life superior to others' ways of life is their detachment from worldly, temporal things and their correlative focus on heavenly, eternal things.[111] More explicitly, Chrysostom exhorts his own congregation by defining virtue as the ability to see the invisible realities: "Virtue is to despise all human things, to keep in front of one's mind at each hour the things to come, to be excited by no present things but to know that every human thing is a shadow and a dream, or even something cheaper than this."[112] This attention to eternal

---

[109]Chrysostom, *Quod nem. laed.* 15 (SC 103bis, 130-34).

[110]Chrysostom, *Hom Matt.* 72.4 (PG 58.672).

[111]Chrysostom, *Comp. reg. et mon.* is a comparison of the monk's poverty and the king's wealth that demonstrates the superiority of the monk's poverty because wealth ensnares one in the cares of the world, whereas poverty frees one to "converse with the angels" (PG 47.387-92). *Adv. opp. vit. mon.* is a series of three homilies designed to demonstrate the superiority of the monastic way of life, and again the key is the monks' poverty, which facilitates the angelic life on earth.

[112]Chrysostom, *In Gen. hom.* 8.6 (PG 53.75). One might argue that Chrysostom's own life does not exemplify "despising all human things" since as a prominent preacher and later bishop he was

realities is what enabled Job to suffer well because Job knew that his suffering was not true harm but was even for his good. The heavenly orientation, which requires holding loosely temporal things, if not scorning them altogether, is what enables a person to be virtuous.

The ability to keep one's mind on eternal things is also one of the ways Chrysostom tells his congregation to avoid sin and to resist the devil's temptations. He preaches,

> If [a person] ponders . . . the temporality of the things that seem bright here, no different from grass and dying more quickly than the flowers of spring—if we continually move these thoughts within ourselves and remember those who were the most virtuous, the devil will not be able to overcome us easily, even if he should make a thousand attempts, nor will he even be able to begin to conquer us.[113]

To his catechumens Chrysostom says to follow the example of the martyrs, who "abandoned all the things on earth and gazed with the eyes of faith on the King of heaven. . . . They changed their thoughts to heaven and paid no attention anymore to anything they could see. . . . They sketched for themselves the fire of Gehenna and thus strengthened their reason."[114] When contending with temptation, be it from passions or from demons, Chrysostom tells his audience to "be just like a corpse toward the things of this life and, as if a corpse, to take no active interest in the things that damage the soul's salvation."[115] A virtuous person keeps her mind on eternal things, which facilitates resistance to the devil and obedience to God.

This insistence on seeing the larger picture and keeping external circumstances and suffering in perspective sounds very Stoic.[116] For Epictetus, we

---

constantly entangled in political affairs and controversies. In the final book of *De sac.* Chrysostom explains that the role of the priest is to deal with the affairs of the world on behalf of his people. These entanglements are his duty as bishop. He writes, "For the Priest ought not only to be thus pure as one who has been dignified with so high a ministry, but very discreet, and skilled in many matters, and to be as well versed in the affairs of this life as they who are engaged in the world, and yet to be free from them all more than the recluses who occupy the mountains" (*De sac.* 6.4). Chrysostom's understanding of detachment for a heavenly orientation is not about throwing away all earthly things but about holding them loosely. This is seen in Chrysostom's call to emulate the monks. They are to live on earth as if in heaven. But they still live on earth.

[113]Chrysostom, *In Ioh. hom.* 9.2 (PG 59.72-73).
[114]Chrysostom, *Cat.* 7.18-19 (SC 50bis, 238).
[115]Chrysostom, *In Gen. hom.* 8.6 (PG 53.75).
[116]There are, of course, significant differences between Chrysostom and the Stoics. The point here is that there are resonances and that these resonances help us understand better what Chrysostom is doing.

saw, virtue consists in attending to the things that are *eph hēmin*, which come down to only the use of one's impressions. One has no control over life circumstances, but one can control one's reaction to them. Chrysostom, too, uses *eph hēmin* this way, saying that life is full of hardship, but that *eph hēmin keitai ta tēs aretēs kai ta tēs kakias* (ἐφ᾿ ἡμῖν κεῖται τὰ τῆς ἀρετῆς καὶ τὰ τῆς κακίας).[117] Making one's life worthy (*axia*, ἀξία) of the baptismal gifts, that is, keeping oneself pure, is what God has made *eph hēmin*.[118] In fact, in *In epistulam ad Ephesios hom.* 23, what is *eph hēmin* is the ability to see one's struggles on earth as temporary and therefore to store up treasures in heaven.[119] The goal of such a perspective is different for Chrysostom, however. For Stoics, controlling what is *eph hēmin is* virtue and leads to human flourishing in this life by being in accord with Nature.[120] For Chrysostom, though, the heavenly perspective facilitates virtue, is the mark of a virtuous person, and leads to salvation.

Chrysostom places a distinct emphasis on contrasting virtue with external circumstances or earthly things, such as wealth or health, which Chrysostom says people are prone to associate with virtue. When people see a healthy, successful person, Chrysostom says, people tend to assume that person is virtuous. Chrysostom argues instead that virtue is located within a human being in a way not unlike Paul's discussion of the "inner man." Chrysostom explains that Judas had every external circumstance in his favor and yet was not virtuous: "Neither his being of the twelve nor his call helped him, since he did not have a γνώμη [*gnōmē*] inclined to virtue."[121] Chrysostom also writes that wealth "does not usually make any one more skilled, wiser, or more capable, nor more intelligent, nor more useful, not more benevolent, not superior to anger or gluttony, not above pleasure. It does not form anyone to be moderate, does not teach a person to be humble, does not introduce or plant in his soul any other piece of virtue."[122] Virtue is not

---

[117]Chrysostom, *In Act. apost. hom.* 47.3 (PG 60.331).
[118]Chrysostom, *In Ioh. hom.* 10.3 (PG 59.76).
[119]Chrysostom, *In Eph. hom.* 23.3 (PG 62.168).
[120]Stoics are also concerned with providing a basis for the virtuous state, and Chrysostom is not concerned with civic virtue, even as he seeks the heavenly πολιτεία on earth. Chrysostom's vision of the heavenly πολιτεία is not a state controlled by the church but a church that lives in the world in accord with its heavenly citizenship.
[121]Chrysostom, *Quod nem. laed.* 11 (SC 103bis, 114).
[122]Chrysostom, *Quod nem. laed.* 7 (SC 103bis, 94-96).

about a person's situation but about something in her soul, a disposition or orientation toward eternity.

The phrase "piece of virtue" (*meros tēs aretēs*, μέρος τῆς ἀρετῆς) in the above quotation suggests that virtue is somehow composite, made up of pieces. Chrysostom uses a similar idea elsewhere, as in *In Iohannem hom.* 16: "[Pride] is enough for all the virtue of the soul to be destroyed completely, even if it finds almsgiving, prayer, fasting, whatever."[123] Various individual virtues reside in a person's soul and together make a person virtuous by composing the virtue of that soul. In another of the *In Iohannem homiliae*, Chrysostom says that chastity or abstention from stealing do not of themselves make a person virtuous. The whole life must be upright. So a person who is chaste but is so only for vainglory or his reputation is not truly virtuous.[124] In this way it sounds as though Chrysostom believes virtue to be an all-or-nothing state. A person either is virtuous or she is not. Given Chrysostom's intensity and moral certitude in the pulpit, it is easy to hear his words this way.[125]

Yet the phrase is "piece of virtue." It is possible for people to have part of virtue or, given Chrysostom's lists, for people to have specific virtues. In *De statuis hom.* 20.8, Chrysostom uses this phrase again: "[The Ninevites], once having heard, were upright; but we, though we have heard many times, do not repent. They were perfect in virtue; we do not have even a piece of virtue."[126] This suggests that, there are three possibilities regarding one's virtue: it is possible to have "perfect" or "complete" (*holoklēros*, ὁλόκληρος) virtue; part of virtue (*meros aretēs*, μέρος ἀρετῆς); or not a single part, none (*oude meros aretēs*, οὐδὲ μέρος ἀρετῆς). In another place Chrysostom uses a more poetic image, saying that fasting has "the last part in the choir of virtue."[127] Here Chrysostom is refuting those who think fasting alone is sufficient for salvation; he says that other virtues like virginity, almsgiving, and humility are more important. In commenting on Abraham, Chrysostom preaches,

[123]Chrysostom, *In Ioh. hom.* 16.4 (PG 59.106).
[124]Chrysostom, *In Ioh. hom.* 28.2 (PG 59.164).
[125]One thinks of his own asceticism and continual quest to find the most stringent forms, eventually damaging his own health, or of his moral certitude in denouncing sins, including the empress's, from the pulpit.
[126]Chrysostom, *De stat.* 20.8 (PG 49.210).
[127]Chrysostom, *In Matt. hom.* 46.4 (PG 58.480-81).

The virtue of the just resembles a treasure containing a huge and unspeakable wealth. Just as if someone was able to take even a small part from it he would gain for himself much luxury, so also you will find happening in the virtue of the patriarch. See how nearly every day we put before you some teaching from the narrative about him, giving you a feast of plenty without ever being able to explain adequately the slightest part of his good deeds [*katōrthōmenōn*, κατωρθωμένων] even today, such is the abundance of his virtue.[128]

None of these is exactly the same, but they get at a theme. Virtue can be greater or less in individuals. Abraham has so much virtue that Chrysostom can treat a part of it every day and still not say very much about the smallest bit of his virtue. Further, individual virtues are better or worse, and single virtues are not alone sufficient for salvation. Virtue is composite for Chrysostom, and people may have a part, even as Chrysostom often says things that make virtue an all-or-nothing state.

The quotation about the Ninevites is most instructive. Complete or perfect virtue is possible, but some people have only part, and others have none. Like in this quotation, Chrysostom spends a lot of time in his corpus exhorting his congregants to virtue, chastising them for specific sins, and showing the monks to be exemplars of virtue, those who live angelic lives now. These practices indicate that, though virtue is possible for all, Chrysostom does not see many who are yet virtuous.[129] Most of Chrysostom's rhetoric is about the struggle for virtue that defines the Christian life, which suggests that Christians are on the way to virtue, that they have "pieces" of virtue and attempt to gain more, always reaching for perfect virtue.[130]

VIRTUE AND DEMONS

There is one more aspect of *proairesis*, *gnōmē*, and virtue to explore: in which context Chrysostom uses which term and with what frequency. In his whole corpus *proairesis* appears about 800 times, whereas *gnōmē* appears 1400 times,

---

[128]Chrysostom, *In Gen. hom.* 36.1 (PG 53.332).

[129]This is also similar to the Stoic ideal of the sage. Though it is possible for anyone to be a sage, there are in reality very few.

[130]Louis Meyer describes Chrysostom's understanding of spiritual growth as that of a plant from a seed or the building of a house on a foundation, where the seed or the foundation is baptism. Louis Meyer, *Saint Jean Chrysostome, maître de perfection chrétienne* (Paris: Beauchesne, 1933), 130-32.

though because *gnōmē* has a broader range of meaning, this is not surprising.[131] They appear together in the same sentence 60 times. Chrysostom
employs *autexousios* only 50 times.[132] Though Chrysostom uses *proairesis*
frequently in all his works, with a special fondness for it in his homilies on
the Pauline epistles, it is his word of choice when discussing why humans
ought not fear the devil.[133] A person's *proairesis* is the reason for her boldness;
she knows that if she safeguards her *proairesis* and exercises it well, not even
the devil can keep her from the kingdom of heaven. Most often Chrysostom
wants the congregation to protect and use their *proairesis* rather than their
gnōmē. In the parable of the sheep and goats, Chrysostom claims *proairesis*
is the cause of a person's end, be it heaven or hell.[134] When scolding the
theatergoers who are absent from worship, Chrysostom says the reason they
are gone and others are present is that they have a different *proairesis*. Those
absent allowed themselves to be deceived by the devil.[135] To those who would
blame demons for their sin, Chrysostom preaches, "Recognize the cause of
the sin, and you will find that it was no one other than yourself who sinned.
Everywhere there is need of a good προαίρεσις [*proairesis.*]"[136]

That *proairesis* is Chrysostom's choice for discussing demons and their
relation to a person's virtue means it is the word that links Chrysostom's
demonology and anthropology. The "chosenness" of an action makes it
either vice or virtue, and Chrysostom often employs demonological rhetoric
to remind his audience of this. Reminding his congregation that they are in
a wrestling match with the devil is often, though not always, Chrysostom's
method for encouraging his people to remember that they are self-
determining and can choose virtue over vice, Christ over the devil. Looking

---

[131]Laird argues convincingly that γνώμη is the core of a person. Chrysostom also uses γνώμη to
describe the part of a person involved in real love and friendship, as in "that [love] which is
sincere is not merely in words, but arises from the disposition, the γνώμη, and fellow-feeling."
Chrysostom, *In 1 Tim. hom.* 2.1 (PG 62.509; Laird, *Mindset, Moral Choice and Sin*, 32-33).

[132]This is particularly noteworthy because where most other ancient writers used αὐτεξούσιος,
Chrysostom used προαίρεσις or γνώμη. For instance, Justin claims an αὐτεξούσιος for angels,
and Tatian argues that demons want to cause the αὐτεξούσιος of humans to choose evil. For an
excellent survey of the use of αὐτεξούσιος up through Maximus the Confessor's works, see
William Telfer, "*Autexousia*," *JTS* 8, no. 1 (1957): 123-29.

[133]Though it is Chrysostom's most frequent choice for speaking about resistance to the devil,
προαίρεσις is not Chrysostom's *exclusive* choice. He does use γνώμη on occasion.

[134]Chrysostom, *De diab. tent.* 2.3 (SC 560bis, 174).

[135]Chrysostom, *De diab. tent.* 2.1 (SC 560bis, 154-56).

[136]Chrysostom, *De diab. tent.* 2.2 (SC 560bis, 168).

at these passages of rhetoric about demons, *De diabolo tentatore* in particular, highlights Chrysostom's anthropology. Where the theodicies of his predecessors and contemporaries mention only human responsibility for sin and Satan's role in the fall, Chrysostom brings the devil to the forefront of his argument.

Chrysostom's demonology is key to understanding his anthropology precisely because, in contrast to other theologians, he explicitly speaks about demons in his anthropology.[137] In arguing that neither demons nor human nature nor God himself is the cause of sin and evil in the world, but a human's *proairesis*, Chrysostom situates himself in a long tradition of theodicy that finds the origin of evil in the creature's self-determination. Chrysostom writes, "For if the head, death itself, has its root and foundation from sin, much more do most of our diseases also. Since from there we became those who suffer, our very capability of suffering did itself originate there."[138] In fact, Chrysostom claims the devil has *proairesis* also, the poor exercise of which caused his own fall: "Let the devil be allowed to be exceedingly wicked, not by *physis*, but by *proairesis*."[139] This argument is part of the project to explain the origins of evil without implicating God that is common in the fourth century. In order to show a continuity with tradition, I will briefly examine the accounts of Methodius (d. 311 CE) and Gregory of Nyssa (334–395 CE). Methodius is one of the first figures to systematize the language of self-determination, and Nyssa demonstrates the assumption of that language in theodicies of the mid-fourth century.

Methodius's *Peri tou autexousiou* (*Autex.*), often translated *On Free Will* and better translated as *On Self-Determination*,[140] is a dialogue about the origin of evil that concludes that evil begins with God's gift of self-determination (*autexousios*) and Adam and Eve's choice to exercise their *autexousioi* in disobedience to God's command. In a statement that sounds like Chrysostom preaches, Methodius writes, "There is nothing evil by nature."[141] He further

---

[137]Most notably for our purposes here, Methodius and Gregory of Nyssa, though in their discourses on anthropology neither Irenaeus nor Origen speaks of demons as much as Chrysostom does.
[138]Chrysostom, *In Matt. hom.* 27.2 (PG 57.345).
[139]Chrysostom, *De diab. tent.* 1.2 (SC 128-32).
[140]As noted in the introduction, I am avoiding use of "free will" because of the connotations and baggage the term picked up after the Augustine-Pelagius debates; instead I use "self-determination."
[141]Methodius, *Autex.* 65.5 (PO 22.789; ANF 6:362).

claims, "It is in designing his hatred against humanity that he became the devil by his own προαίρεσις [*proairesis*]."[142] Because God has created all things, nothing is evil by its very nature, not even the devil. Therefore, all evil comes only from the freedom of the creature, who can choose to disobey God. He also argues that *proairesis*, given to humans by God, is the locus of their moral responsibility.[143] Methodius claims, "The first human was made αὐτεξούσιον [*autexousion*], that is, free [*eleutheron*], from whom his descendants have inherited the same freedom [*eleutheria*]."[144] To have been created free is for the good of the human; it is what allows for praise and blame, for if God had created humans to serve him of necessity (*anankē*), they would only be instruments of God, doing what God wished. Were that true, "no longer would they receive recompense worthy of their προαίρεσις [*proairesis*]."[145] There is no responsibility if there is no freedom, and so God has given freedom, created humans self-determining (*autexousion*) in order that they may choose to obey God and receive reward for their obedience. They may also choose to disobey God.[146]

By the time Gregory of Nyssa writes his *Oratio catechetica*, Methodius's vocabulary is standard. Gregory argues that God created human beings with independence and self-determination (*adespoton kai autexousion*, ἀδέσποτον καὶ αὐτεξούσιον), which is the mark of having been made in God's image.[147] Similar to Chrysostom, Gregory further argues that God cannot be the author of evil because if he were, it would be impossible to blame or punish vice since vice would then be God's fault. Therefore, Gregory argues, evil must be the result of the human's choice, made freely: "Nothing of evil had its origin from the Divine will [*boulēmatos*, βουλήματος] at the beginning, for evil would be outside blame if God were set down as its creator and father,

---

[142]Methodius, *Autex.* 91.5-6 (PO 22.815).

[143]"If [humanity] were made as any of the elements, or those things which render a similar service to God, he would cease to receive a reward befitting [προαίρεσις], and would be like an instrument of the maker; and it would be unreasonable for him to suffer blame for his wrong-doings, for the real author of them is the one by whom he is used." Methodius, *Autex.* 73.7-10 (PO 22.797; ANF 6:362).

[144]Methodius, *Autex.* 71.4-5 (PO 22.795).

[145]Methodius, *Autex.* 73.7-9 (PO 22.797).

[146]Obedience or disobedience was the only choice. There was not some preexistent evil they were to resist, "but obeying God or not obeying was the only cause; for this [God] wished τὸ αὐτεξούσιον." Methodius, *Autex.* 77.5 (PO 22.801).

[147]Nyssa, *Or. catech.* 5 (SC 453bis, 168).

but somehow evil was planted within, then being united with the προαίρεσις [*proairesis*], whenever there is some retreat of the soul away from the good."[148] Again, it is the human's *proairesis* that determines moral responsibility.

This discussion has shown that Methodius began to use an anthropological vocabulary in a particular way. Nyssa, his catechism dated sometime between 381 and 387, either just before or just as Chrysostom begins his ministry in Antioch,[149] demonstrates the prominence of such thought and vocabulary in the late fourth century.[150] In Chrysostom's discussions of the origin of evil, he also uses this vocabulary and these ideas in the same way: to indicate humanity's God-given self-determination. Chrysostom primarily uses this language in his biblical homilies with a particular concentration in his *Homiliae in Genesim*. In one place Chrysostom writes that one can see "already" the *autexousion tēs proaireseōs* of Adam in his naming of the animals, implying that God created Adam with this particular independence of choice.[151] According to Chrysostom, the reason for this creation of human beings as *autexousion* is the issuance of reward and punishment: "For this reason God from the beginning equipped this creature [the human] with αὐτεξούσιον [*autexousion*]. For if it were not this way, there would be no need to punish him when he broke the command nor would he be worthy of praise for keeping it."[152] Moreover, *proairesis* is the locus of moral responsibility. Chrysostom tells his congregation, "In every case [of behavior], the προαίρεσις [*proairesis*] is κυρίαν [*kyrian*]." "Recognize the cause of the sin, and you will find that it was no one other than yourself who sinned. Everywhere there is need of a good προαίρεσις [*proairesis*]."[153]

Chrysostom is using the established vocabulary of theological anthropology, but he is not merely repeating his predecessors. In the context of discussions on the origin of evil, Chrysostom prefers to focus on *proairesis* over *autexousion*. In *De diabolo tentatore, De prophetiarum obscuritate hom.* 3,

---

[148]Gregory of Nyssa, *Or. catech.* 5 (SC 453bis, 168).

[149]Scholars are not in consensus regarding the date of the *Or. catech.* For a discussion of the various possibilities, see SC 453bis, 125-30.

[150]An additional witness to the tradition is Nemesius, whose *On the Nature of Man* is dated sometime in the 390s (Chrysostom is preaching in Antioch from 386 to 397, then in Constantinople from 397 to 407), uses αὐτεξούσιος twenty-five times and προαίρεσις fifty-nine times.

[151]Chrysostom, *In Gen. hom.* 14.5 (PG 53.117).

[152]Chrysostom, *In Gen. hom.* 16.5 (PG 53.132).

[153]Chrysostom, *De diab. tent.* 2.1 (SC 560bis, 158); 2.2 (SC 560bis, 168).

Quod nemo laeditur nisi a seipso, and *Commentarius in Iob*—the four works are the locus of much of his theodicy—*autexousios* does not appear once. Chrysostom's focus in those works is the human's *proairesis*. The faculty is assumed to be self-determining, as it is clear that the key attribute of *proairesis* is a lack of compulsion from outside forces.

The most significant difference Chrysostom introduces, however, is the addition of so much demonic rhetoric. Methodius and Gregory of Nyssa may have touched on demons in their theodicies, but Chrysostom brings them to the fore.[154] Chrysostom's *De prophetiarum obscuritate hom.* 3 argues that evil is neither the fault of demons nor of God, but of humans. He does so by defining true evil, circumscribing the devil's powers, and calling his audience to understand their own role in evil. *De diabolo tentatore* repeats these ideas. Chrysostom here argues that demons are powerless and cannot cause sin and that humans are alone responsible for their actions. He encourages his audience to be virtuous by saying that the devil and his demons cannot prevent people from exercising their *proairesis* for virtue. *Quod nemo laeditur nisi a seipso*, perhaps Chrysostom's most explicit theodicy, speaks of demons less than in other places, but they are still present as Chrysostom writes that true harm is harm to the soul, injury of a person's virtue, and not even the devil is able to injure a person's virtue.[155] Whereas Methodius includes the devil to say that the devil's envy of humanity led to his tempting Adam and Eve to disobey God, which is the origin of evil in the world, Chrysostom refers to the devil to show there is nothing that can keep a Christian from a virtuous life if she is inclined to live it. The devil is the worst-case example, a way to say that if the devil cannot injure a person's virtue, nothing can.

Where his predecessors, in their works on the origin of evil, spoke primarily of a person's responsibility for the presence of sin and evil in the world—as well as the devil's role in the fall—Chrysostom, in his works on the subject, spoke primarily of a human's continued responsibility for her sins. Sin is true evil, and sin is compelled neither by demons nor by God nor by human nature but is chosen by a person, usually because of his negligence regarding

---

[154]Even in Augustine's *Lib.*, a work of similar genre to Methodius's *Autex.*, Augustine does not talk about the devil until the end. Scholars date *Lib.* with a beginning composition date of 387–388 and an ending date between 391 and 395, all of which is during Chrysostom's tenure at Antioch.

[155]Chrysostom, *Quod nem. laed.* 3, 5 (SC 103bis, 70, 82).

the devil's temptations and deceptions. Demons are an integral part of Chrysostom's anthropology because he defines a Christian as a person living in struggle against the devil and his demons. In one of his letters to Olympias, Chrysostom praises her for being an example to others in her "wrestlings of virtue," saying that she demonstrates gender and lack of bodily strength to be no hindrance to virtue.[156] Chrysostom defines these wrestlings further: "Sparring with demons continuously, you won countless victories, but you received not one blow, but you stand unharmed in the midst of a storm of darts."[157] In a more explicit example, Chrysostom's *Catecheses ad illuminandos* provide catechumens with what they must know about the Christian life they are poised to enter, and he uses two images to do this: marriage to Christ and combat with the devil.[158] Of this combat Chrysostom writes, "These thirty days are like the practices and gym exercises in some wrestling school. Let us learn in this time to overcome that wicked demon. For we are about to strip for that [struggle] after the baptism."[159] He also preaches,

> The time before this has been a wrestling-school and a gym, and falls were forgiven. But from today on, the stadium is open, the contest is set, the spectators have taken their seats. Not only humans are watching the wrestling but the host of angels as well. . . . The Lord of angels presides as judge.[160]

In his first homily on John, Chrysostom tells his congregation to remember that those who are baptized made promises to Christ about avoiding the devil's pomps. They renounced Satan and must not look in his direction again.[161] Chrysostom further explains this renunciation in one of his prebaptismal instructions: "Did you see the account of the agreement? After the renunciation of the wicked one and of all the actions that are important to the evil one, again you prepare to say: 'And I enter your service, Christ.'"[162] To renounce Satan is to join oneself forever to Christ.

---

[156]Chrysostom, *Ep. ad Olymp.* 12.1.d (SC 13bis, 324).

[157]Chrysostom, *Ep. ad Olymp.* 12.1.d (SC 13bis, 322).

[158]That Chrysostom introduces both images together in his first catechetical homily implies that he does not see the images as mutually exclusive. Rather, they together define the Christian life. In fact, in the rites of initiation, the renunciation of Satan comes immediately before the formal adhesion to Christ. When one renounces Satan, one chooses Christ.

[159]Chrysostom, *Illum. cat.* 1.16 (SC 366bis, 144).

[160]*Cat.* 3.8-9 (SC 50bis, 155-56).

[161]In this instance, Satan is found particularly at the theater. Chrysostom, *In Ioh. hom.* 1.4 (PG 59.29-30).

[162]Chrysostom, *Cat.* 2.21 (SC 50bis,145).

The connection Chrysostom has made between demonology and anthropology—his use of demonological discourse to highlight human self-determination—is something the monastic tradition does.[163] We saw in chapter two the similarity between Chrysostom's demonology and the demonology put forth by both Egyptian and Syrian asceticism. Both have a distinct emphasis on the demons' powerlessness, defined as an inability either to cause true (that is, moral) harm or to cause physical damage without permission from God. Both the monks and Chrysostom warn their audiences to be vigilant at all times so that they may resist the devil's attacks; both argue that a demon can only incite sin if a person cooperates with it. Both emphasize the inability of demons to cause moral harm over the audience's fear of the demons' ability to cause physical harm. Finally, and most importantly, both the authors of monastic literature and Chrysostom define the Christian life as a struggle against the devil in constant pursuit of virtue.

Chrysostom, then, is creating a synthesis. In using the vocabulary of theological anthropology established by theologians, Chrysostom is situating himself within their tradition. He is using not merely the language his congregation is using but that which has been established and assumed by the writers of his own time. To his congregation's concerns about the suffering they see, their fear of demons, their excuses for their lack of virtue, Chrysostom answers as his traditional theologian forebears would have, by saying that humans are morally responsible. His method, however, and his manner of highlighting this responsibility, is to draw on the demonologically cast anthropology of the monks.

Understanding that Chrysostom is synthesizing a theological tradition with an ascetic tradition is vital to understanding his (abundant) talk of virtue. For instance, in some places where Chrysostom speaks of virtue, he does so assuming that virtue is easy, or is a simple matter of choice, as when he preaches, "If we are willing, [virtue] is very easy."[164] We understand the depth of that choice by looking at those passages where Chrysostom exhorts his congregation to

---

[163] Any of the following similarities on its own is not enough to demonstrate Chrysostom's awareness of ascetic demonologies, but in aggregate the likelihood increases that Chrysostom knows and uses the monastic tradition.

[164] Chrysostom, *In 1 Cor. hom.* 14.4 (PG 61.118).

stop making the devil an excuse and to take control of their own virtue, to choose Christ over the devil.

The details of these arguments reveal some of the foundational assumptions with which Chrysostom builds his arguments in other homilies. For instance, Chrysostom writes, "It is easy to change and to become good and subject to God."[165] Chrysostom has argued, even in this very homily, that no one is evil by nature. Therefore, it is possible to become good, that is, to do good consistently. But Chrysostom also says here that it is easy, which many might consider a false statement. It can be very hard to do good and to be subject to God when evil is so enticing. Yet Chrysostom has spoken on this too. The devil does tempt and even deceive, but Chrysostom maintains that the devil cannot compel. It is the person's choice whether he will allow himself to be deceived and act on his temptation or whether he will choose virtue instead. It is "just" a matter of choice, or decision, and that is easy enough. Moreover, Chrysostom continues in his homily, "The wrestling matches are easy so that you may win the contest, not so that you may lay down to sleep or abuse the greatness of this grace by your laziness, to wallow again in the mire you were in before."[166] He argues the same thing in the *Catecheses ad illuminandos*: "In our struggle with the devil, Christ does not stand impartial but is wholly on our side. . . . He anointed us with the oil of joy; he bound the devil with unbreakable chains in order to bind him hand and foot for the struggle."[167]

Knowing that virtue is a matter of choice and that the choice is between following Christ or giving in to the devil helps us understand more fully and more faithfully what Chrysostom means when he says, "It is easy for a man to change his ways. . . . Virtue is . . . easy and well-known by everyone."[168] Though one may find discussions of anthropology and virtue in Chrysostom's corpus that do not refer to demons, he does refer to them frequently and in key places. These discussions of demons, anthropology, and virtue are not only in comments here and there in Chrysostom's corpus or as a part of subarguments in homilies; they are the subject of whole sermons and

---

[165]Chrysostom, *In Rom. hom.* 13.6 (PG 60.516).
[166]Chrysostom, *In Rom. hom.* 13.7 (PG 60.517).
[167]Chrysostom, *Cat.* 3.8-9 (SC 50bis, 155-56).
[168]Chrysostom, *In Matt. hom.* 23.5 (PG 57.314).

treatises like *Quod nemo laeditur nisi a seipso* and *De diabolo tentatore*, as well as forming one of the major themes of Chrysostom's *Catecheses ad illuminandos*. The latter in particular demonstrates the significant role of demons in the Christian life as Chrysostom describes it. These homilies and passages are essential for understanding Chrysostom's anthropology. They highlight a larger narrative from which Chrysostom works, one of Christ and the devil battling for humans' salvation.

CONCLUSION

In discussing virtue, Chrysostom most often uses the terms *proairesis* and *gnōmē*, and their function is to establish human freedom and self-determination. For Chrysostom, humans are neither good nor evil by nature. They are created with a free *proairesis*, which entails moral responsibility since only freely chosen acts can be punished or rewarded and therefore named vice or virtue. God expects humans to exercise their *proairesis* for virtue, defined as "the precision of true doctrine and the right way of life."[169] Chrysostom encourages this choice for virtue with biblical exemplars like Adam and Eve, whose existence in Eden is the paradise to which humans aspire. We, like them, aim to have a greater attachment to eternal things than to temporal things. With this disposition, a person is able to see circumstances as they truly are and to know what real harm looks like. Seeing things properly, then, makes virtue easier because the choice is clear.

One way Chrysostom often encourages virtue is by discussing demons. He tells his congregants that they are more powerful than demons and should not allow themselves to be taken in by any diabolic tricks but should resist, and, in the struggle, strengthen their virtue. In this way demonological discourse highlights Chrysostom's theological anthropology and provides a more profound understanding of how virtue works for Chrysostom. He casts his anthropology in demonological terms as in the ascetic tradition but also uses the technical anthropological language of theologians. Chrysostom's blending of these traditions shows his understanding of the Christian life to be one of struggle for virtue, and he preaches this message often and in language his congregation knows because virtue is an integral aspect of salvation.

---

[169]Chrysostom, *Quod nem. laed.* 3 (SC 103bis, 70).

Chrysostom's Soteriology

I n c o n t r a s t t o t h e f e a r s a n d e x c u s e s of his congregation, Chrysostom preaches that demons and the devil himself cannot truly harm a human being. Human beings are free and self-determining and thus responsible for their actions and choices, their sin and virtue. At the heart of this is Chrysostom's emphasis on a person's *proairesis* (προαίρεσις) as the locus of moral responsibility. The *proairesis* is that which Chrysostom urges his audience to use when they are tempted by the devil and that which determines whether a person sins or acts virtuously. The *proairesis* is free, and only because it is free can a person be virtuous. That it is free, as Chrysostom argues, means that a person *can* be virtuous.

Now I follow Chrysostom's argument to its end. Because a person *can* be virtuous, God *requires* her to be virtuous. Virtue is what makes a person worthy of the kingdom at the final judgment. God judges us on our virtue and decides whether we are worthy, though we are not alone in our endeavor to be virtuous. Christ helps us, but the responsibility lies finally with us.

Chrysostom believes and preaches that salvation requires our participation and we are judged on the basis of that participation because we are free, but he never preaches this message so succinctly as I have put it here. For this reason I must, as with other areas of Chrysostom's theology, weave together the strands of Chrysostom's thought. A passage from Chrysostom's *Homiliae in Genesim* 8.6 highlights especially well the elements of this argument: the freedom to be virtuous, God's expectation that one will be virtuous, and virtue as the basis of God's judgment. For this reason, I structure this chapter as an exegesis of Chrysostom's *Homiliae in Genesim* 8.6, though I will at times need to step away from the passage and treat larger themes from the text since 8.6 reflects ideas and themes Chrysostom articulates in many other works. The key issue that will remain before us is that our self-determination needs to result in virtuous lives. God does not exempt us from virtue; he requires it. We have thus far seen that Chrysostom's speech about demons insists that demons cannot harm or damn a person and that a person can resist them because her *proairesis* is free. This chapter examines Chrysostom's further belief that God does not save a person unilaterally, also because she is free. We will see that for Chrysostom, a person is in one respect responsible for her own salvation.

HOMILIAE IN GENESIM 8.6

Therefore, let us not think too little of our salvation. For nothing is as important as virtue, beloved. For this virtue snatches us out of Gehenna in the coming age and gives us the enjoyment of the kingdom of heaven, and in our present life it establishes us as superior to all those who attempt to plot vainly and rashly—not only human beings, but the very demons as well—and it even makes us stronger than the enemy of our salvation—I mean the devil. What, then, could be equal to virtue, when it makes those who pursue it superior not only to plotting humans but also to the demons? Virtue is to despise all human things, to keep in front of one's mind at each hour the things to come, to be excited by no present things but to know that every human thing is a shadow and a dream, or even something cheaper than this. Virtue is to be just like a corpse toward the things of this life and, as if a corpse, to take no active interest in the things that damage the soul's salvation, but only to be alive and take active interest in spiritual things, as Paul also said: "I am alive, though it is no longer me but Christ alive in me."

And therefore, beloved, since we have put on Christ, let us do all things in that way, and do not grieve the Holy Spirit. Therefore, when we are troubled by passion or untimely desire or anger or rage or envy, let us consider the one who dwells in us, and let us banish further every such thought. Let us be in awe of the excess of grace offered to us by God and let us bridle all the passions of the flesh, so that, having contended lawfully in this short and mortal life, we may be worthy of those great crowns in the day to come—a frightening day for sinners but a day longed for by those who have put on virtue—and that we may be found worthy of those ineffable goods, by the grace and loving-kindness of our Lord Jesus Christ, to whom with the Father and the Holy Spirit be glory, power and honor, now and forever, for ages of ages. Amen.[1]

This passage is the final section of Chrysostom's eighth homily on Genesis. The first seven homilies have been reflections on Genesis 1:1-25. Homily 8 begins as a reflection on Genesis 1:26-27, and Chrysostom's focus throughout the homily is on the place of the human being in creation. According to Chrysostom, the fact that God created humans to rule over the rest of creation indicates that humans have the highest place in creation. Chrysostom further argues that being made in God's image refers to the control humans have over created things, rather than being made in the physical form of God, as some would say. Then Chrysostom discusses rescuing from the devil's traps those who would oppose God (those who say God has a physical form), the importance of teaching others for the sake of their salvation, the importance of living well as part of that teaching, and fasting and almsgiving as virtuous acts that snatch us from the fires of Gehenna. Chrysostom then draws all these themes together, concluding the homily with this summary passage on the importance of virtue. As with all of Chrysostom's many

---

[1]Chrysostom, *In Gen. hom.* 8.6 (PG 53.75-76). Μὴ τοίνυν καταφρονῶμεν τῆς ἑαυτῶν σωτηρίας. Οὐδὲν γὰρ ἀρετῆς ἴσον, ἀγαπητέ· αὕτη γὰρ ἡμᾶς καὶ ἐν τῷ μέλλοντι αἰῶνι τῆς γεέννης ἐξαρπάζει, καὶ τῆς βασιλείας τῶν οὐρανῶν ἡμῖν τὴν ἀπόλαυσιν χαρίζεται, καὶ ἐν τῷ παρόντι βίῳ πάντων ἀνωτέρους καθίστησι τῶν μάτην καὶ εἰκῇ ἐπιβουλεύειν ἐπιχειρούντων, καὶ οὐκ ἀνθρώπων μόνον, ἀλλὰ καὶ αὐτῶν τῶν δαιμόνων, καὶ τοῦ ἐχθροῦ τῆς σωτηρίας τῆς ἡμετέρας, τοῦ διαβόλου λέγω, ἰσχυροτέρους ἀπεργάζεται. Τί οὖν ἂν εἴη ταύτης ἴσον, ὅταν μὴ μόνον τῶν ἀνθρώπων τῶν ἐπιβουλευόντων, ἀλλὰ καὶ τῶν δαιμόνων ἀνωτέρους ποιῇ τοὺς αὐτὴν μετιόντας; Ἀρετὴ δέ ἐστι τὸ πάντων τῶν ἀνθρωπίνων ὑπερορᾶν, τὸ τὰ μέλλοντα ἐφ' ἑκάστης ὥρας φαντάζεσθαι, τὸ πρὸς μηδὲν τῶν παρόντων ἐπτοῆσθαι, ἀλλ' εἰδέναι, ὅτι πάντα τὰ ἀνθρώπινα σκιά ἐστι καὶ ὄναρ, καὶ εἴ τι τούτων εὐτελέστερον. Ἀρετή ἐστι τὸ καθάπερ νεκρὸν οὕτω διακεῖσθαι πρὸς τὰ τοῦ βίου τούτου πράγματα, καὶ πρὸς μὲν τὰ λυμαινόμενα τὴν τῆς ψυχῆς σωτηρίαν, ὡσανεὶ νεκρὸν ὄντα, οὕτως εἶναι ἀνενέργητον, πρὸς δὲ τὰ πνευματικὰ μόνον ζῆν καὶ ἐνεργεῖν, καθάπερ καὶ Παῦλος ἔλεγε· Ζῶ δὲ, οὐκέτι ἐγώ, ζῇ δὲ ἐν ἐμοὶ ὁ Χριστός.

Καὶ ἡμεῖς τοίνυν, ἀγαπητοὶ, ὡς τὸν Χριστὸν ἐνδεδυμένοι, οὕτως ἅπαντα πράττωμεν, καὶ μὴ λυπῶμεν τὸ Πνεῦμα τὸ ἅγιον. Ὅταν οὖν ἐνοχληθῶμεν ὑπὸ πάθους, ἢ ἐπιθυμίας ἀτόπου, ἢ ὀργῆς, ἢ θυμοῦ, ἢ βασκανίας, ἐννοῶμεν τὸν ἐν ἡμῖν ἐνοικοῦντα, καὶ φυγαδεύωμεν πόρρω πᾶσαν τὴν τοιαύτην ἐνθύμησιν. Αἰδεσθῶμεν τῆς παρὰ τοῦ Θεοῦ παρασχεθείσης ἡμῖν χάριτος τὴν ὑπερβολήν, καὶ χαλινώσωμεν πάντα τῆς σαρκὸς τὰ πάθη, ἵνα, νομίμως ἀθλήσαντες ἐν τῷ βραχεῖ τούτῳ καὶ ἐπικήρῳ βίῳ, τῶν μεγάλων ἐκείνων στεφάνων ἀξιωθῶμεν ἐν τῇ μελλούσῃ ἡμέρᾳ ἐκείνῃ, τῇ φοβερᾷ μὲν ἡμῖν τοῖς ἁμαρτωλοῖς, ποθεινῇ δὲ τοῖς τὴν ἀρετὴν ἐνδεδυμένοις, καὶ καταξιωθῶμεν τῶν ἀπορρήτων ἐκείνων ἀγαθῶν, χάριτι καὶ φιλανθρωπίᾳ τοῦ Κυρίου ἡμῶν Ἰησοῦ Χριστοῦ, μεθ' οὗ τῷ Πατρὶ, ἅμα τῷ ἁγίῳ Πνεύματι, δόξα, κράτος, τιμὴ, νῦν καὶ ἀεὶ, καὶ εἰς τοὺς αἰῶνας τῶν αἰώνων. Ἀμήν.

homily-ending exhortations to virtue, this one is also intimately related to the content of the sermon, which is done for the salvation of his congregation, and not merely an add-on as part of Chrysostom's broader moralism.

Let us not think too little of our salvation. The first sentence tells Chrysostom's congregation that we have some measure of responsibility for our salvation. The question is what a person can (or must) do for her salvation. Not to think too little of salvation could mean that a person must do everything within her power to gain salvation as something to be attained only in the future.[2] Certainly, this is an aspect of Chrysostom's thought, but his thought is more complex. This phrase "not think too little" (*mē kataphronōmen*, μὴ καταφρονῶμεν) can also suggest that salvation is something that has already occurred, something human beings have and must attend to continually in order that they not lose it.[3] I noted in chapter two that Chrysostom sometimes says that the devil is attempting to "throw us out of heaven," suggesting that we are already in heaven, have already been saved.[4] *Mē kataphronōmen* is clearly a verb of present action; the object, the intent, what a person can do, and what salvation is are all things we will explore through the rest of the passage as Chrysostom describes them. What is important here is that the onus of action is on the audience.[5] *We* must not think too little of our salvation. From the beginning of the passage there is something a person can (or must) do to be saved.

Nothing is as important as virtue. This is a strong statement. The first thing to understand about this claim is what Chrysostom means by virtue. Several clauses down in the passage Chrysostom gives a definition: "Virtue is to despise all human things. . . . Virtue is to be just like a corpse toward the things

---

[2]I use the phrase "within her power" to evoke the echoes of ἐφ᾽ ἡμῖν we have explored in the previous two chapters. Further, ἐφ᾽ ἡμῖν is one of the phrases Chrysostom uses to speak about the human contribution to salvation.

[3]Μὴ καταφρονῶμεν need not have salvation as its object, and it is not a technical term. A search of the *TLG* reveals that Chrysostom uses the phrase and the word (καταφρονῶμεν) more frequently than any of his predecessors (fifty-four times as opposed to Basil's two, Origen's two, and Gregory of Nazianzus's two). Chrysostom occasionally uses it to exhort his congregants to attend to their salvation, as in this passage, but he uses καταφρονῶμεν just as often to exhort the audience to despise earthly pleasures, as in *Adv. opp. vit. mon.* 2.3 (ὅταν μὴ σώματος αὐτοῖς μόνον, ἀλλὰ καὶ τῆς ψυχῆς ἀπολλυμένης καταφρονῶμεν). Καταφρονῶμεν is one of Chrysostom's verbs of exhortation. The verb καταφρονέω appears ten times in the New Testament and twenty-four times in the LXX, but never in any technical sense.

[4]Chrysostom, *In Eph. hom.* 22.3 (PG 62.159).

[5]The onus is also on the speaker, since he says "we," not "you."

of this life." We saw in the preceding chapter that virtue is living in obedience to God and that the key to being virtuous is a heavenly orientation that leads to the proper exercise of one's *proairesis*. This heavenly orientation is precisely the despising of the temporal in preference of the eternal that Chrysostom defines as virtue in 8.6. We also saw that the life of virtue is one of struggle against the devil, another element brought up in 8.6 ("[Virtue] makes us stronger than the enemy of our salvation"). Therefore, when Chrysostom says, "nothing is as important as virtue," he means that nothing is as important as the heavenly orientation that leads to a successful struggle to be obedient to God. Similarly, when later in the passage Chrysostom preaches that the time to come is "longed for by those who have put on virtue," he means that the obedient who have exercised their *proairesis* well and won against the devil have reason to look forward to the judgment in the time to come.

The second question about this statement is what Chrysostom wants his audience to understand by "nothing." The context is salvation: the initial "for" (*gar*, γάρ) of the second sentence links it to the first about not neglecting salvation, and the succeeding *gar* explains the relationship between virtue, hell, and the kingdom. Therefore the statement means, "Nothing is as important as virtue [for salvation]." But this is a bold claim, and it must face two challenges. First, is Christ not more important than virtue for salvation? I discuss this point below, which leads to a proper understanding as, "Nothing [a human can do] is as important as virtue [for salvation]." Second, in other homilies in which Chrysostom speaks about the human's necessary contribution to salvation, virtue is not the only contribution. Often Chrysostom insists on faith as well.

In *In epistulam ad Romanos hom.* 9, Chrysostom preaches,

> Contemplate with me how everywhere Paul puts down these two things: both what is up to him [Christ], and what is up to us. The things that [Christ] does are varied, many, and different. For he died on our account, he reconciled us, he brought us near, and he gave us unspeakable grace. But we brought our faith alone.[6]

An investigation of Chrysostom's use of "faith" (*pistis*, πίστις) will show that by *pistis* Chrysostom means an active response to God's work that believes and trusts the work as true and significant for one's life. By *pistis* Chrysostom

---

[6]Chrysostom, *In Rom. hom.* 9.2 (PG 60.468).

often means that the person believes that God has done what the church says God has done and is who the church says God is. For instance, in the *Catecheses ad illuminandos*, faith is a confession and understanding of orthodoxy: "Therefore, you contribute your fair share and make a strong confession of faith in him, not only with your lips but also with your understanding."[7] Chrysostom goes on to say, "Faith, then, is the foundation of piety," and he spends several paragraphs summarizing the articles of faith as outlined in the Nicene-Constantinopolitan Creed.[8]

When commenting on Ephesians 2:8-9 ("For by grace you have been saved through faith, and this is not your own doing; it is the gift of God—not the result of works, so that no one may boast"), which seems to exclude human action as a way to salvation, Chrysostom preaches,

> In order then that the greatness of the good works given may not raise you too high, see how he keeps you in check: "By grace you have been saved," he says, "Through faith." Then, again, so that our αὐτεξούσιος [*autexousios*] not be ruined, he also adds our part [in the work].[9]

In this instance, grace is God's work, but faith belongs to the human as protection of human *autexousios*. God's commitment to human freedom is the foundation for Chrysostom's insistence on a human portion of salvation. However, Chrysostom continues in the homily to explain that faith, human contribution though it is, is also a gift of God:

> The work of faith is not our own. He said, "It is the gift of God, not from works." Shouldn't faith be sufficient to save us? No, he says, but God, lest he should save us empty and without work, required this. He says that faith saves, but through God. For since God wished it, faith saved.[10]

Again Chrysostom articulates a tension as he attempts to preserve both the necessity of God's action and the importance of human freedom.

The prevalence of Chrysostom's insistence on faith in his corpus establishes it as a significant part of Chrysostom's thought.[11] Yet in many places

---

[7]Chrysostom, *Cat.* 1.19 (SC 50bis, 118). See also *In Rom. hom.* 9.2, 30.

[8]Chrysostom even names Arius and Sabellius as those who "desire to destroy sound doctrines" (*Cat.* 1.22; SC 50bis, 119), leaving no doubt regarding Chrysostom's own commitment to orthodoxy.

[9]Chrysostom, *In Eph. hom.* 4.2 (PG 62.33).

[10]Chrysostom, *In Eph. hom.* 4.2 (PG 62.33).

[11]In addition to the passages quoted above, the subject of Chrysostom's *De incomprehensibili dei natura* series is the necessity of having orthodox faith. For a sample of other instances of

Chrysostom says that God requires virtue in addition to faith, that faith is not enough. Chrysostom tells his audience,

> Even if we have complete faith and knowledge of the Scriptures, if we are desolate and naked of the leadership from life, there is nothing preventing us from being thrown into the fire of hell and being consumed forever by the unquenchable flame.[12]

This is similar to Chrysostom's declaration in 8.6 that "nothing is as important as virtue. . . . Virtue snatches us out of Gehenna in the coming age and gives us the enjoyment of the kingdom of heaven."[13] Though Chrysostom often speaks of faith as the human's contribution to salvation without reference to virtue, and though a person must have orthodox faith to be saved, these further statements indicate that faith alone is not enough for salvation. A person must add her virtue. When Chrysostom says, "nothing is as important as virtue [for salvation]," he means no other human contribution is as important as virtue. Faith is essential, but virtue is as well, and virtue is even more important or more decisive for salvation than is faith because virtue snatches us from hell and bestows on us the kingdom.

Virtue snatches us out of Gehenna . . . Here Chrysostom offers a glimpse of what virtue *does*, and the first function of virtue regards the world to come. One's virtue determines one's place in the age to come. Chrysostom uses the verb "snatches" (*exarpazei*, ἐξαρπάζει) here, as though one is not in heaven but in hell, and virtue is able to snatch a person out of the clutches of hell that cling and drag a person down. Elsewhere, however, Chrysostom says that the devil is attempting to cast us out of heaven.[14] He also preaches that laziness (*rhathymia*, ῥαθυμία) throws a person down from heaven, and Chrysostom tells the newly baptized that they are now citizens of heaven and need to show they are worthy of it.[15] Given Chrysostom's commitment to the Christian's heavenly residence, the best understanding of this statement is

---

Chrysostom's insistence on faith, see Chrysostom, *In Rom. hom.* 13.7; *Cat.* 4.10; *In Ioh. hom.* 10.3, 84.3; and *In Eph. hom.* 2.2.

[12]Chrysostom, *In Ioh. hom.* 6 (PG 59.62).

[13]Chrysostom, *In Gen. hom.* 8.6 (PG 53.75).

[14]Chrysostom, *In Eph. hom.* 22.3 (PG 62.159).

[15]Chrysostom, *De poen. hom.* 1.2 (PG 49.279); *Cat.* 7.12 (SC 50bis, 235): "Hasten, he says, to transfer your whole mind there where you are registered as citizens, and determine to do the things which can show that you are worthy of your citizenship [in heaven]."

that Gehenna, or the residents of Gehenna, since it was made for the devil
and his demons and Chrysostom refers to the devil as the enemy of salvation,
makes attempts to bring humans to it. The devil and his demons tempt and
deceive, as we saw in chapter two, but they are unable to cause true injury to
a person because true injury, sin, occurs only by choice. If a person chooses
virtue, that virtue will keep a person out of Gehenna, however much the
devil attempts to deliver him to hell. Virtue will snatch the person out of the
devil's grip. Should a person neglect her virtue, Gehenna will succeed and
drag a person out of her heavenly residence and into hell.

This future function of virtue also reveals that salvation is about heaven
and hell. In *Homiliae in Genesim* 7 Chrysostom makes a statement that adds
depth to the one in 8.6: "Let us . . . not neglect our own salvation, and let us
give all attention to a godly way of life, knowing that on this most of all we
will either be condemned or be deemed worthy of loving kindness from
him."[16] Here again the congregation is encouraged to attend to salvation,
and we saw in the previous chapter that one way Chrysostom defines virtue
is as obedience to God, or "living a life of God's wanting." Thus, here again
virtue is the way a person attends to her salvation. What *Homiliae in
Genesim* 7 adds is that our virtue is the basis of God's judgment. We have
seen Chrysostom's preoccupation with recompense and know that God's
judgment sends either to hell or to heaven, and Chrysostom makes it clear
that virtue is the determining factor. Therefore, virtue snatches from Gehenna and bestows the kingdom because at the judgment God deems the
virtuous worthy of the kingdom.

One question this statement leaves open is how much virtue one needs
in order to be worthy or to be snatched from Gehenna. Chrysostom does
not say. Most of Chrysostom's rhetoric suggests that either one is virtuous
or one is not, but he does sometimes mention that it is possible for a person
to have a part (*meros*, μέρος) of virtue. Moreover, Chrysostom encourages
his congregation to be virtuous and recognizes that people change, which
suggests that virtue is dynamic rather than static; it is something one pursues,
even when one is virtuous. Chrysostom's understanding of virtue sees it as
a continuous choice because virtue is choice rather than nature, which is

---

[16]Chrysostom, *In Gen. hom.* 7.7 (PG 53.69).

immutable. It is a choice to be obedient to God and to resist the devil. This understanding leaves no room for the question, "How much virtue is enough virtue to stay in heaven?" There is no "enough"; one must continue to choose virtue over vice until the judgment, especially if the devil is still attacking with temptations and deceptions.

Can everyone be saved? The answer appears to be yes.[17] Chrysostom goes so far as to claim, "If we are willing, [virtue] is very easy."[18] In every sermon Chrysostom exhorts his audience to be virtuous, whether he uses *aretē* (ἀρετή) or tells people to give alms or to stop going to the races, he encourages his congregants to live a life of obedience to God. Chrysostom also gives his congregation examples. Job exemplifies resistance to the devil; Paul displays conversion and faithfulness in everything. Like Gregory of Nyssa in the *Life of Macrina*, which makes Macrina the example of a true philosophical, Christian life, Chrysostom tells his congregation to be like the monks in the mountains outside Syria. They are living the angelic life, and Christians need to live the same angelic life in the cities. The difference is that whereas Gregory wants the true Christian to become a monk removed from society, Chrysostom tells his congregants to become like the monks *where they are*. They are to have the same heavenly orientation as the monks but do not need to go to the mountains to do it; they need to have that orientation in the cities.[19]

Chrysostom urges his people to be virtuous because virtue is possible. He also urges them often because virtue is a choice, and it is not a one-time choice. Finally, Chrysostom preaches virtue because it is the basis of God's judgment. The stakes are high, so Chrysostom must tell his congregation. They can only choose well if they understand the choice and the consequences.[20]

---

[17]By "everyone" I mean only humans. We saw in chap. 2 that Chrysostom rejects the idea that Satan can be saved.

[18]Chrysostom, *In 1 Cor. hom.* 14.4 (PG 61.118).

[19]The one difference Chrysostom concedes is that non-monks can marry. Chrysostom also explains that the angelic life is easier for monks than non-monks because monks have many fewer distractions in the mountains than Christians do in the city: "Avarice will be conquered more easily, not by the person who is caught in the midst of worldly activity, but by the one who lives in the mountains" (Chrysostom, *Adv. opp. vit. mon.* 3.15; PG 47.375; David G. Hunter, trans., *A Comparison Between a King and a Monk; Against the Opponents of the Monastic Life: Two Treatises* [Lewiston, NY: Mellen, 1988], 160-61).

[20]This is a significant point of contrast between Chrysostom and his Stoic sources. We saw in both chaps. 4 and 5 that Chrysostom uses Stoic moral psychology, but Chrysostom comes to a

In our present life [virtue] establishes us as superior . . . Being virtuous has benefit not only in the future but also "in our present life." Virtue gives superiority over "plotting humans" and also the demons. Plotting humans suggests futility.[21] The tenor of this passage suggests an antagonism by using words like "superior" (*anōteros*, ἀνωτέρος) and "stronger" (*ischyroteros*, ἰσχυροτέρος). At the very least these superlatives imply ranking, if not competition. Beyond these words, though, Chrysostom mentions demons as well as human beings, and his congregation knows that demons seek to harm. Pairing humans with demons here indicates that the humans who plot do so maliciously. And virtue makes a person superior to both. No one who attempts to cause injury can do so; the plots are futile because humans and demons are unable to harm human beings. A person can only harm himself. Again, this is Chrysostom's point that the demons cannot damn; the *proairesis* is free to resist them effectively.

Chrysostom does not only mention humans and demons, though. He also maintains that virtue renders a person stronger than the devil, the enemy of salvation. We have seen how the devil attempts to thwart salvation at every turn. In the context of this passage it becomes clear what kinds of attacks on salvation he makes. We saw that both faith and virtue are essential for salvation, though Chrysostom only discusses virtue here.[22]

---

different conclusion about the way it plays out in life. The Stoics thought sages to be rare, and though they taught often about the path to virtue, they did not expect their audiences to be fully virtuous. Even so, Stoic philosophers urged their audiences to pursue virtue because even if they did not become virtuous, this way of life would make them happier. In contrast, Chrysostom expects that his congregants can indeed become virtuous. That he spends so much time exhorting to virtue may imply that he does not see enough of his audience virtuous yet, but he preaches so that they may become so. For Chrysostom there is no consolation in attempting to be virtuous; one must *be* virtuous to be saved.

[21]It is also fair to say that for Chrysostom there are things with which a person busies her life that have no eternal significance. Often Chrysostom hints that having a heavenly perspective is part of being vigilant against the devil's schemes, and that "laziness" (ῥαθυμία) is the prime cause of sin, as in the discussion of Adam's expulsion from paradise. Chrysostom's interlocutors ask, "What then? . . . Didn't [the devil] injure Adam and trip him up and cast him out of paradise?" Chrysostom answers, "Not the devil, but the laziness [ῥᾳθυμία] of the one who was injured, and his lack of temperance and vigilance" (*Quod nem. laed.* 4 [SC 103bis, 74]). See also *In Ioh. hom.* 36.2: "What, then, is the creator of evil? What else but the laziness of the προαιρέσις?" (PG 59.206).

[22]Elsewhere in his corpus Chrysostom elucidates the devil's attacks on faith, which consist of instigating misinterpretations of Scripture or false doctrine: "In this way many destructive doctrines are introduced into our life, the lazier people persuaded by the devil to give a twisted report the contents of the Scriptures" (*Dom., non est in hom.* 2 [PG 56.156]). In *De incompr.*

The devil attacks a person's virtue. In some places the devil's wiles are obvious. The devil may tempt a person to attend the theater or the race-track instead of worship, or he may suggest they need their money too much to be able to give alms. Elsewhere, though, Chrysostom speaks of the devil's sabotaging of virtue as more insidious. Destruction is the devil's foremost aim:

> Nothing, nothing is the devil so eager about as to persuade the human spirit of this, that he is neither liable to punishment in sinning nor deserving of praise and crown in virtue, so that he may release the hands of the zealous, quench enthusiasm, incite the apathy of the faint-hearted and increase their laziness.[23]

The core of Chrysostom's exhortations to virtue is that virtue leads to the kingdom because God punishes sinners but rewards the virtuous. Chrysostom's understanding of compensation is what funds his account of human freedom and self-determination, which are necessary for an act to be either sinful or virtuous. According to the quotation above, then, the devil is doing his best to destroy a person's virtue at its source.

Against all these attacks, however, a person is stronger than the devil and superior to demons. Her virtue or her pursuit of virtue makes her stronger, according to *Homiliae in Genesim* 8.6. The devil does his best to cause injury to a person's virtue, but a person is stronger and can defeat the devil, keeping her virtue intact. In 8.6, virtue (or a continuous choice for virtue) makes a person superior to anything that would keep her from being virtuous. This is not to say that one must have virtue before one can be superior to those who try to hinder one's virtue. We saw in the previous chapter that for Chrysostom a human's *proairesis*—or *gnōmē* (γνώμη)—is all that is necessary for a person to triumph over even the devil's attempts to lead into vice. *Proairesis* or *gnōmē* is the gift of self-determination God has given humanity. Yet Chrysostom also tells his audience the devil is like a punching bag. Struggling against the devil makes a person stronger, more virtuous.[24] This

---

hom. 2, Chrysostom claims that the Anomeans are caught in the devil's snare and deception: "Praying for them and calling on the human-loving God . . . to free them from this deceit and snare of the devil" (*De incompr. hom.* 2.55 [SC 28bis, 184]).

[23]Chrysostom, *Dom., non est in hom.* 2 (PG 56.156).

[24]This benefit to humans is, for Chrysostom, the reason God allows the devil to remain on earth. See *De diab. tent.* 1.1-2 (SC 560bis, 126).

suggests that the more a person chooses virtue, the easier the struggle to choose virtue becomes.[25]

Chrysostom often exhorts his listeners to remember that they are themselves responsible for their sins, to remember that they have *proairesis*. This remembering is supposed to help them recall that they can resist the devil and therefore must. For all he tries to injure a person's virtue and in so doing bring her down with him to hell, the devil can be defeated by one's choice of virtue over vice.

Virtue is to despise all human things . . . First Chrysostom exhorts his people not to think too little of their salvation, speaking about virtue and its strength. Virtue snatches a person from hell and bestows enjoyment of the kingdom; virtue makes a person superior to demons and the devil in this world. Now Chrysostom wants to be clear about what it is to be virtuous. This was the question in the previous chapter, and here the themes appear again: virtue as a heavenly orientation, a preference for the eternal over the temporal, a continuousness ("each hour of the day"), and even a Stoic or Platonic influence. These themes fit within the overall scheme of Chrysostom's soteriology. When Chrysostom says "virtue" in 8.6, we understand all that we discovered about virtue in the previous chapter. Moreover, this account of virtue is what Chrysostom is telling his congregation it can and must be because of self-determination.

Virtue is to be just like a corpse . . . Here Chrysostom continues his description of virtue. It begins much like the sentence before it with an encouragement to ignore the temporal and embrace the eternal, but with his quotation of Paul the passage shifts. What has been a passage about what a person can do to attend to his salvation—be virtuous—becomes now about more than the person himself. It is now about a person inhabited by Christ.

Chrysostom's use of the corpse image may be pagan language, or it may be drawing on Romans 6. Both are distinct possibilities for Chrysostom, and, in fact, he may be using both, though it is more likely that here Chrysostom's thoughts are driven by Paul's words. On the pagan side, Marcus Aurelius writes, "'You are a little soul carrying around a corpse,' as Epictetus said."[26]

---

[25]Even this present function of virtue is future-oriented, for the reason a person seeks to be virtuous is to be worthy of the kingdom of heaven.
[26]Aurelius, *Meditations* 4.41.1.

The term, *nekros* (νεκρός), is the same in both Epictetus and Chrysostom, but Chrysostom is not using corpse language in precisely the same way as Epictetus. For one thing, Epictetus is commenting on the relationship between body and soul, and by his description of the body as a *nekros* he indicates the uselessness of the body. It is not neutral but cumbersome, which is implied by the verb "carrying" (*bastazon*, βαστάζον). For Chrysostom, however, the body is neutral rather than negative. The body is not a lifeless mass of flesh to be dragged around but the instrument of the soul, working with the soul to do good deeds.[27] Moreover, the body cannot be evil because God created it, and God created nothing evil.

Another difference is that, though both are metaphorical statements, Chrysostom's metaphor is about a person's attitude rather than about the body-soul relationship. To "be just like a corpse" is a choice, or an active posture; to carry around a corpse is a sentence. The attitude about which Chrysostom speaks, however, may be drawing on the image from Epictetus. For the Stoic, the soul is the locus of the self; the body is an encumbrance, senseless to the world. Chrysostom similarly gives much importance to the soul as leading the body, and here urges that a person choose to be insensible to the "the things of this life." Whereas Epictetus tells his audience that they are in fact souls dragging corpses, Chrysostom urges his people to act thus. Even as he does not have the same negative view of the body as Epictetus, Chrysostom does find the image useful for explaining Christians' disposition toward this life. Furthermore, much as Epictetus does, Chrysostom places virtue and vice in the soul, rather than the body. Given his Stoic leanings and focus on the irrelevance of earthly things, Chrysostom may have Epictetus's language in mind.

The other likely source of the corpse image for Chrysostom is Romans 6, where Paul discusses a Christian's participation in Christ's death and resurrection in baptism. In his homily on this passage, Chrysostom also uses corpse language. He says, "Just as the one who is dead is freed from sinning in the future, being a corpse, so also is the person who comes up from baptism. Since he died there once and for all, it is necessary for him to remain dead to sin altogether."[28] Again the word is *nekros*, and again the

---

[27]Chrysostom, *In Rom. hom.* 13.2-3 (PG 60.509-11).
[28]Chrysostom, *In Rom. hom.* 11.1 (PG 60.485).

idea is to act like a corpse, that is, unaffected and unmoved. We spoke about what it might be to be a corpse with respect to the affairs of this life, but Chrysostom also tells his listeners to be like a corpse in relation to "things that damage the soul's salvation." What damages salvation for Chrysostom but sin? In a more explicit example, Chrysostom uses the same language in his *Catecheses ad illuminandos*, telling his catechumens,

> What now do you have in common with the present life? . . . You died, that is, you have become corpses in sin; once and for all you renounced the present life. . . . Therefore do not work for the things of this life as though you were living, but be as if you died and are corpses.[29]

Finally, in 8.6, in the same sentence as the corpse expression, Chrysostom quotes Paul in Galatians, indicating that Scripture in general and Paul in particular are at the forefront of his mind. It is most probable that Chrysostom is speaking of ideas he has gained from philosophy in language he takes from Paul. It is difficult to know whether Chrysostom knew the quotation from Epictetus discussed above, and even if he did, Chrysostom does not adopt the same kind of thinking regarding the body-soul relationship. However, the soul as responsible and the attention to what constitutes true good are important features of Stoic thinking. The language gained from Paul about being dead to sin helps Chrysostom articulate his point in the context of Christianity and Christ's work. A person is only able to be a corpse to what threatens salvation when he has participated in Christ's death through baptism.

Something similar is true of resurrection for Chrysostom:

> Having believed that Christ died and that he was raised, therefore you must also believe your own [death and resurrection]. . . . For if you shared in death and burial, much more you will share in resurrection and life. . . . After the future resurrection has been set before us, [Paul] demands of us another resurrection, the new way of life [*politeian*, πολιτείαν], which is borne in our present life by a change of our habits.[30]

Christ's resurrection not only establishes the future resurrection; it also raises Christians to a new life in the present, their life of virtue. This metaphorical resurrection is a real occurrence. Chrysostom believes that in baptism the

---

[29]Chrysostom, *Cat.* 7.22 (SC 50bis, 240).
[30]Chrysostom, *In Rom. hom.* 10.4 (PG 60.480).

Christian dies to old habits and will live a different life after baptism: "Christ lives in me." The possibility of Christian virtue is a result of Christ's prior work on behalf of human beings.

Before we can further explore this thought, a word is necessary about terminology. We have noted the shift in *Homiliae in Genesim* 8.6 from an emphasis on what a person does for salvation to Christ's role in salvation, and these are the two parts of what scholars have often referred to as Chrysostom's "synergistic" soteriology and what I will call his cooperative soteriology. Chrysostom makes statements, as in 8.6, that emphasize a human responsibility for salvation, but he also makes statements that emphasize God's responsibility. For instance, in *In epistulam ad Galatas commentarium* 1 Chrysostom writes that, by God's calling, Christ "reconciled to us and gave it as a gift, for we were not saved out of works done in righteousness."[31] In many other places, Chrysostom makes the dual role explicit, such as in *In epistulam ad Romanos hom.* 9.2: "Contemplate with me how everywhere Paul puts down these two things: both what is up to him [Christ], and what is up to us."[32] His *In epistulam ad Hebraeos hom.* 12.3 observes, "All things depend on God, but not so that our αὐτεξούσιον [*autexousion*] is harmed. . . . It is up to us [*eph hēmin*, ἐφ᾽ ἡμῖν], and it is up to him [*eph autō*, ἐφ᾽ αὐτῷ]."[33] It is clear that Chrysostom understands salvation to be a divine-human cooperation.

Scholars have long noted this divine-human cooperation set out in Chrysostom's soteriology: Louis Meyer's second chapter is an outline of the Christian's incorporation into Christ and his subsequent efforts to become perfect,[34] and Chrysostomus Baur states the matter in terms of grace and free will, writing that Chrysostom's position is, "If we do what lies in us, God will also do what lies in him."[35] Susan Donegan also uses "grace and free will" to describe the character of Chrysostom's soteriology: "The very ability to receive salvation is a matter of both grace and free will."[36]

---

[31]Chrysostom, *In Gal. comm.* 1.6 (PG 61.621).

[32]Chrysostom, *In Rom. hom.* 9.2 (PG 60.468).

[33]Chrysostom, *In Heb. hom.* 12.3 (PG 63.99).

[34]Louis Meyer, *Saint Jean Chrysostome, maître de perfection chrétienne* (Paris: Beauchesne, 1933).

[35]Chrysostomus Baur, *John Chrysostom and His Time*, trans. M. Gonzaga (Westminster, MD: Newman, 1959), 1:360. I find Baur's characterization unhelpful because of the history of this vocabulary after Chrysostom, which leads to a mischaracterization of Chrysostom's thought.

[36]Susan Donegan, "St John Chrysostom: An Argument for a Greater Appreciation of His Theology of Salvation," *Diakonia* 23 (1990): 24. As with Baur, the characterization of Chrysostom's thought

There is another strand of scholarship, however, that labels Chrysostom's cooperative soteriology "synergistic." Demetrios Trakatellis characterizes Chrysostom's *In epistulam ad Romanos hom.* this way: "From the very beginning to the very end of his exegesis on Romans, Chrysostom is eager to maintain a principle of synergy."[37] Panayiotis Papageorgiou offers this definition in his dissertation:

> This working together of the human efforts and the grace of God is the process which leads to the salvation and ultimately the perfection of man in "the image and likeness" of God and is called by Chrysostom, and the other Greek fathers before him, συνεργία [*synergia*].[38]

Papageorgiou then argues that the *synergia* between the human will and the will of God is "the most critical element required for the salvation of man."[39] Christopher Hall, drawing on Trakatellis, titles a section of his essay on Chrysostom's *In epistulam ad Romanos hom.* "Προαίρεσις [*Proairesis*] and the Chrysostomic Synergism," and writes, "Chrysostom's comments on Matthew's Gospel clearly reflect a synergism that is also present throughout Chrysostom's exegesis of Romans. Metropolitan Demetrios Trakatellis draws our attention to a number of key comments in Chrysostom's exegesis where the synergism between the grace of God and the προαίρεσις [*proairesis*] of human beings is evident."[40] Hall at least is specific about the synergism, explaining that the cooperation is between grace and *proairesis*.

This choice to use the adjective *synergistic* of Chrysostom's soteriology is understandable, but it is a misleading term. Chrysostom himself uses *synergia*

---

as a dichotomy of "grace and free will" is imprecise because of the history these terms acquired after Chrysostom. However, one understands what Donegan means, and her own use does not map later debates onto Chrysostom's thought.

[37]Demetrios Trakatellis, "Being Transformed: Chrysostom's Exegesis of the Epistle to the Romans," *GOTR* 36 (1991): 215.

[38]Panayiotis E. Papageorgiou, "A Theological Analysis of Selected Themes in the Homilies of St. John Chrysostom on the Epistle of St. Paul to the Romans" (PhD diss., Catholic University of America, 1995), 88. Papageorgiou cites only Gregory of Nyssa for the use of συνεργία in Greek fathers prior to Chrysostom, though Papageorgiou does mention Clement of Alexandria when discussing Werner Jaeger's *Two Rediscovered Works of Ancient Christian Literature: Gregory of Nyssa and Macarius* (Leiden: Brill, 1954). Most of Papageorgiou's lengthy footnote on this subject concerns secondary scholarship.

[39]Papageorgiou, "Theological Analysis," 88.

[40]Christopher A. Hall, "John Chrysostom," in *Reading Romans Through the Centuries: From the Early Church to Karl Barth*, ed. Jeffrey P. Greenman and Timothy Larsen (Grand Rapids: Brazos, 2005), 48.

to describe salvation only once and does not use the verb form *synergeō* in any specific manner.[41] By the term—noun, verb, or other derivative—he usually means only "working together" or even "assistance."[42] In Chrysostom's usage the term is not restricted to a divine-human relationship. When describing creation, Chrysostom emphasizes that creation happened by the word of God alone, not from human labors, nor "*synergia* from oxen," nor anything else.[43] In one place Chrysostom uses the noun in a discussion of salvation, writing, "If he has chosen you for salvation, he will not cheat you, nor will he abandon you to be completely destroyed. But lest he lead you to laziness this way, and lest they, thinking everything is of God, should themselves sleep, see how he also demands συνεργία [*synergia*] from them."[44] Note here the emphasis is on the human's cooperation with God, not God's with the human.

It is clear that *synergia* is not a technical term for Chrysostom; at most it is a useful description of the working together that God and humans do for salvation. Furthermore, Chrysostom does not give any indication regarding the psychology of *synergia*. When Chrysostom says that Jacob had God's *synergia* in receiving Isaac's blessing or in making Laban favorable toward him,[45] Chrysostom does not speculate about precisely *how* God assisted

---

[41]Chrysostom, *In 2 Thess. hom.* 5 (PG 62.493). Papageorgiou claims that a passage from *In Gen. hom.* 53.2 finds Chrysostom using συνεργία to discuss salvation: "Consider . . . how everything was from above. For when we bring things from ourselves, we also enjoy abundantly cooperation from God. For lest we be lazy or give up, he wishes also for us to contribute something, in order that in this way we may show our part. And it is not that everything comes as help from above, but it is necessary also for us to contribute something. Nor again is everything demanded from us, knowing our excessive weakness, but portraying his characteristic love, and wishing to take something as a starting-point to demonstrate his characteristic prodigality, he waits for what we bring of ourselves" (PG 54.466). Though it is true that this language, especially that of "contribution" (εἰσφέρω), is similar to Chrysostom's discussions of salvation, in this homily, Chrysostom is discussing Jacob and Rebecca's deception of Isaac (Gen 26). There is nothing in the text to suggest that Chrysostom has salvation in mind. Instead, he seems to be speaking of the divine-human cooperation that is the established way of things. God will not do all the good for us; we must act as well.

[42]For example, "Before the creation of the elements, to his word and to that command the earth gave up all the seed, needing nothing other than cooperation [συνεργίαν]" (*In Gen. hom.* 5.4; PG 53.52); or, in the prologue to the *In Rom. hom.*, explaining the order of Paul's letters and the identity of Archippus, Chrysostom writes, "He received the cooperation [συνεργὸν] in the letter to Philemon of the appeal on behalf of Onesimus" (*In Rom. hom.* prologue; PG 60.393); or even, "Now, God helping us, let us carry on to set the word before you" (*In Matt. hom.* 12.2; PG 57.204).

[43]Chrysostom, *In Gen. hom.* 5.4 (PG 53.51).

[44]Chrysostom, *In 2 Thess. hom.* 5.1 (PG 62.492-93).

[45]Chrysostom, *In Gen. hom.* 53.1 (PG 54.465); 55.2 (PG 54.481).

Jacob.[46] Therefore, when scholars use *synergism* to describe Chrysostom's soteriological system, they ignore the fact that Chrysostom himself does not use the term as technical soteriological vocabulary. His description of salvation is more idiomatic, preferring to use "God's things" and "our things" (*ta theou/ta hēmōn*, τὰ θεοῦ/τὰ ἡμῶν or *ta para theou/ta par hēmōn*, τὰ παρὰ θεοῦ/τὰ παρ᾽ ἡμῶν), "contribution" (some form of *eispherō*, εἰσφέρω), or even that which is "up to us" or "up to him" (*eph hēmin/epi tōi Theō*, ἐφ᾽ ἡμῖν/ἐπὶ τῷ Θεῷ), which suggests that God does something and humans do something and together this brings about salvation.[47] The usual English word for this arrangement is *cooperation*, so for ease of reading I use this term when describing the divine-human relationship that is part of Chrysostom's soteriology. I mean by *cooperation* nothing more than what I have outlined in this paragraph.

Having established our terminology, there is one more issue to discuss before we return to our examination of *Homiliae in Gen.* 8.6. In the passage under consideration we have only the indication that salvation requires both God's action and human action, not a reason why this is the case. Elsewhere

---

[46]In contrast, Gregory of Nyssa uses συνεργέω, its derivatives, and a handful of other, related terms (e.g., συμμαχέω, σύνερχομαι) in a technical capacity to refer to the interplay between grace and human freedom that results in Christian perfection. For instance, he writes, "When a just act and grace of the Spirit come together in this, they fill the soul into which they come with a blessed life" (Gregory of Nyssa, *On the Christian Mode of Life*, GNO 8.1.46-57; FC 58:131). Gregory also writes, "Govern yourselves thus as you are going to ascend to a high power and glory through cooperation [συνεργίᾳ] with the Spirit" (*On the Christian Mode of Life*, GNO 8.1.87). There has been discussion of Gregory's use of the term since Werner Jaeger discovered *De instituto Christiano* and published his monograph on it in 1952 (Jaeger, *Two Rediscovered Works of Ancient Christian Literature*). Ekkehard Mühlenberg concludes that, though Jaeger appears to be right, this does not necessarily make Nyssa a semi-Pelagian (Ekkehard Mühlenberg, "Synergism in Gregory of Nyssa," ZNW 68 [1977]: 104). See also Verna E. F. Harrison, *Grace and Human Freedom According to St. Gregory of Nyssa*, rev. ed. (Lewiston, NY: Mellen, 1992). Nyssa uses συνεργία as a specific theological term; Chrysostom does not.

[47]For instance, "He purchased our part, our salvation, and he gave us a deposit in the meantime. Why did he not give us the whole immediately? Because we did not do the whole work. We believed; this is a beginning, and he himself gave a deposit. When we show our faith through works, then he will bestow everything" (Chrysostom, *In Eph. hom.* 2.2 [PG 62.18-19]). Also, "Not everything is up to us, but some things are up to us, and some are up to God. For choosing the most beautiful things, being willing, and being eager, and enduring all toil, it is from our purpose. But these things leading to perfection, and not to let them fall, and to go toward the goal of right actions, is grace from above" (Chrysostom, *Dom., non est in hom.* 4 [PG 56.160]). See also Chrysostom, *In Eph. hom.* 4.2; *Ad Theod.* 2.6; *In Matt. hom.* 50.2 (for τὰ θεοῦ/τὰ ἡμῶν or τὰ παρὰ θεοῦ/τὰ παρ᾽ ἡμῶν); *Ne tim. hom.* 2.4; and *In Rom. hom.* 26.4 (εἰσφέρω).

in Chrysostom's corpus he explains what he understands to be God's reasoning for designing salvation as a cooperation:

> [Paul] says, "In love, having preordained us." For this [preordination] comes
> not from efforts, nor from good works of ours, but from love; and yet not of
> love alone, but also of our virtue.[48] For if indeed from love alone, it would be
> necessary for all to be saved; but again, if from our virtue alone, then his
> coming [the incarnation] was superfluous, and all his economic works. But it
> is from neither his love alone, nor from our virtue, but from both.[49]

The first question here is what Chrysostom understands Paul to mean by
"preordination" (*proorixō*, προορίζω). Ephesians 1:4-5 says that God preordained us for adoption as children. Chrysostom equates this adoption
with salvation, noting here that both God's love and human virtue are necessary for a person to be saved (*sōzō*, σώζω), and two sentences later he
preaches, "Virtue would not save anyone unless there is also love."[50] That
Paul uses "preordained" implies to Chrysostom that out of love God decided
before any human effort that humans should be saved and adopted as God's
children. Chrysostom is not specific about when God made this determination (before what?), but only says it happened "from the beginning"
(*anōthen*, ἄνωθεν). The point is that God's love must precede human virtue,
even as both are necessary.

Chrysostom explains why it would be problematic for salvation to be
either love or virtue alone. First, Chrysostom has a commitment to the truth,
accuracy, and pedagogical nature of Scripture, and Scripture speaks of Gehenna as a place of torment. Therefore, not everyone is saved. If not everyone
is saved, then salvation cannot be a matter of God's love alone. Second, if
salvation comes from virtue alone, then the incarnation would be pointless.

There is one other element that may lead to Chrysostom's assertion that
salvation is not only about God's love since that would require salvation for
all. During the last part of Chrysostom's tenure at Antioch and during his
entire time as bishop of Constantinople, the Origenist controversies were

---

[48]We generally think of virtue as good works, but Chrysostom's statement here indicates that
  virtue is something other than good works. Virtue is indeed both human efforts and good works,
  as these two are opposed to God's love in the first clause of the sentence and virtue to God's love
  in the second.
[49]Chrysostom, *In Eph. hom.* 1.2 (PG 62.12).
[50]Chrysostom, *In Eph. hom.* 1.2 (PG 62.12).

engulfing the church. Moreover, Chrysostom was himself involved in one particular Origenist controversy as bishop.[51] One of Origen's ideas denounced by Epiphanius in the first wave of controversy is that even the devil will be returned to glory; that is, the devil could be saved.[52] Chrysostom himself rejects this idea explicitly when he writes, "The devil was good from the beginning, but he fell through laziness and despair into such evil that he was never able to recover again."[53] We saw that, for Chrysostom, the devil also has a *proairesis* and that he is thus responsible for his own fall. Should God override the devil's *proairesis* to save him, then God could override a human's as well, and this would trample on human freedom. The devil is but the extreme case in the argument, however. The controversy questioned the claim that God saves all, and for Chrysostom to say that salvation is a matter

---

[51]Chrysostom's affiliation with the controversy is clear. When Theophilus drove the Origenists out of the desert, some of them (known as the Long Brothers or the Tall Brothers) sought refuge in Constantinople under Chrysostom, which gave an opportunity for Theophilus to make charges against Chrysostom, leading to his eventual exile and death. The Long Brothers held strictly to God's incorporeality (against the anthropomorphism of some monks), but there is no evidence that they believed any of Origen's controversial ideas. Though it is unclear exactly what the Long Brothers believed, all accounts hold that they were orthodox on trinitarian matters and were willing to reject Origen's views on the Son and Spirit that were no longer acceptable. The issue was one of politics rather than theology, instigated by Theophilus (Elizabeth A. Clark, *The Origenist Controversy: The Cultural Construction of an Early Christian Debate* [Princeton, NJ: Princeton University Press, 1992], 105-6). For a thorough account of Chrysostom's involvement with the Long Brothers, see J. N. D. Kelly, *Golden Mouth: The Story of John Chrysostom—Ascetic, Preacher, Bishop* (London: Duckworth, 1995), 191-202. Though Chrysostom's involvement here occurs after he has preached his series of homilies on Ephesians, his role and notoriety in the church make it likely that he would have been aware of the Origenist controversies before his explicit involvement. For a full account of the Origenist controversies, see Elizabeth Clark's aforementioned seminal work, *Origenist Controversy*.

[52]Elizabeth Clark (*Origenist Controversy*) argues that there are more factors in play in the controversies than Origen's words alone, but that is irrelevant with regard to Chrysostom. He was involved with the controversy and attempted to preach orthodoxy against whatever heretical opinions appeared, whether those opinions were due to Theophilus's problems with Nitrian monks, Epiphanius's iconoclastic tendencies, or Jerome's encounter with Jovinian (as Clark proposes).

[53]Chrysostom, *De poen. hom.* 1.2 (PG 49.279). It is unclear where Chrysostom gets the idea that the devil fell beyond redemption since neither Lk 10:18 nor any comment on the verse by earlier Fathers suggests that the fall was beyond redemption. It may be that Chrysostom is holding to orthodox doctrine and infusing this into the text. He also has a fondness for Mt 25:31-46, where the Evangelist writes that hell was prepared "for the devil and his angels" (Mt 25:41) but heaven for humans. This text suggests to Chrysostom that the devil belongs in hell. On Chrysostom's fondness for this passage, see Randolf Brändle, "Jean Chrysostome—L'importance de Matth. 25,31-46 pour son éthique," *VC* 31 (1977): 47-52; and Robert Allen Krupp, *Saint John Chrysostom, a Scripture Index* (Lanham, MD: University Press of America, 1984), 129-30, where Krupp notes that Chrysostom quotes the passage 132 times.

not only of God's love but also of human virtue is to distance himself from the Origenist controversies.

Since we have put on Christ, let us do all things in that way ... For Chrysostom, God plays the primary role in salvation. God's contribution to salvation is prior to the human's and makes the human contribution possible. We see this here: "Since we have put on Christ, let us do all things in that way. ... Let us be in awe of the excess of grace offered to us by God." We act after having put on Christ, and we act out of regard for the grace already offered to us. Chrysostom thus indicates that there are two moments of salvation: the already done and the ongoing, and Christ is involved in both. We will look first at what Christ has already done for salvation and then at what Christ continues to do.

Absent from 8.6 altogether are the mechanics of how Christ causes salvation. These mechanics are less clear in Chrysostom's works than in other patristic authors, though he fits within the range of favored explanations.[54] Some, like Clement of Alexandria, conceived of Christ as a role model or as the true teacher who instructs humans in the way that leads from sin to freedom and life.[55] Another popular way to explain what Christ did was to say with Athanasius that Christ's death fulfills the death required by Adam's sin.[56] Irenaeus is famous for explaining that Christ recapitulates, or even reverses, Adam's fall.[57] Origen is keen to speak about Christ's defeat of the devil, the prince of this world, and uses language of ransom. Christ offered himself to the devil as ransom for all humanity and then cheated the devil of himself.[58] I have noted particular proponents of each explanation, but it is not so simple as to say that each of these authors conceived of Christ's work in only one way. All the theologians mentioned spoke about Christ's redemptive work in many related ways; Athanasius's *On the Incarnation*

---

[54]An excellent overview of patristic soteriologies can be found in J. N. D. Kelly, *Early Christian Doctrines*, 5th rev. ed (London: A. C. Black, 1977), 163-88, 375-400. A more recent summary is in Ronald E. Heine, *Classical Christian Doctrine: Introducing the Essentials of the Ancient Faith* (Grand Rapids: Baker Academic, 2013), 116-28.

[55]Clement of Alexandria, *Paedagogus*. Book 1 lays out Clement's understanding of Christ as teacher.

[56]Athanasius, *On the Incarnation* 4.

[57]A representative quotation comes from Irenaeus, *Haer.* 3.18.1: "He commenced afresh the long line of human beings, and furnished us, in a brief, comprehensive manner, with salvation; so that what we had lost in Adam—namely, to be according to the image and likeness of God—that we might recover in Christ Jesus" (*ANF* 1:446).

[58]Origen, *Cels.* 7.17; *Comm. Matt.* 16.8.

alone uses all of these models to explain what Christ did. This list is meant to be representative rather than exhaustive.

Chrysostom's own way of discussing Christ's work is also complex and uses a few different images. Christ "fettered" the devil; the devil overreached and brought punishment on himself when he tried to take the innocent Christ.[59] The devil's destruction is a result of his choice, as was his fall, as is the destruction (damnation) of humans who are not virtuous. All comes down to choice.

At other times Chrysostom employs language of reconciliation. Chrysostom argues in *In epistulam II ad Corinthios hom.* 11, commenting on 2 Corinthians 5:19, that God was the one who first reached for reconciliation: "Who was the maltreated one? Himself. Who was the first to want reconciliation? Himself."[60] The need for reconciliation is due to human *proairesis*. The human choice to sin caused the rift, yet God is the first to reach out. Chrysostom begins to explain how that reconciliation was achieved, and it was not from human effort. He preaches,

> God is the one who works the whole, who reconciled the world through the Only-Begotten. And how did he reconcile it to himself? . . . Forgiving their sins; for there was no other way. . . . But even though our sins were so big, not only did he not demand justice, he even reconciled.[61]

God reconciles by forgiving sins. This is not by decree only, however, for Chrysostom says it is through the Only-Begotten. Forgiveness occurs through Christ. Though this passage is no more specific, other comments Chrysostom makes give us a better picture of his thought on this point.

In short, we are reconciled to God through the incarnation, death, and resurrection of Jesus Christ.[62] Chrysostom's thoughts on the incarnation are

---

[59]Chrysostom, *Cat.* 3.9 (SC 50bis, 156); *In Ioh. hom.* 67.3 (PG 59.373).
[60]Chrysostom, *In 2 Cor. hom.* 11.2 (PG 61.477).
[61]Chrysostom, *In 2 Cor. hom.* 11.2 (PG 61.477).
[62]Though this project focuses only on Chrysostom's soteriology, it is important to note that soteriology and Christology are inextricably linked. How Chrysostom understands who Christ is affects how he thinks about what Christ has done (and how he was able to do it) for humanity, just as is true of any other theologian. Chrysostom's comments about the person of Christ are fewer than his comments about Christ's work in the world and for humanity, though Christ's work both reveals and is dependent on Christ's person. For a rich exploration of Chrysostom's Christology, especially as it relates to broader Antiochene Christologies, see Lawrence R. Barnard, "Christology and Soteriology in the Preaching of John Chrysostom"

often about the incarnation as the prime example of God's *synkatabasis* (συγκατάβασις) toward human beings.⁶³ The incarnation displays God's *synkatabasis* and loving-kindness in the way he comes to those who could neither understand nor come to him in any other way.⁶⁴ Regarding the resurrection, Chrysostom emphasizes the way Christ's resurrection sets a model for human resurrection, which is both a future reality as well as a metaphor for conversion, as in the quotation about baptism in the previous section. All three moments of Christ's life are important and together bring a person to God, but when Chrysostom speaks of the reconciliation of humans to God, he speaks most often about Christ's death as the event that accomplishes salvation.

Chrysostom preaches, "He proclaimed our salvation with their [those who crucified Jesus] transgressions. For after the blow the blows of our salvation gushed forth from there."⁶⁵ On the efficacy of Christ's death for eternal life, Chrysostom tells his audience, "Christ himself being in death, he in this way overcame it so as to raise up those who were already held

---

(ThD thesis, Southwestern Baptist Theological Seminary, 1974); Melvin E. Lawrenz, "The Christology of John Chrysostom," in *Studia Patristica: Cappadocian Fathers, Chrysostom and His Greek Contemporaries, Augustine, Donatism and Pelagianism*, ed. E. A. Livingstone, vol. 22 (Leuven: Peeters, 1989), 148-53; and Lawrenz, *The Christology of John Chrysostom* (Lewiston, NY: Mellen, 1996).

⁶³For a detailed look at the role of συγκατάβασις in Chrysostom's theology, see David Rylaarsdam, "The Adaptability of Divine Pedagogy: *Sunkatabasis* in the Theology and Rhetoric of John Chrysostom" (PhD diss., University of Notre Dame, 2000). Robert C. Hill prefers to translate συγκατάβασις as "considerateness" in Chrysostom's usage because it does not carry the pejorative connotation that "condescension" does. Hill also argues that the incarnation as the ultimate συγκατάβασις of God is Chrysostom's hermeneutical framework. See Robert C. Hill, "Chrysostom's Terminology for the Inspired Word," *Estudios bíblicos* 41 (1983): 367-73; Hill, "On Looking Again at *sunkatabasis*," *Prudentia* 13 (1981): 3-11. Mary W. Tse also follows this thought in her "Συγκατάβασις and Ακρίβεια—the Warp and Woof of Chrysostom's Hermeneutics: A Study Based on Chrysostom's Genesis Homilies," *Jian Dao* 15 (2001): 1-17.

⁶⁴For instance, "What is this συγκατάβασις? It is when God is not seen as he is but in the way one incapable of seeing him is able to look upon him. In this way God reveals himself, accommodating the revelation to the weakness of vision of those who see him" (*De incompr. hom.* 3.15 (SC 28bis, 176).

⁶⁵Chrysostom, *In Matt. hom.* 88.1 (PG 58.776). God (and Christ) used human wickedness for salvation, just as Chrysostom urges his congregation to use the devil for salvation. Chrysostom says the devil tried to deceive people by having Christ crucified with two thieves, but this strategy was foiled and used to make salvation more clear. Chrysostom preaches, "The devil's plot became stale and everything got upturned on his own head. . . . Not only, then, did [Christ] not diminish his glory by the crucifixion, but he even increased it not a little" (Chrysostom, *In Ioh. hom.* 85.1 [PG 59.460]). Everywhere Chrysostom seeks to show that those things that seem to be harmful can be tools for salvation.

down by it."[66] He also preaches, "Unspeakable is the power of the cross. . . . It was more inconceivable that by dying he should do away with death than that he should not die at all."[67] Christ's death is the source of eternal life for humans. In order to spend eternity in the kingdom of heaven, one must first be eternal. Christ's death defeats death and makes mortal human beings immortal.[68]

Another passage adds a dimension to the effect of Christ's death. In *In epistulam ad Hebraeos hom.* 16, Chrysostom says that Christ's death fulfills the death deserved by humans:

> See how he became a mediator, bringing words from [God] and bringing [them to us], carrying them from the Father to us, and adding his own death. We had offended, and we ought to have died; he [Christ] died on our behalf and made us worthy of the trust [*diathēkēs*, διαθήκης].[69] By this is the trust sure, in that from now on it is not made for the unworthy. Indeed, at the beginning, he [God] made his dispositions as a father to his sons; but since we had become unworthy, there was no longer need of a trust, but of punishment.[70]

Chrysostom here uses language of being "worthy" and "unworthy" (*axios*, ἄξιος, and *anaxios*, ἀνάξιος), which he does with unparalleled frequency. As in the statements where a person is rewarded with the kingdom or punished with Gehenna, here a person is either punished for unworthiness or receives her inheritance for worthiness. In this case, however, unlike in cases where Chrysostom puts the choice of reward or punishment, heaven or hell, in his congregation's hands, Christ is the one who makes us worthy. When Chrysostom puts the choice in his congregation's hands, he is assuming they have

---

[66]Chrysostom, *In Ioh. hom.* 5.3 (PG 59.58).

[67]Chrysostom, *In 1 Cor. hom.* 4.1 (PG 61.31).

[68]For a more detailed discussion of the possible atonement theories Chrysostom endorsed, see Barnard, "Christology and Soteriology in the Preaching of John Chrysostom," 153–210; and Melvin E. Lawrenz, "The Christology of John Chrysostom" (PhD diss., Marquette University, 1987), 177–200. Both authors conclude that Christus victor is the most accurate description of Chrysostom's beliefs but allow for elements of other theories, in particular, the ransom theory. The primary difficulty with both authors, though Barnard is the more egregious offender, is that they apply theories to Chrysostom's thought anachronistically rather than describing Chrysostom's understanding. Though they rigorously investigate his understanding, they spend too much time and effort attempting to overlay more recent theories onto Chrysostom.

[69]Διαθήκης is the word used for "covenant" in the New Testament and the LXX.

[70]Chrysostom, *In Heb. hom.* 16.1 (PG 63.123-24). The *In Heb. hom.* are thought to have been preached very late, likely the winter of 402–403, and only published from shorthand notes after Chrysostom's death (J. N. D. Kelly, *Golden Mouth*, 133).

already been made worthy by Christ, as in *In epistulam ad Hebraeos hom.* 16, and that they are choosing to make themselves unworthy. We had, in Adam, become unworthy of what God offered, but Christ restored our worthiness. Now, having been restored, because of the freedom God gives us as humans, we can choose to be unworthy again.

This flow is clear in the passage from *Homiliae in Genesim hom.* 8.6: "Since we have put on Christ, let us do all things in that way, and do not grieve the Holy Spirit."[71] We have been made worthy, and if we put on Christ like a baptismal robe, we want to remain worthy. Then Chrysostom urges, "Let us be in awe of the excess of grace offered to us by God . . . so that, having contended lawfully . . . we may be worthy of those great crowns."[72] In both homilies, he states that the grace has been offered, Christ has acted, and then we are to strive, that is, to be found worthy.

Having been made worthy by Christ's action, Chrysostom also insists that we act as those who have put on Christ. In *Homiliae in Genesim hom.* 8.6 Chrysostom tells the audience to "consider the one who dwells in us." He is not specific about who the "the one" is. He has just said that we put on Christ and quoted Paul's line that Christ lives in us. He has also told us not to grieve the Holy Spirit. In either case, it is this person to whom we are to look when we are tempted. Elsewhere Chrysostom is more explicit about the role God, without specifying which member of the Trinity, plays in the Christian's ongoing struggle for virtue. After discussing the necessity of the human contribution and zeal for salvation in *Expositiones in psalmos* 121.2, Chrysostom preaches, "[God] is your defender . . . your ally, your help. . . . He will make a stand by your right hand so that you may be invincible, so you may be active, so you may be strong, so you may be powerful, set up a trophy, sustain victory, since it is most of all in this that we shall do everything."[73] God has not left us alone in our attempts to be worthy.

---

[71]Chrysostom, *In Gen. hom.* 8.6 (PG 53.75).

[72]Chrysostom, *In Gen. hom.* 8.6 (PG 53.75).

[73]Chrysostom, *Exp. in ps.* 120.2 (121.2) (PG 55.346). The PG of Chrysostom's *Exp. in ps.* follows the LXX numbering of Psalms (as Chrysostom would have been using the LXX); Hill renumbers them to follow the MT. The numbers I give are for the PG, with Hill's in parentheses. The Psalms commentary is traditionally located during Chrysostom's years in Antioch, but beyond this a date is not offered. Many scholars have suggested a date of 387 for the commentary on Ps 41 in particular but place the rest of *Exp. in Ps.* in the mid to late Antiochene period. Wendy Mayer, *The Homilies of St John Chrysostom: Provenance, Reshaping the Foundations* (Rome: Pontifical Oriental Institute, 2005), 266.

Chrysostom argues more specifically that virtue itself is a cooperation between God and a human being in *In Matthaeum. hom.* 82: "A person's willingness [*prothymia*, προθυμία] is not sufficient, unless there is some beneficial tipping of the scale from above; and that again we gain nothing by the tipping of the scale from above, if there is not a willingness. . . . For from these two things virtue is woven."[74] Both God's and the human's action are necessary. We also see this theme in Chrysostom's panegyrics for the apostle Paul. Prompted by Paul's own sufferings of imprisonments, shipwrecks, and the like, Chrysostom argues that nothing Christ commanded is impossible: "If we would contribute as large a share of willingness as we have, then God would weigh in the balance heavily for us, and thus we shall all become unassailable to all the terrors attacking us."[75]

In the *Catecheses ad illuminandos*, Chrysostom makes it clear that Christians are not alone in their struggle with the devil, that enemy of salvation who aims to injure one's virtue:

> The Lord of angels presides as judge. This is not only an honor for us, but also a security. For when the one who laid down his life for us judges the wrestling match, what kind of honor is this? How much security? In the Olympic games the judge stands impartial from the competitors, favoring neither the one nor the other, but waiting for the result. . . . In our struggle with the devil, Christ does not stand impartial but is wholly on our side. . . . He anointed us with the oil of joy; he bound the devil with unbreakable chains in order to bind him hand and foot for the struggle. And if I slip, he reaches out his hand, lifts me up when I fall, and sets me on my feet again.[76]

Note again that Christ's work is past in that he has bound the devil before we entered the arena, and that work is present in that Christ is still on our side, raising us when we fall. Christ has defeated the devil, that is, made it possible for humans to resist him, and he also continues to help humans to

---

[74]Chrysostom, *In Matt. hom.* 82.4 (PG 58.742). An example of a situation where Chrysostom sees this working is Joseph's resistance of the advances of Potiphar's wife. He writes, "This man, after doing what he could and demonstrating his struggle for chastity with great intensity, enjoyed much help from on high and had victory in the struggle by cooperation [συμμαχίας] from God's right hand" (*In Gen. hom.* 62.4 [PG 54.538]).

[75]Chrysostom, *De laud. Paul. hom.* 6.3 (SC 300bis, 264-66). English from Margaret M. Mitchell, *The Heavenly Trumpet: John Chrysostom and the Art of Pauline Interpretation* (Tübingen: Mohr Siebeck, 2000), 476.

[76]Chrysostom, *Cat.* 3.8-9 (SC 50bis, 155-56).

resist and defeat the devil themselves. Therefore, when there are temptations, to "untimely desire or anger or rage or envy," that is, when there is a choice between vice and virtue, Christ helps us when we choose virtue. Christ already reconciled us and now helps us to remain worthy.

The onus, however, remains on the human choice, however much God helps. Without imploring God, Chrysostom charges the audience, "Since we have put on Christ, let us do all things in that way, and do not grieve the Holy Spirit. . . . Let us banish further every such [evil] thought." In another of the *Homiliae in Genesim*, Chrysostom states, "The grace of God has made us stronger than steel and entirely invincible, if we want."[77] For all of Chrysostom's statements that humans are able to resist the devil (and ought to) because of their *proairesis*, he also says that it is God's grace that makes a person invincible. Grace is the operative element, though according to this statement, a person must desire to be made strong and invincible. This hints at how Chrysostom sees the cooperation working. God does all the heavy lifting, and God's grace is operative and effective, but a human must want to be invincible. God will not force his grace on us; God created humans with freedom and self-determination. Chrysostom paints God as a gentleman who offers everything but stands aside waiting for permission to give, wooing but never coercing.

***Having contended lawfully* . . .** This is the reason Chrysostom urges his congregation to be aware of their free *proairesis*, to use that freedom to be virtuous, to remember what Christ has done, and to know that Christ still helps them if they are willing. Chrysostom wants his congregation to be crowned and to "be found worthy" "in the day to come." We saw earlier that the "coming age" is the world of Gehenna and the kingdom and that God, at the judgment, sends people to one or the other on the basis of their virtue. That theme is here again. Referring to "a frightening day for sinners but a day longed for by those who have put on virtue" is not unlike maintaining that "virtue snatches us out of Gehenna in the coming age and gives us the enjoyment of the kingdom of heaven." A passage that began as an exhortation for the congregants to take responsibility for their virtue became a reminder of Christ's work and help in the pursuit of virtue, and now Chrysostom has

---

[77]Chrysostom, *In Gen. hom.* 4.2 (PG 53.40).

returned at the end to make it clear that virtue is a person's own responsibility. One must be found worthy.

We see similar language in the first of Chrysostom's *Catecheses ad illuminandos*: "As many of you as have been considered worthy of being granted citizenship here, come forward with much kindness and put behind you all the things you had done already and demonstrate the change in your whole thought."[78] God has deemed the catechumens worthy of all his gifts, and their virtue is a response to this. Once a person has been found or made worthy by God's invitation in Christ's reconciling work, one should prove that one is indeed worthy of those gifts and act like the citizen of heaven one is.[79]

A statement that nuances the picture we have in *Homiliae in Genesim* 8.6 and is supported by *Catecheses ad illuminandos* 1 comes from Chrysostom's *In epistulam I ad Corinthios hom.* 1: "God wished to save us in this way. For we did nothing right, but through the will of God we have gained salvation; and since he thought it good, not because we were worthy, we were called."[80] Here Chrysostom says that salvation has nothing to do with any kind of worth the human has. This, however, refers only to Christ's initial work, just like the worth language in the passage from *In epistulam ad Hebraeos hom.* 16. The past tense "were" (aorist *ēmen*, ἤμεν) differentiates the text I have just quoted from all of Chrysostom's exhortations for the people to be worthy or to be found worthy at the judgment, which are present tense. Attaining salvation not because we were worthy means that there is no intrinsic worth in the human being such that it was necessary for God to call him to salvation, as though he deserved it. Instead, God called in spite of the unworthiness brought on by Adam's disobedience, and after having been called in such a way, one is meant to be worthy because one has been deemed and made worthy.

One final image is helpful for understanding what virtue does for a person in the world to come. Several times in the *Catecheses ad illuminandos*

---

[78]Chrysostom, *Cat.* 1.18 (SC 50bis, 117-18).

[79]Chrysostom does not elaborate on what kind of citizenship he means, but he has just finished quoting Paul (Eph 5:27), and Paul in Phil 3:20 speaks about a Christian's citizenship in heaven. Moreover, Chrysostom's frequent use of heavenly πολιτεία language suggests that the citizenship conferred by baptism is the citizenship of heaven.

[80]Chrysostom, *In 1 Cor. hom.* 1.1 (PG 61.13).

Chrysostom tells his catechumens to keep clean the garment they put on at baptism: "I encourage you who have just been deemed worthy of the divine gift to show great caution and to guard carefully the clean and spotless spiritual garment given to you."[81] The catechumens have again been "deemed worthy" (*axioō*, ἀξιόω). God's esteeming worthy precedes a person's remaining worthy or, in this case, remaining clean and spotless. A few lines down from this, Chrysostom preaches, "It is much better to have concern and thought for your radiance now so as to remain in purity continually and receive no stain."[82] Here Chrysostom's robe metaphor is linked explicitly to living in purity; the spotless robe is the spotless life. In *Catecheses ad illuminandos* 4 Chrysostom urges, "You put on the new [garment] and have such a radiance as to shine with the rays of the sun. Contemplate how you may maintain the shining beauty of this same garment."[83] The garment is both literal and metaphorical. Chrysostom refers at the literal level to the white baptismal garment the neophytes put on following their baptism, which symbolizes the marriage robe.[84] This they are to keep clean, though the context of the passage makes it clear that Chrysostom means this metaphorically. The robe is also a symbol of their virtue, their new way of life as Christians, and it is this virtue that needs to be kept clean and pure.

Alluding to the parable of the wedding banquet in Matthew 22:1-14, where a guest is discovered without the proper wedding attire and ejected from the feast, Chrysostom tells the catechumens, "You are called to a wedding, beloved; do not come wearing filthy clothes, but take an appropriate dress to the wedding."[85] In Chrysostom's commentary on this parable in *In Matthaeum. hom.* 69, he explains that the garment in question is the soul, which can only be adorned properly with good works.[86] Elsewhere Chrysostom uses this parable to explain that those who are not properly attired with

---

[81]Chrysostom, *Cat.* 5.24 (SC 50bis, 212).

[82]Chrysostom, *Cat.* 5.26 (SC 50bis, 213).

[83]Chrysostom, *Cat.* 4.22 (SC 50bis, 193).

[84]The baptism as marriage is one of Chrysostom's primary images in his *Cat.*

[85]Chrysostom, *Illum. cat.* 2.2 (PG 49.234).

[86]Chrysostom, *In Matt. hom.* 69.3. In fact, Chrysostom tells his audience that the monks in their "garments of hair" are those properly attired for the feast, not kings who wear purple: "If you are able to open the gates of the mind, and to look at their soul, and all the decorations within, you would fall down on the ground, not bearing the shine of their beauty, and the dazzling radiance of those clothes, and the lightning brightness of their knowledge" (*In Matt. hom.* 69.3 [PG 58.652]).

virtue will be ejected from the kingdom of heaven, as in *Expositiones in psalmos* 143:

> Those who are living in sin are like that. . . . Even if they are beaming in garments and other finery, their condition is no better than those who died once and are in darkness, but even much more severe, as much as one condition is an action of φύσις [*physis*], the other an accusation of προαίρεσις [*proairesis*]. There is a darkness coming, about which Scripture says, "Pick him up and throw him into the outer darkness" [Mt 22:13].[87]

For Chrysostom, virtue is like the baptismal robe. God deems a person worthy to wear it, that is, worthy of his grace and salvation, but it is the person's responsibility to keep the robe clean, or to remain worthy. Without a spotless robe, that is, without a virtuous soul, a person is not worthy to remain at the wedding banquet, the kingdom of heaven. Virtue makes one worthy of the kingdom, or, in the words of *Homiliae in Genesim* 8.6, worthy of unspeakable goods and crowned with that marvelous crown.

CONCLUSION

Chrysostom begins *Homiliae in Genesim* 8.6 with an exhortation to his audience: "Let us not think too little of our salvation." It is therefore clear that, for Chrysostom, there is something the audience can do to attend to its salvation, and Chrysostom tells them what that is: be virtuous. God has made human beings free and given each a *proairesis*. Because they are free, it is possible for them to be virtuous. Then, because it is possible to be virtuous, God requires that they be virtuous. Only virtue will make them worthy of the kingdom of heaven when they stand before God at the judgment.

Chrysostom was concerned that his congregation know that both the devil and his demons are unable to cause any harm to human beings. Demons cannot cause them to sin, and demons cannot damn them. However much the devil deceives or tempts, a person is free and able to resist—and therefore must. Chrysostom's project, however, is larger than this. It is not only about a person's ability to resist demons but about her responsibility to do so. His project is about a person's responsibility to be virtuous. Not only can demons not damn, but God does not save unilaterally. A person cannot

---

[87]Chrysostom, *Exp. in ps.* 142.3 (143.3) (PG 55.451).

expect to be saved unless she add some effort of her own. God requires our virtuous victory over the devil. God does not leave a person alone in her effort. Christ reconciled her to God, made her worthy, and continues to help her remain worthy should she desire it, but the responsibility to be virtuous is hers alone, which means that the responsibility for her salvation is also hers alone.

Conclusion

IMPLICATIONS FOR THE CHURCH TODAY

T HIS BOOK HAS, on its surface, been about John Chrysostom's demonology. What are demons, where do they come from, and how do they
interact with human beings, according to Chrysostom? In his answers to
these questions, Chrysostom is in many ways similar to his predecessors. A
survey of the demonologies of pagans, Jews, and Christians of the fourth
century established a broad context for Chrysostom's work, and it became
clear that the world of late antiquity was populated by spirits: some good,
some evil, some ambiguous. This world was characterized by a general fear
of the physical harm that could befall a person from evil demons who caused
illness, poverty, pregnancy complications, and even death. It was not a debilitating fear, however, but a way of life. In response to the demonic threat,
people employed amulets, magic bowls, and magical papyri to protect themselves and their families from the danger of demonic action. People of all
stripes in the fourth century participated in such magic as a part of life. It
was what one did.

Chrysostom, however, responds to this fearful way of life by telling his
congregation that they do not understand demons at all. If they did, they
would not be afraid. The details of Chrysostom's demonology show that,
when it comes to the origin and nature of demons, Chrysostom believes the
devil to be a spiritual creature made good by God in the beginning who fell
from his position because of pride and the demons to be angels similarly

created good who fell with him. This happened before the creation of the rest of the world. The devil and his demons are incorporeal, spiritual beings created good and possessing a *proairesis* (προαίρεσις), which allowed for their fall. Though Chrysostom explains these finer points of demonology, he does so rarely and only with occasional comments; his primary concern is with the limits of demonic activities and correcting his congregation's misunderstanding of those limits.

Chrysostom has a habit of warning his congregation against laziness (*rhathymia*, ῥαθυμία) when it comes to the devil. The devil is always working, using deception and wiles, enticing with words and clever tricks, to convince a person to sin. Sometimes the devil even attacks physically, as in the case of Job. However, this is where Chrysostom tells his congregation that they misunderstand. The devil does wish to destroy human beings, but amulets and magic bowls are unnecessary, for the destruction the devil has in mind is spiritual, and a person is able to resist.

Truth and Appearances

The first thing Chrysostom does in his attempt to rectify his congregation's mistaken assumptions about demons is to explain the difference between true and apparent evil, or true and apparent harm. The congregants, he says, believe that demons are governing the world because of all the suffering they see. They believe that demons are causing harm. Chrysostom tells his congregants that the demons may, in fact, be causing the suffering they experience, but this suffering is not true harm. It is only apparent harm. True harm is harm done to the soul, and the soul is impervious to all harm except that inflicted by the person on herself: sin. Sin is harm to one's virtue, soul, and salvation. All other suffering—illness, poverty, physical injury, even death—is not evil, not truly injurious. Therefore, though demons can cause suffering, they cannot cause true injury.

The congregation has failed to appreciate the limitations of demons, and these limits are the core of Chrysostom's exhortation. If demons are causing suffering and apparent harm, it is only with God's permission. Demons cannot do whatever they please; they must receive permission from God. Here Chrysostom's demonology begins to be informed by his anthropology. Chrysostom explains that the devil cannot cause a person to sin (though not for lack of trying). God has made each person free and self-determining and has endowed each person with a *proairesis*. Because the *proairesis* is free, neither the devil nor God can compel a person to choose one action over another; the choice is entirely within her power (*eph hēmin*, ἐφ᾽ ἡμῖν). Further, because the *proairesis* is *eph hēmin*, the *proairesis* is the seat of moral responsibility, what makes an action virtuous or vicious.

Chrysostom places high importance on virtue because he understands virtue to be an essential aspect of salvation. Human beings are free and thus able to be virtuous. Because they *can* be virtuous, God requires them to be virtuous, and God does not leave people alone in their attempts to be virtuous. God makes salvation possible in Christ and offers human beings the gift of entrance into the kingdom, but humans must also cooperate with God's work and bring their own contribution, their virtue, in order to walk through the kingdom's gates. Virtue is what makes people worthy of the kingdom of heaven when they stand before God at the judgment.

Chrysostom tells his people that sin is their own fault and virtue their own responsibility, regardless of what the devil and his demons are doing. The devil is the enemy of salvation, and every Christian is locked in a struggle with this enemy. The Christian enters the arena in her baptism, and the devil does everything in his power to drag a person into hell. Thus, this struggle against the devil for virtue is what defines the Christian life. Chrysostom articulates his soteriology by means of demonology. Chrysostom's rhetoric about demons highlights the self-determination of human beings and their resulting moral responsibility. Chrysostom in turn uses self-determination and moral responsibility to exhort his congregation to be virtuous, which is the state of all human beings that God intends.

The preceding account of demons, virtue, and salvation implies that, as Chrysostom understands the world, humans have a measure of responsibility for their salvation, and demons highlight this responsibility. Though God has done, and continues to do, the major part of the work, God requires his people to put up a fight:

> This is why [God] wants you to work a little: so that the victory may be yours too. And just as a king desires his son to be in the line of battle, and be seen, so that a trophy can be given to him, even though [the king] himself achieves everything: so too does God act in the war against the devil. In return [God]

asks only one thing from you—that you show genuine enmity against him. If you present him with this, he will finish off the whole war.[1]

Salvation is a war against the devil, who tries at every step with every device available to him to keep Christians from the kingdom of heaven that God has prepared for them. Therefore, when Chrysostom urges his congregation to be virtuous, he is encouraging them to take responsibility for their salvation and fight against the devil. They can do something about their salvation, and they must.

CONTRIBUTIONS TO THE CHURCH

The account provided here is important in its own right as we look to understand better John Chrysostom and his thought, but history should not be left solely to the past. Chrysostom has much to say to our present church if we will listen. And so I end this account with a few thoughts about what Chrysostom's message can contribute to modern Christianity.

Cultural assumptions. First, to Protestant, post-Reformation ears, Chrysostom's narrative of virtue and the Christian life can sound like earning our salvation or a works righteousness that we have been taught Martin Luther freed us from. I dare say it is more complicated than that, and not only because the narrative about Luther is rather more complicated than that. It would never have occurred to Chrysostom to ask questions about whether his account encourages a works righteousness of some kind. Even Augustine's controversies with the Pelagians over grace, free will, and original sin occurred after Chrysostom's death.[2] Chrysostom is squarely within the realm of accepted discourse on salvation in his own time. No one was suggesting anything about merit or earning salvation. Such things were unthinkable to the Christians of Chrysostom's time, and evaluating Chrysostom's theology with modern categories and judgments is a complex endeavor.

---

[1]Chrysostom, *In Matt. hom.* 16.11 (PG 57.254).

[2]Though just barely, as Chrysostom died in 407, and Pelagius arrived in Rome sometime in the first decade of the fifth century. Augustine's writings against the Pelagians concentrated about 415–420. For more on Chrysostom's relation to Pelagian categories, see Peter B. Ely, "Chrysostom and Augustine on the Ultimate Meaning of Human Freedom," *Ultimate Reality and Meaning* 29, no. 3 (2006): 163-82; Robert C. Hill, "A Pelagian Commentator on the Psalms?," *ITQ* 63 (1998): 263-71; and Anthony Kenny, "Was St. John Chrysostom a Semi-Pelagian?," *ITQ* 37 (1960): 16-29.

The same is true for evaluating theology across cultures. I can no more make Ghanaian Christians North American than I can make Chrysostom a modern. There are assumptions and categories at work in each culture's expressions of theology, and therefore there are questions, concerns, and constructions that simply do not occur to one culture or another. For this reason, evaluating one culture's theology with the categories and judgments of another is at least complex if not altogether unfair. As Christianity becomes ever more global, it is important that conversations between cultures happen, but it is also important that all parties in a conversation listen and understand what assumptions and categories underlie each party's thought. Only in recognition of this can we have fruitful conversation.

Global deliverance and the limits of prosperity. One place where attention to cultural assumptions is especially prescient is in conversations about demonology. This is the second area where this study has a contribution to make to modern Christianity. Some Christians see suffering in the world and say that real demons are causing this suffering. Demons are the reason for a woman's miscarriage or a friend's depression or even a person's adultery. To them Chrysostom says, "Yes, demons are real. And a demon might be behind a miscarriage. But it also might not. As for their adultery, a demon can do no more than tempt and deceive. A demon does not cause sin. Use the demons. Fight against them and become more virtuous for the sake of your salvation!" There are Christians in the United States as well as in the growing Christianity of the Global South who ascribe to deliverance, a theology that sounds very much like the beliefs of Chrysostom's own congregants about demons.

Ministers in the deliverance movement argue that demons "oppress" or "afflict" human beings and are the cause of suffering, evil, and even sin in the world.[3] The solution to demonic oppression is deliverance, a kind of

---

[3]Oppression is different from possession. Whereas in a possession a demon hijacks the human's mental faculties, in oppression the demon is "regarded as simply influencing the lives of victims in negative ways" (Kwaku Dua-Agyeman, *Covenant, Curses, and Cure* [Kumasi, Ghana: Payless Printing Press, 1994], 5). See also J. Kwabena Asamoah-Gyadu, "Mission to 'Set the Captives Free': Healing, Deliverance, and General Curses in Ghanaian Pentecostalism," *International Review of Religion* 93 (2004): 395-396; Opoku Onyinah, "Deliverance as a Way of Confronting Witchcraft in Contemporary Africa: Ghana as a Case Study," in *Spirit in the World: Emerging Pentecostal Theologies in Global Contexts*, ed. Veli-Matti Kärkkäinen (Grand Rapids: Eerdmans, 2009), 191; and Derek Prince, *They Shall Expel Demons: What You Need to Know About*

low-level exorcism.[4] Get rid of the demon, and the financial troubles, cancer, or even adultery will cease. In this theology, all suffering or misfortune is caused by demons, which are given the right to afflict a person through any number of "doorways" such as sin, trauma, or ancestral curses.[5] The way to rid a person of these demons—and therefore his suffering or misfortune—is to perform a deliverance. The basic form of this act involves the pastor discerning and naming which spirits are oppressing the person (the "demon of lust" or "demon of laziness" or "demon of cancer," for instance), the pastor and other ministers laying hands on the afflicted person, praying for the person's release, watching for any manifestations of the demon as they fight to stay in (screaming, writhing, coughing), and then a command from the pastor for the demon to leave "in Jesus' name," at which point the demon will leave, often through some bodily orifice in the form of sneezes, vomiting, or the like.[6] All of this is common in charismatic branches of global Christianity, and is in fact a major reason why Christianity is growing in those regions.[7]

Demons—Your Invisible Enemies (Grand Rapids: Chosen Books, 1998), 103. For more on this distinction, see J. Kwabena Asamoah-Gyadu, *African Charismatics: Current Developments Within Independent Indigenous Pentecostalism in Ghana*, Studies of Religion in Africa 27 (Leiden: Brill, 2005), 167; and Prince, *They Shall Expel Demons*, 6-17.

[4]For an overview of deliverance, see J. Kwabena Asamoah-Gyadu, "Conquering Satan, Demons, Principalities, and Powers: Ghanaian Traditional and Christian Perspectives on Religion, Evil, and Deliverance," in *Coping with Evil in Religion and Culture: Case Studies*, ed. Nelly van Doorn-Harder and Lourens Minnema (Amsterdam: Rodopi, 2008), 85-103; Stephen Hunt, "Managing the Demonic: Some Aspects of the Neo-Pentecostal Deliverance Ministry," *Journal of Contemporary Religion* 13 (1998): 215-30; and Nigel Scotland, "The Charismatic Devil: Demonology in Charismatic Christianity," in *Angels and Demons: Perspectives and Practice in Diverse Religious Traditions*, ed. Peter G. Riddell and Beverly Smith Riddell (Nottingham: Apollos, 2007), 84-105. For a manual on deliverance, see Prince, *They Shall Expel Demons*.

[5]For full lists, see Asamoah-Gyadu, "Mission to 'Set the Captives Free,'" 691; Dua-Agyeman, *Covenant, Curses, and Cure*, 5; Onyinah, "Deliverance as a Way of Confronting Witchcraft," 191; and Prince, *They Shall Expel Demons*, 103.

[6]For a description of the process, see Asamoah-Gyadu, *African Charismatics*, 187-88; Prince, *They Shall Expel Demons*, 70; as well as the sources in note 4 above.

[7]The accepted narrative is that when missionaries from mainline traditions presented Christianity to traditional African groups, for instance, the missionaries stirred up fear by calling the traditional gods "demons" but then not providing any sort of relief from the suffering or fear resulting. In contrast, Pentecostal missionaries and other charismatic movements presented a way to be delivered from these fears in concrete ways with deliverance theology. It met the culture and took seriously the enchanted worldview it found there. See Opoku Onyinah, who writes, "By the introduction of a personalized devil and the association of the gods with demons, the missionaries strengthened the belief in witchcraft, yet they failed to provide for the holistic needs of the people. For the Ghanaian, these images were real life-threatening forces." Onyinah, "Deliverance as a Way of Confronting Witchcraft in Contemporary Africa," 185.

Chrysostom is an excellent conversation partner for deliverance ministers, as he shares several of their assumptions about the world, in particular the belief that the world is populated by spirits. Indeed, Chrysostom would recognize in deliverance ministers similar fears to those of his own congregants. Both groups fear that demons are running the world and causing suffering or even sin. Chrysostom would respond to the deliverance practitioners and ministers much the same way he responded to his own congregants: they assume demons are far more powerful than they really are. Moreover, they fear demons when they should truly fear their own conduct. Chrysostom's demonological discourse applies to the deliverance movement as well.[8] By engaging in conversation with Chrysostom, it becomes clear that deliverance ministers believe all suffering to be evil and even that demons can cause sin. Chrysostom insists that suffering is not in itself evil and that sin is our own responsibility. Just as Chrysostom's demonology reveals his anthropology and soteriology, so too does deliverance demonology. Both assume a particular understanding of salvation.

The other side of the deliverance coin is the prosperity gospel. This, too, is prominent worldwide and particularly strong in the growing Christianity of the Global South. According to the prosperity gospel, suffering is a sign of God's disfavor or even sin in a person's life. True Christians are materially wealthy and healthy in the here and now. Chrysostom's insistence that it is not outward wealth or circumstances that make a person virtuous speaks to this tendency. Chrysostom says that Job was virtuous both when he was wealthy and when the devil had taken everything from him.[9] Judas had everything going for him, all the right external circumstances, and he was not virtuous.[10] For Chrysostom, virtue in those cases was about resisting the devil's temptations and choosing obedience to God. In fact, Chrysostom often argues that the more wealth a person has, the harder it is to be virtuous.[11] Just as with deliverance theology, a conversation with Chrysostom

---

[8]This claim requires some nuance, to be sure, but that is another project in itself. For more on a hypothetical conversation between Chrysostom and deliverance practitioners, see my essay: Samantha L. Miller, "The Devil Did Not Make You Do It: Chrysostom's Refutation of Modern Deliverance Theology," in *Revisioning John Chrysostom: New Approaches, New Perspectives*, ed. Chris L. de Wet and Wendy Mayer (Leiden: Brill, 2019), 613-37.

[9]Chrysostom, *Comm. in Iob* 1.1 (SC 346bis, 88).

[10]Chrysostom, *Quod nem. laed.* 11 (SC 103bis, 114).

[11]This is Chrysostom's argument in *Comp. reg. et mon.* He makes a similar argument throughout *Ad. opp. vit. mon.*, and the virtue of poverty and almsgiving is Chrysostom's theme in *De poen. hom.* 1-9.

shows the prosperity gospel to have particular anthropological and soteriological concerns.

This is significant because the Western, noncharismatic branches of the church need ways to speak with the charismatic branches in the West as well as in the Global South. Christianity is growing in the Global South, and the forms that are growing most rapidly are the charismatic branches that subscribe to deliverance and the prosperity gospel. Chrysostom offers those of us unfamiliar with demonological discourse a way to engage these traditions. Chrysostom's talk of demons is not about what they are, where they come from, or whether they are real; Chrysostom's talk of demons is about moral responsibility, virtue, and salvation. The same is true about Chrysostom's talk of wealth: it is about virtue and salvation, not only about God's favor or the absence of demons. Chrysostom offers us a bridge on which to engage the whole body of Christ. This could be especially important for denominations that have churches globally. How do the United Methodist annual conferences of California, Texas, and New Jersey remain a united church with those conferences in Ghana, South Africa, and Brazil? We begin by recognizing that everyone is invested in their theology because virtue and salvation are at stake.

ACTIVE FAITH

The same thing is true of debates within the Western church. If we cannot treat demonology without treating soteriology, what other discussions or debates are we having that entail soteriology? This is the third contribution to modern Christianity. Chrysostom insists on an active faith where God has acted first and acted effectively for humanity's salvation. God's love for us comes before anything we do, and Christ died and rose for us before we did anything. Still, Chrysostom says that we need to add our faith and our virtue to what God in Christ has already done. In fact, he preaches, following Paul, that our baptism unites us to Christ's resurrection as much as to his death, and Christ's resurrection is what enables us to live virtuously in the present.[12] If we listen to him, we hear from Chrysostom that we do not have

---

[12]For instance, "For if you shared in death and burial, much more you share in resurrection and life. . . . He himself, having set before us the one to come, demands of us another resurrection, the new πολιτεια, the one brought about in the present life by a change of ways. For when the

a passive faith; we have an active one. As Christians, we do not simply sit around resting on what Christ has done for us and waiting for heaven. Chrysostom tells us that we need to participate in our ongoing salvation, perhaps even working it out "with fear and trembling" (Phil 2:12). The threat that the devil "prowls around" like a roaring lion (1 Pet 5:8) is one Chrysostom takes seriously. He urges his congregation to be proactive. If their faith is merely passive, they will be taken down by demons who tempt and deceive, and they may follow the devil straight to hell. By fighting, remembering that Christ is on our side and has rigged the contest, we can stand tall and win. We can take an active interest in our own salvation and show ourselves worthy of what Christ has already done out of his love for us. Chrysostom's message is that Christ has saved us not only for a future heaven but for a virtuous life now.

ON FIGHTING THE DEVIL AND NOT DEMONIZING OTHERS

This narrative that Chrysostom tells is as important today as it was in his own time. We, too, need to be found glowing with the sweat of virtue. At some level, Christians recognize this. Most of our battles in the church today are about our behavior, or in some cases theological description of behavior, and most of the arguments, at their core, are about how behavior affects salvation. Some call certain behaviors sins and argue that Scripture teaches that those who live in sin will not enter the kingdom of heaven. That is, some argue for people to be virtuous and worthy of the kingdom of heaven. Others argue that particular behaviors are not sins and therefore will not keep a person out of the kingdom of heaven. Still others argue that, sin or not, God's love and Christ's action overwhelm our behavior, welcome us all into the kingdom of heaven, and thus make our virtue irrelevant. Few describe the arguments as debates about virtue, even as some recognize that they are arguing about salvation, and yet this is what they are.

If we can listen, Chrysostom offers some important insights. Some people speak about demons as real beings trying to lead Christians or even all of society astray. Some people argue that Satan is controlling this political

---

fornicator becomes chaste, and the greedy one merciful, and the savage tame, even there is a resurrection. . . . When you hear about a new life, search for a great change." Chrysostom, *In Rom. hom.* 10.4 (PG 60.480).

leader or that religious figure, that real demons are behind the culture's move to embrace abortion or homosexuality, and this will lead to the destruction of the world. To them Chrysostom says, "Yes, demons are real, and yes, the devil does aim to destroy humanity. But he is only deceiving and tempting; the devil cannot cause anyone to sin. If you resist, he cannot win. Do not blame the devil for your sins or even for the sins of your culture. Take responsibility." Chrysostom preached that demons were indeed tempting and deceiving, but it is human beings who sin. Chrysostom did not deal in euphemisms. He called sin sin wherever he saw it, including in the empress. Yet when he denounced the sin, he encouraged the human being. There was an admonition to stop the sinful behavior, whether going to the theater or taking advantage of the poor, but then also exhortation to choose virtue. Chrysostom gave his audience courage for the battle with demons and a vision of being found worthy of Christ. However stern, Chrysostom's rhetoric was never hateful. He aimed to persuade his congregants to virtuous lives.[13]

Other Christians are less certain about whether demons are real, but too often they demonize their opponents and enemies all the same. Some would claim that those who oppose abortion and gay marriage must be evil. They are trying to hurt human beings, deny people their God-given dignity, and destroy our society. To these people Chrysostom responds, "Whatever suffering they cause, it is not true harm. They cannot harm your soul. But you can. Every time you demonize a person, every time you give in to your anger and say more than you should, every time you fail to love your neighbor, you injure your own soul. You soil your baptismal robe and become less worthy of your salvation."

The United States has become increasingly polarized, harboring a climate of hatred and an unwillingness to listen, not only politically but also among churches. Denominations like my own United Methodist Church are ripping themselves apart over ethical issues. At the root of much of this climate is fear. In particular, it is a fear of the other, or of the unknown and how the other will affect my current way of life. Chrysostom says not to fear the other

---

[13]Admittedly, sometimes his mode of persuasion was to incite the fear of hell, though this is still not hateful speech and is driven by his love for his people. See Samantha L. Miller, "The Hellish Homiletic Practices of Billy Graham and John Chrysostom," *Worship* 91 (2017): 300-317.

because no one else can harm a person's soul, only the person himself. Christ has loved and redeemed each person, and we ourselves are the only ones who can damage that because the only thing that damages it is sin. Since humans are free and self-determining, since they have exercise of their own *proairesis* (προαίρεσις), each person is responsible for his own sin. It is not the suffering that causes true harm, according to Chrysostom, but our reaction to that suffering. When we fear the other and lash out in hatred, we fear the wrong thing and cause grave harm to ourselves. Chrysostom would have us be loving, joyful, peaceful, patient, kind, gentle, and self-controlled in our interactions with those with whom we disagree.[14] In this way we can be virtuous as we work out together with our brothers and sisters in Christ how we are called to live in the already and not-yet kingdom of God.

All these debates are on the surface about behavior or theological descriptions of behavior, but they get so heated because people's deeply held understandings of salvation are operative in their arguments. Arguments about ethics are ultimately arguments about theological anthropology, ecclesiology, and soteriology. The debates about gay marriage, for example, are debates about what constitutes sin, but the next level of debate is how God's action overcomes sin and how much our behavior affects our salvation. The same is true of arguments about abortion. We often argue about sin because we worry about salvation. Recognizing our assumptions and talking about the issues we believe to be at stake could lead us forward in conversation instead of keeping us in stalemate.

What began as an exploration of Chrysostom's demonology has taken us through the realm of anthropology and into soteriology. The three fields are intertwined for Chrysostom in a single enterprise such that a study of Chrysostom's demonology is by necessity a study of his anthropology and soteriology, and this movement is useful for modern ecclesial conversations. Demons are not so frightening as Chrysostom's congregation believes. In fact, demons can be used to attain salvation, a tool whereby a person may be found worthy of the kingdom: "Behold even the devil has become a cause [*aitios*, αἴτιος] of salvation."[15] The more the devil tries to harm her virtue, the

---

[14]At least, Chrysostom's argument would have us be thus. He himself was not particularly known for being gentle or patient.

[15]Chrysostom, *De diab. tent.* 1.4 (SC 560bis, 140).

more the vigilant Christian will profit. When he considers hoarding his money, he will remember that he is stronger than the devil and choose to give alms instead. When she considers forsaking church attendance in favor of the theater or the races, she will remember that she is not subject to the devil and choose worship instead. When he considers blaming his sin on the devil or slandering a political opponent, he will choose to take responsibility and speak gently. She will strengthen her virtue and become even more superior to the enemy of her salvation as she climbs this circular stairway to heaven. He will himself be found vigorous and glowing with the sweat of one who is worthy of the gifts he has received, worthy to enter the kingdom of heaven.

Bibliography

Chrysostom

Critical Editions

Daniélou, Jean, Anne-Marie Malingrey, and Robert Flacelière, eds. *Sur l'incompréhensibilité de Dieu*. 2nd ed. SC 28. Paris: Cerf, 1970.

Dumortier, Jean, ed. *A Théodore*. SC 117. Paris: Cerf, 1966.

Malingrey, Anne-Marie, ed. *Lettres à Olympias*. SC 13. Paris: Cerf, 1947.

———. *Lettre d'exil à Olympias et à tous les fidèles (Quod nemo laeditur)*. SC 103. Paris: Cerf, 1964.

Peleanu, Adina, ed. *Homélies sur l'impuissance du diable*. SC 560. Paris: Cerf, 2013.

Piédagnel, Auguste, ed. *Panégyriques de S. Paul*. SC 300. Paris: Cerf, 1982.

Piédagnel, Auguste, and Louis Doutreleau, eds. *Trois catéchèses baptismales*. SC 366. Paris: Cerf, 1990.

Sorlin, Henri, and Louis Neyrand, eds. *Commentaire sur Job*. SC 346. Paris: Cerf, 1988.

Wenger, Antoine, ed. *Huit catéchèses baptismales*. SC 50. Paris: Cerf, 1957.

Greek of Chrysostom for which there is no critical edition comes from the PG:

Patrologia graeca [= Patrologiae Cursus Completus: Series Graeca]. Edited by J.-P. Migne. 162 vols. Paris, 1857–1886.

Translations

Christo, Gus George, trans. *On Repentance and Almsgiving: St. John Chrysostom on Repentance and Almsgiving*. FC 96. Washington, DC: Catholic University of America Press, 1998.

Goggin, Sr. Thomas Aquinas, trans. *Commentary on Saint John the Apostle and Evangelist: Homilies 1-47*. FC 33. New York: Fathers of the Church, 1957.

———. *Commentary on Saint John the Apostle and Evangelist: Homilies 48-88*. FC 41. New York: Fathers of the Church, 1960.

Hall, Christopher Alan. "John Chrysostom's 'On Providence': A Translation and Theological Interpretation." PhD diss., Drew University, 1991.

Harkins, Paul W., trans. *Baptismal Instructions*. ACW, Works of the Fathers in Translation, 31. Westminster, MD: Newman Press, 1963.

———. *Discourses Against Judaizing Christians*. FC 68. Washington, DC: Catholic University of America Press, 1979.

Hill, Robert C., trans. *Homilies on Genesis 1–17*. FC 74. Washington, DC: Catholic University of America Press, 1986.

———. *Homilies on Genesis 18–45*. FC 82. Washington, DC: Catholic University of America Press, 1990.

———. *Homilies on Genesis 46–67*. FC 87. Washington, DC: Catholic University of America Press, 1992.

———. *Old Testament Homilies*. 3 vols. Brookline, MA: Holy Cross Orthodox Press, 2003.

———. *St. John Chrysostom Commentary on Job*. SJC: CS 1. Brookline, MA: Holy Cross Orthodox Press, 2006.

———. *St. John Chrysostom Commentary on the Psalms*. Brookline, MA: Holy Cross Orthodox Press, 1998.

Hunter, David G., trans. *A Comparison Between a King and a Monk; Against the Opponents of the Monastic Life: Two Treatises*. Lewiston, NY: Mellen, 1988.

Laistner, M. L. W. *Christianity and Pagan Culture in the Later Roman Empire; Together with an English Translation of John Chrysostom's Address on Vainglory and the Right Way for Parents to Bring Up Their Children*. James W. Richard Lectures in History for 1950–1951. Ithaca, NY: Cornell University Press, 1951.

Neville, Graham, trans. *Six Books on the Priesthood*. Crestwood, NY: St. Vladimir's Seminary Press, 1996.

Papageorgiou, Panayiotis, trans. *Homilies on Romans*. Brookline, MA: Holy Cross Orthodox Press, 2013.

Schaff, Philip, ed. *A Select Library of the Nicene and Post-Nicene Fathers of the Christian Church [First Series]*. Vols. 9-14. Grand Rapids, MI: Eerdmans, 1956.

OTHER PRIMARY SOURCES

Critical Editions

Akademie der Wissenschaften in Göttingen. *Septuaginta: Vetus Testamentum Graecum*. Göttingen: Vandenhoeck & Ruprecht, 1931.

Athanasius of Alexandria. *Vie d'Antoine*. Edited and translated by G. J. M. Bartelink. SC 400. Paris: Cerf, 1994.

Bobichon, Philippe, ed. *Justin Martyr, Dialogue avec Tryphon: Édition critique*. 2 vols. Fribourg: Academic Press, 2003.

Butler, Edward Cuthbert, ed. *The Lausiac History of Palladius: A Critical Discussion Together with Notes on Early Egyptian Monachism*. Nendeln, Liechtenstein: Kraus Reprints, 1967.

Cicero, Marcus Tullius. *Cicero on the Emotions: Tusculan Disputations 3 and 4*. Translated and with commentary by Margaret Graver. Chicago: University of Chicago Press, 2002.

Gregory of Nyssa. *Traité de la virginité*. Edited and translated by Michel Aubineau. SC 119. Paris: Cerf, 1966.

Origen. *Traité des principes*. Edited and translated by Henri Crouzel and Manlio Simonetti. 5 vols. SC 252-53, 268-69, 312. Paris: Cerf, 1978–1984.

Greek from other authors where there is no critical edition comes from either Migne's PG listed above, the Loeb Classical Library (volumes listed below under translations), or from the Patrologia Orientalis:

Methodius. *Le De autexusio de Méthode d'Olympe: Version slave et texte grec*. Edited by André Vaillant. PO 22, fasc. 5. Paris: Firmin-Didot, 1930.

Translations

Aristotle. *The Athenian Constitution: The Eudemian Ethics; On Virtues and Vices*. Translated by H. Rackham. LCL 285. Cambridge, MA: Harvard University Press, 1935.

———. *Nicomachean Ethics*. Translated by H. Rackham. LCL 73. Cambridge, MA: Harvard University Press, 1934.

Athanasius. *The Life of Antony*. Translated by Tim Vivian and Apostolos N. Athanassakis with Rowan A. Greer. Kalamazoo, MI: Cistercian, 2003.

Athenagoras. *Legatio and De resurrectione.* OECT. Oxford: Clarendon, 1972.

Augustine. *Treatises on Marriage and Other Subjects.* Translated by Charles T. Wilcox. FC 27. Washington, DC: Catholic University of America Press, 1955.

Basil. *Saint Basil: Ascetical Works.* Translated by Monica Wagner. FC 9. Washington, DC: Catholic University of America Press, 1950.

Boeft, J. den. *Calcidius on Demons: (Commentarius Ch. 127–136).* Leiden: Brill, 1977.

Charlesworth, James H., ed. *Old Testament Pseudepigrapha.* 2 vols. Garden City, NY: Doubleday, 1983–1985.

Clarke, Emma C., John M. Dillon, and Jackson P. Hershbell, eds. *Iamblichus: De mysteriis.* Leiden: Brill, 2004.

Danby, Herbert, trans. and ed. *The Mishnah.* Oxford: Clarendon, 1933.

Diogenes Laertius. *Lives of Eminent Philosophers.* Translated by R. D. Hicks. Vol. 2, bks. 6-10. LCL 185. New York: Putnam's Sons, 1925.

Dupont-Sommer, André, trans. *The Essene Writings from Qumran.* Cleveland: World, 1962.

Epictetus. *Discourses and Selected Writings.* Translated and edited by Robert Dobbin. New ed. Penguin Classics. London: Penguin, 2008.

———. *Discourses, Books 1-2.* Translated by W. A. Oldfather. LCL 131. Cambridge, MA: Harvard University Press, 1925.

———. *Discourses, Books 3-4; Fragments; the Encheiridion.* Translated by W. A. Oldfather. LCL 218. Cambridge, MA: Harvard University Press, 1928.

Epstein, Isidore, ed. *The Babylonian Talmud.* 18 vols. London: Soncino, 1961.

Evagrius Ponticus. *The Praktikos & Chapters on Prayer.* Translated by John Eudes Bamberger. Cistercian Studies 4. Spencer, MA: Cistercian, 1970.

Fowler, Harold North, W. R. M Lamb, Robert Gregg Bury, and Paul Shorey, eds. *Plato in Twelve Volumes.* LCL. Cambridge, MA: Harvard University Press, 1967–1995.

Gellius, Aulus. *Attic Nights.* Translated by John C. Rolfe. Vol. 2, bks. 6-13. LCL 196. Cambridge, MA: Harvard University Press, 1927.

Gregory of Nazianzus. *Festal Orations: Saint Gregory of Nazianzus.* Translated by Nonna Verna Harrison. Crestwood, NY: St. Vladimir's Seminary Press, 2008.

———. *On God and Man: The Theological Poetry of St. Gregory of Nazianzus.* Translated by Peter Gilbert. Crestwood, NY: St. Vladimir's Seminary Press, 2001.

Holmes, Michael W., ed. and rev. *The Apostolic Fathers: Greek Texts and English Translations.* Translated by J. B. Lightfoot and J. R. Harmer. 2nd ed. Grand Rapids: Baker Books, 1999.

Marcus Aurelius. *Meditations.* Translated by Gregory Hays. New York: Modern Library, 2002.

Neusner, Jacob, ed. *The Talmud of Babylonia: An American Translation.* 36 vols. BJS. Chico, CA: Scholars Press, 1984–1994.

Origen. *On First Principles: Being Koetschau's Text of the* De principiis. Translated by G. W Butterworth. 1936. Reprint, Gloucester, MA: Peter Smith, 1973.

Palladius. *The Lausiac History.* Translated by Robert T. Meyer. ACW 34. New York: Newman, 1965.

Philo. *On the Cherubim. The Sacrifices of Abel and Cain. The Worse Attacks the Better. On the Posterity and Exile of Cain. On the Giants.* Translated by F. H. Colson and G. H. Whitaker. LCL 227. Cambridge, MA: Harvard University Press, 1929.

Porphyry. *On Abstinence from Killing Animals.* Translated by Gillian Clark. Ithaca, NY: Cornell University Press, 2000.

Roberts, Alexander, and W. H. Rambaut, trans. *Ante-Nicene Christian Library.* Edinburgh: T&T Clark, 1868–1872.

Rubenson, Samuel. *The Letters of St. Antony: Monasticism and the Making of a Saint.* Minneapolis: Fortress, 1995.

Seneca. *Epistles.* Trans. Richard M. Gummere. Vol. 3, Epistles 94-124. LCL 77. Cambridge, MA: Harvard University Press, 1996.

Seneca. *Moral Essays.* Translated by John W. Basore. Vol. 1. LCL 214. Cambridge, MA: Harvard University Press, 1928.

Tertullian. *Disciplinary, Moral, and Ascetical Works.* Translated by Rudolph Arbesmann, Emily Joseph Daly, and Edwin A. Quain. FC 40. Washington, DC: Catholic University of America Press, 1959.

———. *Tertullian: Apologetical Works, and Minucius Felix: Octavius.* Translated by Rudolph Arbesmann, Emily Joseph Daly, and Edwin A. Quain. FC 10. New York: Fathers of the Church, 1950.

Theodore of Mopsuestia. *The Commentaries on the Minor Epistles of Paul.* Translated by Rowan A. Greer. Leiden: Brill, 2011.

Theodoret of Cyrrhus. *A History of the Monks of Syria.* Translated by R. M. Price. Cistercian Studies 88. Kalamazoo, MI: Cistercian, 1985.

Ward, Benedicta, trans. *The Sayings of the Desert Fathers: The Alphabetical Collection.* Cistercian Studies 59. Kalamazoo, MI: Cistercian, 1975.

Wright, Wilmer Cave France, ed. *The Works of the Emperor Julian.* Vol. 2. LCL 29. Cambridge, MA: Harvard University Press, 1913.

SECONDARY SCHOLARSHIP

Algra, Keimpe. "Stoics on Souls and Demons: Reconstructing Stoic Demonology." In Vos and Otten, *Demons and the Devil*, 71-96.

Allen, Pauline, Wendy Mayer, Lawrence Cross, and B. Janelle Caiger, eds. *Prayer and Spirituality in the Early Church.* Everton Park, Queensland: Australian Catholic University, 1998.

Amirav, Hagit. *Rhetoric and Tradition: John Chrysostom on Noah and the Flood.* Leuven: Peeters, 2003.

Asamoah-Gyadu, J. Kwabena. *African Charismatics: Current Developments Within Independent Indigenous Pentecostalism in Ghana.* Studies of Religion in Africa 27. Leiden: Brill, 2005.

———. "Conquering Satan, Demons, Principalities, and Powers: Ghanaian Traditional and Christian Perspectives on Religion, Evil, and Deliverance." In *Coping with Evil in Religion and Culture: Case Studies*, edited by Nelly van Doorn-Harder and Lourens Minnema, 85-103. Amsterdam: Rodopi, 2008.

———. "Mission to 'Set the Captives Free': Healing, Deliverance, and General Curses in Ghanaian Pentecostalism." *International Review of Mission* 93 (2004): 389-406.

Ayers, James. "John Chrysostom's Doctrine of Conversion." PhD diss., Boston College, 2001.

Barnard, Lawrence R. "Christology and Soteriology in the Preaching of John Chrysostom." ThD thesis, Southwestern Baptist Theological Seminary, 1974.

Barnard, Leslie W. *Justin Martyr: His Life and Thought.* London: Cambridge University Press, 1967.

Barnes, Michel R. "Galen and Antony: Anger and Disclosure." In Livingstone, *Studia Patristica* 30:136-43.

Baur, Chrysostomus. *John Chrysostom and His Time*. Translated by M. Gonzaga. 2 vols. Westminster, MD: Newman, 1959.

Bebis, George S. "Saint John Chrysostom: On Materialism and Christian Virtue." *GOTR* 32 (1987): 227-37.

Bobzien, Susanne. *Determinism and Freedom in Stoic Philosophy*. New York: Clarendon, 1998.

Bohak, Gideon. *Ancient Jewish Magic: A History*. Cambridge: Cambridge University Press, 2008.

Bosinis, Constantine. "Two Platonic Images in the Rhetoric of John Chrysostom: 'The Wings of Love' and 'the Charioteer of the Soul.'" In Young, Edwards, and Parvis, *Studia Patristica* 41:433-38.

Brakke, David. *Demons and the Making of the Monk: Spiritual Combat in Early Christianity*. Cambridge, MA: Harvard University Press, 2006.

———. "The Greek and Syriac Versions of the Life of Antony." *Muséon* 107 (1994): 29-53.

———. "The Making of Monastic Demonology: Three Ascetic Teachers on Withdrawal and Resistance." *Church History* 70 (2001): 19-48.

Brändle, Rudolf. "Jean Chrysostome—L'importance de Matth. 25,31-46 pour son éthique." *VC* 31 (1977): 47-52.

Brenk, Frederick E. *In Mist Apparelled: Religious Themes in Plutarch's Moralia and Lives*. Leiden: Brill, 1977.

———. "'A Most Strange Doctrine': Daimon in Plutarch." *Classical Journal* 69 (1973): 1-11.

Brown, Peter. *Augustine of Hippo: A Biography*. Berkeley: University of California Press, 2000.

———. *The Body and Society: Men, Women, and Sexual Renunciation in Early Christianity*. New York: Columbia University Press, 1988.

———. *The Cult of the Saints: Its Rise and Function in Latin Christianity*. Chicago: University of Chicago Press, 1981.

———. "The Rise and Function of the Holy Man in Late Antiquity." *Journal of Roman Studies* 61 (1971): 80-101.

———. *The World of Late Antiquity: From Marcus Aurelius to Muhammad*. London: Thames & Hudson, 1971.

Burns, J. Patout. "Augustine on the Origin and Progress of Evil." *Journal of Religious Ethics* 16 (1988): 9-27.

Carpenter, Dwayne E. "The Devil Bedeviled: Diabolical Intervention and the Desert Fathers." *American Benedictine Review* 31, no. 2 (1980): 182-200.

Carter, Robert E. "The Future of Chrysostom Studies: Theology and Nachleben." In *Symposion: Studies on St. John Chrysostom*, edited by Panayotis C. Christou, 129-36. Analecta Vlatadōn 18. Thessaloniki: Patriarchal Institute for Patristic Studies, 1973.

Clark, Elizabeth A. *The Origenist Controversy: The Cultural Construction of an Early Christian Debate*. Princeton, NJ: Princeton University Press, 1992.

———. "Sexual Politics in the Writings of John Chrysostom." *AThR* 59, no. 1 (1977): 3-20.

———. "Theory and Practice in Late Ancient Asceticism: Jerome, Chrysostom, and Augustine." *Journal of Feminist Studies in Religion* 5 (1989): 25-46.

Coleman-Norton, P. R. "St. Chrysostom and the Greek Philosophers." *Classical Philology* 25, no. 4 (1930): 305-17.

Coyle, J. Kevin. "Early Monks, Prayer, and the Devil." In Allen, Canning, Cross, and Caiger, *Prayer and Spirituality in the Early Church*, 229-49.

Crenshaw, James L. *Defending God: Biblical Responses to the Problem of Evil*. New York: Oxford University Press, 2005.

Crépey, Cyrille. "La récompense, un thème majeur dans le discours pastoral de Jean Chrysostome." *Revue des sciences religieuses* 83, no. 1 (2009): 97-113.

Daniel, R W. "A Christian Amulet on Papyrus." *VC* 37 (1983): 400-404.

Day, Peggy L. *An Adversary in Heaven: Śāṭān in the Hebrew Bible.* Atlanta: Scholars Press, 1988.

De Bruyn, Theodore S. "Appeals to Jesus as the One 'Who Heals Every Illness and Every Infirmity' (Matt 4:23, 9:35) in Amulets in Late Antiquity." In *Reception and Interpretation of the Bible in Late Antiquity,* edited by Lorenzo DiTommaso and Lucian Turcescu, 65-81. Leiden: Brill, 2008.

———. "The Use of the Sanctus in Christian Greek Papyrus Amulets." In Young, Edwards, and Parvis, *Studia Patristica* 40:15-19.

De La Torre, Miguel A., and Albert Hernández. *The Quest for the Historical Satan.* Minneapolis: Fortress, 2011.

de Wet, Chris L. "Claiming Corporeal Capital: John Chrysostom's Homilies on the Maccabean Martyrs." *Journal of Early Christian History* 2, no. 1 (2012): 3-21.

———. *Preaching Bondage: John Chrysostom and the Discourse of Slavery in Early Christianity.* Oakland: University of California Press, 2015.

———. "The Priestly Body: Power-Discourse and Identity in John Chrysostom's *De Sacerdotio.*" *Religion & Theology* 18 (2011): 351-79.

de Wet, Chris L. and Wendy Mayer, eds. *Revisioning John Chrysostom: New Approaches, New Perspectives.* Leiden: Brill, 2019.

Desprez, Vincent. "Saint Anthony and the Beginnings of Anchoritism." *American Benedictine Review* 43 (1992): 61-81; 141-72.

Dickie, Matthew W. *Magic and Magicians in the Greco-Roman World.* London: Routledge, 2001.

Dobbin, Robert. "Προαίρεσις in Epictetus." *Ancient Philosophy* 11, no. 1 [1991]: 111-35.

Dodds, E. R. *Pagan and Christian in an Age of Anxiety: Some Aspects of Religious Experience from Marcus Aurelius to Constantine.* Cambridge: Cambridge University Press, 1965.

Donegan, Susan. "St John Chrysostom: An Argument for a Greater Appreciation of His Theology of Salvation." *Diakonia* 23 (1990): 21-42.

Dua-Agyeman, Kwaku. *Covenant, Curses, and Cure.* Kumasi, Ghana: Payless Printing Press, 1994.

Ely, Peter B. "Chrysostom and Augustine on the Ultimate Meaning of Human Freedom." *Ultimate Reality and Meaning* 29, no. 3 (2006): 163-82.

Ferguson, Everett. *Demonology of the Early Christian World.* Lewiston, NY: Mellen, 1984.

———. "Origen's Demonology." In *Johannine Studies: Essays in Honor of Frank Pack,* edited by James Eugene Priest, 54-66. Malibu, CA: Pepperdine University Press, 1989.

Finn, Thomas M. *The Liturgy of Baptism in the Baptismal Instructions of St. John Chrysostom.* Washington, DC: Catholic University of America Press, 1967.

Florovsky, Georges. "St John Chrysostom: The Prophet of Charity." *SVTQ* 4, nos. 3/4 (1955): 37-42.

Ford, J. N. "Phonetic Spellings of the Subordinating Particle *d(y)* in the Jewish Babylonian Aramaic Magic Bowls." *Aramaic Studies* 10, no. 2 (July 2012): 215-47.

Frede, Michael. *A Free Will: Origins of the Notion in Ancient Thought.* Edited by A. A. Long. Berkeley: University of California Press, 2011.

Gager, John G., ed. *Curse Tablets and Binding Spells from the Ancient World.* Oxford: Oxford University Press, 1992.

Geller, Markham J. "Eight Incantation Bowls." *Orientalia Lovaniensia Periodica* 17 (1986): 101-17.

———. "Tablets and Magic Bowls." In *Officina Magica: Essays on the Practice of Magic in Antiquity*, edited by Shaul Shaked, 53–72. Leiden: Brill, 2005.

Gignoux, Philippe. "A New Incantation Bowl Inscribed in Syriac (National Museum of Oriental Art, Rome)." *East and West* 34 (1984): 47-53.

Gitler, H. "Four Magical and Christian Amulets." *Studii Biblici Franciscani Liber Annuus* 40 (1990): 365-74.

Goodenough, Erwin R. *The Theology of Justin Martyr.* Jena: Verlag Frommannsche Buchhandlung, 1923.

Gordon, Barry. "The Problem of Scarcity and the Christian Fathers: John Chrysostom and Some Contemporaries." In Livingstone, *Studia Patristica* 22:108-20.

Gould, Josiah B. *The Philosophy of Chrysippus.* Leiden: Brill, 1970.

Hall, Christopher A. "John Chrysostom." In *Reading Romans Through the Centuries: From the Early Church to Karl Barth*, edited by Jeffrey P. Greenman and Timothy Larsen, 39-57. Grand Rapids: Brazos, 2005.

———. "John Chrysostom's 'On Providence': A Translation and Theological Interpretation." PhD diss., Drew University, 1991.

Harrison, Verna E. F. *Grace and Human Freedom According to St. Gregory of Nyssa.* Rev. ed. Lewiston, NY: Mellen, 1992.

Hartney, Aideen M. *John Chrysostom and the Transformation of the City.* London: Duckworth, 2004.

Heine, Ronald E. *Classical Christian Doctrine: Introducing the Essentials of the Ancient Faith.* Grand Rapids: Baker Academic, 2013.

Hill, Robert C. "*Akribeia*: A Principle of Chrysostom's Exegesis." *Colloquium* 14 (1981): 32-36.

———. "Chrysostom's Terminology for the Inspired Word." *Estudios bíblicos* 41 (1983): 367-73.

———. "On Looking Again at *sunkatabasis.*" *Prudentia* 13 (1981): 3-11.

———. "A Pelagian Commentator on the Psalms?" *ITQ* 63 (1998): 263-71.

———.*Reading the Old Testament in Antioch.* Bible in Ancient Christianity 5. Leiden: Brill, 2005.

Holman, Susan R., ed. *Wealth and Poverty in Early Church and Society.* Grand Rapids: Baker Academic, 2008.

Hunt, Stephen. "Managing the Demonic: Some Aspects of the Neo-Pentecostal Deliverance Ministry." *Journal of Contemporary Religion* 13 (1998): 215-30.

Hunter, David G. "Borrowings from Libanius in the *Comparatio Regis et Monachi* of St John Chrysostom." *JTS* 39, no. 2 (1988): 525–31.

———. "Preaching and Propaganda in Fourth Century Antioch: John Chrysostom's *Homilies on the Statues.*" In *Preaching in the Patristic Age*, edited by David G. Hunter, 119-38. New York: Paulist, 1989.

Inwood, Brad. *Ethics and Human Action in Early Stoicism.* New York: Oxford University Press, 1985.

Isaacs, Ronald H. *Ascending Jacob's Ladder: Jewish Views of Angels, Demons, and Evil Spirits.* Northvale, NJ: Jason Aronson, 1998.

Isbell, Charles D. "The Story of the Aramaic Magical Incantation Bowls." *BA* 41, no. 1 (1978): 5-16.

Jaeger, Werner Wilhelm. *Two Rediscovered Works of Ancient Christian Literature: Gregory of Nyssa and Macarius.* Leiden: Brill, 1954.

Janowitz, Naomi. *Magic in the Roman World: Pagans, Jews, and Christians.* New York: Routledge, 2001.

Johnson, Timothy Jay. "Job as Proto-Apocalypse: Proposing a Unifying Genre." PhD diss., Marquette University, 2004.

Kalleres, Dayna S. *City of Demons: Violence, Ritual, and Christian Power in Late Antiquity.* Berkeley: University of California Press, 2015.

———. "Demons and Divine Illumination: A Consideration of Eight Prayers by Gregory of Nazianzus." *VC* 61 (2007): 157-88.

———. "Exorcising the Devil to Silence Christ's Enemies: Ritualized Speech Practices in Late Antique Christianity." PhD diss., Brown University, 2002.

Kanaan, Marlène. "Le diable et les démons chez saint Jean Chrysostome." *Bulletin de littérature ecclésiastique* 113 (2012): 291-302.

Kelly, Henry Ansgar. *The Devil at Baptism: Ritual, Theology, and Drama.* Ithaca, NY: Cornell University Press, 1985.

———. *The Devil, Demonology, and Witchcraft: The Development of Christian Beliefs in Evil Spirits.* A Scott & Collins Book. Garden City, NY: Doubleday, 1968.

———. *Satan: A Biography.* New York: Cambridge University Press, 2006.

Kelly, J. N. D. *Early Christian Doctrines.* 5th rev. ed. London: A. C. Black, 1977.

———. *Golden Mouth: The Story of John Chrysostom—Ascetic, Preacher, Bishop.* London: Duckworth, 1995.

Kenny, Anthony. "Was St. John Chrysostom a Semi-Pelagian?" *ITQ* 37 (1960): 16-29.

Kidd, Ian. "Some Philosophical Demons." *Bulletin of the Institute of Classical Studies* 40, no. 1 (1995): 217-24.

Kondoleon, Christine. *Antioch: The Lost Ancient City.* Princeton, NJ: Princeton University Press, 2000.

Korteweg, Theodoor. "Justin Martyr and His Demon-Ridden Universe." In Vos and Otten, *Demons and the Devil,* 145-58.

Krupp, Robert Allen. *Saint John Chrysostom, a Scripture Index.* Lanham, MD: University Press of America, 1984.

Lacerenza, Giancarlo. "Jewish Magicians and Christian Clients in Late Antiquity: The Testimony of Amulets and Inscriptions." In *What Athens Has to Do with Jerusalem: Essays on Classical, Jewish, and Early Christian Art and Archaeology in Honor of Gideon Foerster,* edited by Leonard V. Rutgers, 393-419. Leuven: Peeters, 2002.

Laird, Raymond. *Mindset, Moral Choice and Sin in the Anthropology of John Chrysostom.* Strathfield, NSW: St Pauls, 2012.

Langton, Edward. *Essentials of Demonology: A Study of Jewish and Christian Doctrine, Its Origin and Development.* London: Epworth Press, 1949.

Lawrenz, Melvin E. "The Christology of John Chrysostom." In Livingstone, *Studia Patristica* 22:148-53.

———. *The Christology of John Chrysostom.* Lewiston, NY: Mellen, 1996.

———. "The Christology of John Chrysostom." PhD diss., Marquette University, 1987.

Leroux, Jean M. "Saint Jean Chrysostome et le monachisme." In *Jean Chrysostome et Augustin,* edited by Charles Kannengiesser, 125-44. Paris: Beauchesne, 1975.

Leyerle, Blake. "John Chrysostom on Almsgiving and the Use of Money." *HTR* 87, no. 1 (1994): 29-47.

Limberis, Vasiliki. "The Eyes Infected by Evil: Basil of Caesarea's Homily, On Envy." *HTR* 84, no. 2 (1991): 163-84.

Livingstone, E. A., ed. *Studia Patristica: Cappadocian Fathers, Chrysostom and His Greek Contemporaries, Augustine, Donatism and Pelagianism.* Vol. 22. Leuven: Peeters, 1989.

———, ed. *Studia Patristica: Biblica et Apocrypha, Ascetica, Liturgica.* Vol. 30. Leuven: Peeters, 1996.

Long, A. A. "Representation and the Self in Stoicism." In *Psychology*, edited by Stephen Everson, 102-20. Companions to Ancient Thought 2. Cambridge: Cambridge University Press, 1991.

Long, A. A., and D. N. Sedley, eds. *The Hellenistic Philosophers.* 2 vols. Cambridge: Cambridge University Press, 1987.

Ludlow, Morwenna. "Demons, Evil and Liminality in Cappadocian Theology." *JECS* 20, no. 2 (2012): 179-211.

Martin, Dale B. *Inventing Superstition: From the Hippocratics to the Christians.* Cambridge, MA: Harvard University Press, 2004.

———. "When Did Angels Become Demons?" *Journal of Biblical Literature* 129, no. 4 (2010): 657-77.

Marx-Wolf, Heidi. "A Strange Consensus: Daemonological Discourse in Origen, Porphyry, and Iamblichus." In *The Rhetoric of Power in Late Antiquity: Religion and Politics in Byzantium, Europe and the Early Islamic World*, edited by Robert M. Frakes, Elizabeth DePalma Digeser, and Justin Stephens, 219-40. London: Tauris, 2010.

———. "Third-Century Daimonologies and the *Via Universalis*: Origen, Porphery and Iamblichus on *diamones* and Other Angels." In Baun, Cameron, Edwards, and Vinzent, *Studia Patristica* 46, 207-16.

Maxwell, Jaclyn L. *Christianization and Communication in Late Antiquity: John Chrysostom and His Congregation in Antioch.* Cambridge: Cambridge University Press, 2006.

Mayer, Wendy. *The Homilies of St John Chrysostom: Provenance, Reshaping the Foundations.* Rome: Pontifical Oriental Institute, 2005.

———. "John Chrysostom and Women Revisited." In *Men and Women in the Early Christian Centuries*, edited by Wendy Mayer and Ian J. Elmer, 211-25. Strathfield, NSW: St Paul's Press, 2014.

———. "John Chrysostom: Extraordinary Preacher, Ordinary Audience." In *Preacher and Audience: Studies in Early Christian and Byzantine Homiletics*, edited by Mary B. Cunningham and Pauline Allen, 105-37. Leiden: Brill, 1998.

———. "Mania and Madness in the Works of John Chrysostom: A Snapshot from Late Antiquity." In *The Concept of Madness from Homer to Byzantium: Manifestations and Aspects of Mental Illness and Disorder*, edited by Hélène Perdicoyianni-Paléologou, 349-73. Amsterdam: Hakkert, 2016.

———. "Monasticism at Antioch and Constantinople in the Late Fourth Century: A Case of Exclusivity or Diversity?" In Allen, Mayer, and Cross, *Prayer and Spirituality in the Early Church*, 275-88.

———. "The Persistence in Late Antiquity of Medico-Philosophical Psychic Therapy." *Journal of Late Antiquity* 8 (2015): 337-351.

———. "Shaping the Sick Soul: Reshaping the Identity of John Chrysostom." In *Christians Shaping Identity from the Roman Empire to Byzantium: Studies Inspired by Pauline Allen*, edited by Geoffrey Dunn and Wendy Mayer, 140-64. Leiden: Brill, 2015.

———. "What Does It Mean to Say That John Chrysostom Was a Monk?" In Young, Edwards, and Parvis, *Studia Patristica* 41:451-55.

Metzger, Bruce M. *Chapters in the History of New Testament Textual Criticism.* New Testament Tools and Studies 4. Grand Rapids: Eerdmans, 1963.

———. "Patristic Evidence and the Textual Criticism of the New Testament." *New Testament Studies* 18, no. 4 (1972): 379-400.

Meyer, Louis. *Saint Jean Chrysostome, maître de perfection chrétienne.* Paris: Beauchesne, 1933.

Meyer, Marvin W., and Richard Smith, eds. *Ancient Christian Magic: Coptic Texts of Ritual Power.* San Francisco: HarperSanFrancisco, 1994.

Mikalson, Jon D. *Greek Popular Religion in Greek Philosophy.* Oxford: Oxford University Press, 2010.

Mikoda, Toshio. "A Comparison of the Demonologies of Origen and Plutarch." In *Origeniana Quinta: Papers of the 5th International Origen Congress, 1989,* edited by Robert J. Daly, 326-32. Leuven: University Press, 1992.

Miller, Samantha L. "'The Devil Did Not Make You Do It: Chrysostom's Refutation of Modern Deliverance Theology," in de Wet and Mayer, *Revisioning John Chrysostom,* 613-37.

———. "The Hellish Homiletic Practices of Billy Graham and John Chrysostom." *Worship* 91 (2017): 300-317.

Mitchell, Margaret M. *The Heavenly Trumpet: John Chrysostom and the Art of Pauline Interpretation.* Tübingen: Mohr Siebeck, 2000.

———. "John Chrysostom." In *The Sermon on the Mount Through the Centuries: From the Early Church to John Paul II,* edited by Jeffrey P. Greenman, Timothy Larsen, and Stephen R. Spencer, 19-42. Grand Rapids: Brazos, 2007.

Montgomery, James A. "A Syriac Incantation Bowl with Christian Formula." *American Journal of Semitic Languages and Literatures* 34 (1918): 137.

Motte, André. "La catégorie platonicienne du démonique." In Ries, *Anges et démons,* 205-21.

Mühlenberg, Ekkehard. "Synergism in Gregory of Nyssa." *ZNW* 68 (1977): 93-122.

Nassif, Bradley. "Antiochene θεωρία in John Chrysostom's Exegesis." In *Ancient & Postmodern Christianity: Paleo-Orthodoxy in the 21st Century; Essays in Honor of Thomas C. Oden,* edited by Kenneth Tanner and christopher A. Hall, 49-67. Downers Grove, IL: InterVarsity Press, 2002.

———. "The 'Spiritual Exegesis' of Scripture: The School of Antioch Revisited." *AThR* 75, no. 4 (1993): 437-70.

Naveh, Joseph, and Shaul Shaked. *Amulets and Magic Bowls: Aramaic Incantations of Late Antiquity.* Jerusalem: Magnes Press, Hebrew University, 1985.

———. *Magic Spells and Formulae: Aramaic Incantations of Late Antiquity.* Jerusalem: Magnes Press, Hebrew University, 1993.

Neusner, Jacob, ed. *The Talmud of Babylonia: An American Translation.* 36 vols. Chico, CA: Scholars Press, 1984–1994.

Nowak, Edward. *Le chrétien devant la souffrance: Étude sur la pensée de Jean Chrysostome.* Paris: Beauchesne, 1973.

Onyinah, Opoku. "Deliverance as a Way of Confronting Witchcraft in Contemporary Africa: Ghana as a Case Study." In *Spirit in the World: Emerging Pentecostal Theologies in Global Contexts,* edited by Veli-Matti Kärkkäinen, 181-202. Grand Rapids: Eerdmans, 2009.

Pagels, Elaine H. "The Social History of Satan, the 'Intimate Enemy': A Preliminary Sketch." *HTR* 84, no. 2 (1991): 105-28.

Papageorgiou, Panayiotis. "Chrysostom and Augustine on the Sin of Adam and Its Consequences." *SVTQ* 39, no. 4 (1995): 361-78.

———. "A Theological Analysis of Selected Themes in the Homilies of St. John Chrysostom on the Epistle of St. Paul to the Romans." PhD diss., Catholic University of America, 1995.

Peleanu, Adina. "Deux séries chrysostomiennes: Sur l'impuissance du diable et sur l'obscurité des prophéties." *Revue d'études augustiniennes et patristiques* 57 (2011): 89-108.

Prince, Derek. *They Shall Expel Demons: What You Need to Know About Demons—Your Invisible Enemies.* Grand Rapids: Chosen Books, 1998.

Quasten, Johannes. *Patrology.* Vol. 3. Utrecht: Spectrum, 1963.

Reed, Annette Yoshiko. "The Trickery of the Fallen Angels and the Demonic Mimesis of the Divine: Aetiology, Demonology, and Polemics in the Writings of Justin Martyr." *JECS* 12, no. 2 (2004): 141-71.

Rexine, John E. "Daimon in Classical Greek Literature." *GOTR* 30, no. 3 (1985): 335-61.

Ries, Julian. "Cultes païens et démons dans l'apologétique chrétienne de Justin à Augustin." In Ries, *Anges et démons,* 337-52.

Ries, Julian, ed. *Anges et démons: Acts du colloque de Liège et de Louvain-la-Neuve, 25-26 novembre, 1987.* Louvain-la-Neuve, Belgium: Centre d'histoire des religions, 1989.

Riley, Hugh M. *Christian Initiation: A Comparative Study of the Interpretation of the Baptismal Liturgy in the Mystagogical Writings of Cyril of Jerusalem, John Chrysostom, Theodore of Mopsuestia, and Ambrose of Milan.* Washington, DC: Catholic University of America Press, 1974.

Rubenson, Samuel. *The Letters of St. Antony: Monasticism and the Making of a Saint.* Minneapolis: Fortress, 1995.

Russell, Jeffrey Burton. *The Devil: Perceptions of Evil from Antiquity to Primitive Christianity.* Ithaca, NY: Cornell University Press, 1977.

———. *Lucifer: the Devil in the Middle Ages.* Ithaca, NY: Cornell University Press, 1984.

———. *Mephistopheles: The Devil in the Modern World.* Ithaca, NY: Cornell University Press, 1986.

———. *Satan: The Early Christian Tradition.* Ithaca, NY: Cornell University Press, 1981.

Rylaarsdam, David. "The Adaptability of Divine Pedagogy: Sunkatabasis in the Theology and Rhetoric of John Chrysostom." PhD diss., University of Notre Dame, 2000.

———. *John Chrysostom on Divine Pedagogy: The Coherence of His Theology and Preaching.* Oxford: Oxford University Press, 2014.

Salem, Claire Elayne. "Sanity, Insanity, and Man's Being as Understood by St. John Chrysostom." PhD diss., Durham University, 2010.

Schreiber, Stefan. "The Great Opponent: The Devil in Early Jewish and Formative Christian Literature." In *Angels: The Concept of Celestial Beings—Origins, Development and Reception,* edited by Friedrich Vinzenz Reiterer, Robias Nicklas, and Karin Schöpflin, 437-57. Berlin: de Gruyter, 2007.

Scotland, Nigel. "The Charismatic Devil: Demonology in Charismatic Christianity." In *Angels and Demons: Perspectives and Practice in Diverse Religious Traditions,* edited by Peter G. Riddell and Beverly Smith Riddell, 84-105. Nottingham: Apollos, 2007.

Shaked, Shaul. "Transmission and Transformation of Spells: The Case of the Jewish Babylonian Aramaic Bowls." In *Continuity and Innovation in the Magical Tradition,* edited by Gideon Bohak, Yuval Harari, and Shaul Shaked, 187-217. Leiden: Brill, 2011.

Shanks, Hershel. "Magic Incantation Bowls." *Biblical Archaeology Review* 33, no. 1 (2007): 62.

Skidmore, Clive. *Practical Ethics for Roman Gentlemen: The Work of Valerius Maximus.* Exeter: University of Exeter Press, 1996.

Smith, Gregory. A. "How Thin Is a Demon?" *JECS* 16, no. 4 (2008): 479-512.

Smith, Jonathan Z. "Towards Interpreting Demonic Powers in Hellenistic and Roman Antiquity." *ANRW* 2.16.1, 425-39.

Smyth, Herbert Weir. *Greek Grammar.* Edited by Gordon M. Messing. Rev. ed. Cambridge, MA: Harvard University Press, 1956.

Sorabji, Richard. "Epictetus on *Proairesis* and Self." In *The Philosophy of Epictetus*, edited by Theodore Scaltsas and Andrew S. Mason, 87-98. Oxford: Oxford University Press, 2007.

Telfer, William. "*Autexousia.*" *JTS* 8, no. 1 (1957): 123-29.

Timotin, Andrei. *La démonologie platonicienne: Histoire de la notion de* daimon *de Platon aux derniers Néoplatoniciens.* Leiden: Brill, 2012.

Tofană, Stelian. "John Chrysostom's View of Reading and Interpreting the Scripture: A Critical Assessment." *Sacra Scripta: Journal of the Centre for Biblical Studies* 6, no. 2 (2008): 165-81.

Trakatellis, Demetrios. "Being Transformed: Chrysostom's Exegesis of the Epistle to the Romans." *GOTR* 36 (1991): 211-29.

———. "Man, Fallen and Restored, in the Teaching of St. John Chrysostom." *Sobornost* 4, no. 10 (1964): 569-84.

Tse, Mary W. "Συγκατάβασις and Ἀκρίβεια—the Warp and Woof of Chrysostom's Hermeneutics: A Study Based on Chrysostom's Genesis Homilies." *Jian Dao* 15 (2001): 1-17.

Ubaldi, Paolo. "Di due citazioni di Platone in Giovanni Crisostomo." *Rivista di filologia e di istruzione classica* 28, no. 1 (1900): 69-75.

Valantasis, Richard. "Daemons and the Perfecting of the Monk's Body: Monastic Anthropology, Daemonology, and Asceticism." *Semeia* 58 (1992): 47-79.

Van Rompay, Lucas. "Some Remarks on the Language of Syriac Incantation Texts." In *V Symposium Syriacum, 1988, Katholieke Universiteit, Leuven, 29-31 août 1988*, edited by René Lavenant, 369-81. Rome: Pontifical Oriental Institute, 1990.

Vos, Nienke, and Willemien Otten, eds. *Demons and the Devil in Ancient and Medieval Christianity.* Supplements to Vigiliae Christianae 108. Leiden: Brill, 2011.

Wilford, F. A. "Daimon in Homer." *Numen* 12 (1965): 217-32.

Wilken, Robert L. *John Chrysostom and the Jews: Rhetoric and Reality in the Late 4th Century.* Berkeley: University of California Press, 1983.

Yamauchi, Edwin M. "Magic Bowls: Cyrus H. Gordon and the Ubiquity of Magic in the Premodern World." *BA* 59 (1996): 51-55.

Young, F., M. Edwards, and P. Parvis, eds. *Studia Patristica: Liturgia et Cultus, Theologica et Philosophica, Critica et Philologica, Nachleben, First Two Centuries.* Vol. 40. Leuven: Peeters, 2006.

———, eds. *Studia Patristica: Orientalia, Clement, Origen, Athanasius, the Cappadocians, Chrysostom.* Vol. 41. Leuven: Peeters, 2006.

Young, Frances M. "Alexandrian and Antiochene Exegesis." In *History of Biblical Interpretation*, edited by Alan J. Hauser and Duane F. Watson, 1:334-54. Grand Rapids: Eerdmans, 2003.

Scripture Index

New Explorations in Theology

Theology is flourishing in dynamic and unexpected ways in the twenty-first century. Scholars are increasingly recognizing the global character of the church, freely crossing old academic boundaries and challenging previously entrenched interpretations. Despite living in a culture of uncertainty, both young and senior scholars today are engaged in hopeful and creative work in the areas of systematic, historical, practical and philosophical theology. New Explorations in Theology provides a platform for cutting-edge research in these fields.

In an age of media proliferation and academic oversaturation, there is a need to single out the best new monographs. IVP Academic is committed to publishing constructive works that advance key theological conversations. We look for projects that investigate new areas of research, stimulate fruitful dialogue, and attend to the diverse array of contexts and audiences in our increasingly pluralistic world. IVP Academic is excited to make this work available to scholars, students and general readers who are seeking fresh new insights for the future of Christian theology.

Volumes Include:

- *Karl Barth's Infralapsarian Theology: Origins and Development, 1920–1953*, Shao Kai Tseng
- *The Reality of God and Historical Method: Apocalyptic Theology in Conversation with N. T. Wright*, Samuel V. Adams
- *A Shared Mercy: Karl Barth on Forgiveness and the Church*, Jon Coutts
- *The Making of Stanley Hauerwas: Bridging Barth and Postliberalism*, David B. Hunsicker